Indian Writings in English

Edited by
Binod Mishra
Sanjay Kumar

ATLANTIC
PUBLISHERS & DISTRIBUTORS (P) LTD

Published by

ATLANTIC

PUBLISHERS & DISTRIBUTORS (P) LTD

7/22, Ansari Road, Darya Ganj,
New Delhi-110002
Phones : +91-11-40775252, 23273880, 23275880, 23280451
Fax : +91-11-23285873
Web : www.atlanticbooks.com
E-mail : orders@atlanticbooks.com

Branch Office
5, Nallathambi Street, Wallajah Road,
Chennai-600002
Phones : +91-44-64611085, 32413319
E-mail : chennai@atlanticbooks.com

Printed in India at Glorious Printers, A-13, D.S.I.D.C., Jhilmil Industrial Area, Delhi-110095

Preface

Enshrined in its vague and obscure roots of nineteenth century, the Indian writing in English has now secured a universal acceptability as it is read, prescribed and discussed in many English speaking countries besides, of course, India, where since the last few decades it has developed into an ever expansive literary activity. Critical endeavours have been staggeringly focused on Indian writing in English. The present anthology assimilates some of the latest perspectives on noted Indian writers who have contributed significantly to the corpus of Indian Writing in English.

The essays in this Volume have been drawn from various scholars from all over India. Their in-depth understanding and candid criticism will be helpful to the budding scholars pursuing their research in the field of Indian writing in English. The anthology will also awaken in them a penchant for alterations going on in Indian ethos through various forms of human consciousness and self-fulfilment. Literature is a landmark of lived and unlived experiences and this anthology is a humble attempt to record such experiences.

In his elaborately probing paper, K.C. Mishra explores the philosophical genus that characterizes Bhabani Bhattacharya's *So Many Hungers*!. The article establishes how the novelist expresses his acute sense of commitment towards his culture and notion by exposing to the reader the divisive guile of the Britishers who colonized Indians not only physically but psychologically as well. The critic also admires the author for having expressed his ideology for the post-colonial India that education in India must incorporate values such as patriotism, harmony and tolerance.

Sathyaraj V. and Joe Verghese Yeldho in their paper analyse Shashi Tharoor's *Riot* as an interplay of fact and fiction. They situate the famous work as something that blurs the existing boundaries between fiction or fact, history or literature, universal or particular and aesthetics or politics.

Mansing G. Kadam defines post-colonialism and delves deep into the intricacies involved in interpreting post-colonial writings. He highlights how post-colonialism becomes an exasperating process when tested on the crucible of critical speculation, inquiry and evaluation. Kadam considers Amitav Ghosh's *The Glass Palace* as a quintessential post-colonial work expressed in the literary creations of the colonized, the non-white minorities all over the world.

In his incisive and elaborate analysis of Raj Kamal Jha's *If You are not Afraid of Heights*, Kanhaiyajee Jha discusses the structural, stylistic and textual nuances that harmonize the elements of compassion and fantasy in the narrative. The essay also highlights how the novelist articulates artistically his sense of reality through loosely held images, which provide to the text an evocative eloquence, and relates it to the post-modernistic tendencies of writing.

Sanjay Kumar in his perceptive critical essay ideates that Indian feminist fiction today has broadened its vision and illustrates how various women fiction writers show this transcendence through their writings. Dr. Kumar gives an exegesis of the works of major women writers, *viz.* Arundhati Roy, Jhumpa Lahiri and Manju Kapur and asseverates that their canvas also delineates the basic human predicament where what matters more than feministic fulminations is the dilemma of choice, struggle and an existential void.

Devika in her paper has made a close examination of Jhumpa Lahiri's award-winning book *Interpreter of Maladies*. She considers Lahiri's stories free from male-female bias and treats them as a depiction of characteristic experiences of Indians living in an alien land.

Shubha Mishra, in her short and concise paper, throws light on the borrowed existence of immigrants in a foreign land as delineated by Jhumpa Lahiri in her two works. Shubha is of the opinion that Lahiri's characters are her own prototypes who ocsillate between ethnicity and exoticism.

Sushila Rathore in her study of Jhumpa Lahiri, brings to the fore the anguish and strife of a *dis*placed Indian woman, who confronts her diasporic destiny in the glittering though alienated land of America. The paper focuses on the grit and determination of Ashima, who combats her predicament despite remaining committed to her cultural and traditional moorings.

Pushpa Lata in her critique of Manju Kapur's *Difficult Daughters*, explores how Virmati, the pivotal figure in the novel, fails in her bid to emancipate herself from the straining clutches of incarcerating patriarchy. The paper traces the protagonist's journey from a semblance of clarity to utter chaos and confusion.

Ashok Kumar in his thought-provoking essay throws light on Manju Kapur's *A Married Woman*. He argues how women can preserve their feminine status and maintain their individuality by entering into a relationship with their own community. The essay also points out women's revenge on men without disturbing their marital status.

Geetha B. traces magical realism in the debut novel *The Last Song of Dusk* by Sidhharth Shanghvi. Her paper considers this novel as a song of dawn that symbolizes different facets of love and friendship with exquisite details and lyrical quality of prose having sublime approach.

Binod Mishra makes a close examination of Anita Nair's *Ladies Coupe* and traces the yearning for self as the root cause of human beings' predicament. The ignorance of self leads to anxiety and sorrow but the realization to attain it can provide a new meaning. Mishra opines that the key to all conflicts and contortions lies in reconciling the adversities with something one can call one's own and nothing can be more refurbishing than resurrecting our self.

S.S. Kanade in his insightful paper considers 'bed as battle-field' in Shobhaa De's *Starry Nights*. He is of the view that De's novels are the documents of sex; the *summum bonum* of life and the negation of it may have disastrous results.

Swarnalatha explores philosophical echoes and eschatological experiences in Manil Suri's *The Death of Vishnu*. She strongly supports the ideology that love is the only remedy for all sorts of tensions either external or internal.

Shivika Verma attempts to project Shobha De as a feminist who fights for the equality of women in a dogmatic, patriarchic Indian society. Ms. Verma shows how De articulates her rebellion much in consonance with the views of some noted feminists like Virginia Woolf, Simon de Beauvoir etc., through a bold projection of their quintessentially explosive and expressive heroines.

Rashmi Bajaj and Aparana Batra in their insightful paper trace the ongoing transition in female psyche in the present-day Indian women poets writing in English. The duo examines many eminent women poets and portray the waves rising in their writings.

In his elaborate article, focusing on Arundhati's *The God of Small Things*, Umed Singh perceptively highlights how both in manner and matter the novel epitomizes Indian sense and sensibility. The critic observes how the novelist asserts through her novel, her artistic independence shattering all linguistic orthodoxies denouncing thereby the hegemonies pertaining to caste, creed, nation and gender.

P.S. Ramana in his scholarly paper closely examines the prevalent critical theory in the interpretation of literature by post-colonial or marginalized writers. He rues the continual hegemonic dominance of the western critical canon and stresses the need to concentrate on the 'book in the language' than 'the language in the book' in order to reappropriate the whole import of the meaning employed in a given text.

We are thankful to all our contributors whose willing co-operation ennobled us in our endeavour. Our special thanks are also registered to our erudite teachers who kept us egging on our mission. We are also indebted to our savant colleagues who gave their sound suggestions from time to time in editing this anthology. Narendra Saini and Ashok Jitawat do deserve a special mention for typing the manuscript patiently. We owe our deep sense of gratitude to Dr. K.R. Gupta, Chairman of Atlantic Publishers and Distributors, who agreed to publish this anthology well in time despite his busy schedule. His faith in us will go a long way in the fruition of our further ventures. His prompt correspondences and his timely advice have helped this book see the light of the day.

Binod Mishra
Sanjay Kumar
—Editors

Contents

1

The Clash of Social Identities in the Post-colonial Indian English Novel: A Study of Bhabani Bhattacharya's *So Many Hungers!**

K.C. MISHRA

So Many Hungers! & The Question of the Post-colonial Tag For It

The post-colonial tag for Bhabani Bhattacharya's first novel *So Many Hungers!* is obvious first because historically the date of the publication of the novel in 1947 October followed the historic winning of Indian Independence in August 1947. The next significant reason is that the theme of the novel is the suffering of the famine-stricken millions of Indians who were deliberately rendered intense under a diabolic colonial rule that knew only to its selfish interests at the exploitation and neglect of the victims who were made to go starving for days before meeting untimely death. This is how the novel deals with the ugliest aspect of the cruel colonial British power as it cared little about the genuine welfare needs of its subject people in India. The third important consideration to use this post-colonial tag for this novel is that the novelist, himself a colonized sufferer, provides an authentic account of experiencing suffering bearing proper and spontaneous sympathies for the famine-victims while spewing venom and fire at the oppressor. In condemnation of the inhuman acts of savage and criminal ignorance of the woes and plights of the

*This Paper was presented at the U.G.C. – National Seminar held on 23-24 Jan., 2005 at Mahila Maha Vidyalaya, Kidwai Nagar, Kanpur (U.P.).

native Indians by the Britishers, the novelist arouses the hatred and disapproval of the humanity of all times against all the nasty ways of colonial oppression. The next important consideration to attract for the novel the post-colonial tag is that the novelist provides a vision and blueprint of a plan of rehabilitation, accommodation and development without which, on getting independence an erstwhile colony would not know how to manage its own affairs. Significantly enough, the novel sells the dream of Freedom, talks of what free India would have on offer to its people, discusses how ruthlessly the struggle for freedom in India is crushed and how leadership in India shows its grit and anti-colonial determination to oust the exploiting foreign rule, describes how nation-wide support is ever on the rise once Gandhi or Nehru are sending out messages of mass-participation in the Satyagraha movement against the British Raj. Ashish Nandy (as in Leela Gandhi 2001) compares Gandhi's role in India's struggle for freedom with Fanon's activities in Algeria and considers Gandhi as an anti-colonial activist of high order. As an anti-colonialist thinker and activist Gandhi's visualizing the need to free India and his vision of the free India are important matters that have been taken up in Bhattacharya's *So Many Hungers*! Besides this, the novel also symbolically deals with the trauma and tragedy of India's partition in the raps and abortion of Kajoli in the hands of the foreign soldier (Mishra 2003) and this very brute force in its ugly display is exposed by Bhattacharya to stress on the Englishman's lack of proper human culture. However, to reduce the antipathy of the situation, the soldier's sending Kajoli for treatment to the hospital has been reported. Bhattacharya suggests how war makes rapist brute of an essential human being and there the attention is drawn to the inhuman atmosphere in which soldiers are made to stay and work away from their own lands and own people. War as a colonial-imperial tool has been condemned in the novel.

In dealing with the disappearance of Samarendra's second son Kunal in Italy during the war period, the novelist has used the allusion of the disappearance of Subhash Chandra Bose

(Mishra 2003). Through the colonial British power's mysterious silence to the utter disregard of the anxiety and concern of an entire subject nation on the issue of Bose's disappearance, Bhattacharya digs up the callousness of the colonial regime in matters of a whole people's deep regard and interest about their family member or their national hero.

It is worthwhile to read *So Many Hungers*! as a "powerful post-colonial text" (Mishra 2003). It is interesting in this context to see how colonialism as a base as well as debasing ideology has inflicted damage on the native Indian culture, society and family relationships. The dangerous tentacles of colonialism have reached the individuals and fuelled in them the aspirations to amass wealth while disregarding the needs of the fellow neighbours in the society. In these identities of various individuals an individual level has undergone unpredictable and even regrettable change. The Bask family that *So Many Hungers*! deals with has for its purposes Devata who stands for Gandhian ways of life and high Indian cultural values. It depicts Samerandra, Devata's son and Rahoul's father, as a greedy and unscrupulous fellow. He has the corruption and unfair wealth-accumulation spirit as a man working to see his gains to the utter disregard of what his father is doing to strengthen the movement for India's freedom. Rahoul's determination to follow Devata is indicative of how youth is fired with the zeal of patriotism after receiving high education even though initial signs were there that the lure of power, prestige, position and reward under the colonial rule would make them collaborators in the expansionist colonialist imperialist project. Rahoul experimenting on the Death-ray would otherwise have ended up in strengthening the colonial might as the possessor of the powerful death-ray. Bhattacharya through Rahoul's example has tried to show the misdirection of youth energy under the colonial powers than invest on death rather that on life. Misuse of scientific research for spreading the empire under colonial rule killing rather than saving is their goal. Power, dictation, possession, exploitation etc. happen to be the colonialist's strategies to help perpetuate the ends of colonialism-imperialism. Not famine, but death and war had attracted the psyche of the British rulers in India. *So Many Hungers*! in a subtle way bears a comment on how colonial criminality of intention and action is basically guided by deliberately misplaced priorities. The novel tries to show how representatives of the Western / European / British culture were actually demonstrating through their actions that essentially they were savages and brutes and despite their much-hyped "civilizing" mission they were an uncultured, uncivilized people. In real terms their kind of ideology and self-oriented self-benefiting biased administrative provisions present them as an ugly people who are inhuman in every consideration.

Portrayal of Characters and the Technique of Creating Social Identities for Post-colonial Situations

The contrast that Bhattacharya creates in terms of characters and the social identities they enjoy vis a vis their various social roles, responsibilities and activities happens to be a unique means by which he suggests what is desirable, what is preferable and what is ideal against what is to be despised, discouraged and discarded. This is an indirect, but powerful way of telling a people as to how carefully and with due calculation of pros and cons involved in the situation they have to choose from among alternatives available such that the goals they cherish and challenges they confront in achieving these goals would be appropriately taken care of. Himself a student of history, Bhattacharya as a Gandhian thinker with a strong conviction that literature should have a definite social purpose is very deeply aware that freedom in being available to his countrymen is going to be both a rich opportunity and strong challenge at one and the same time. In adequate conscious preparedness to face the same could be one historic blunder to avoid which—Bhattacharya here seems to be greatly responsible in his discharge of the writer's duty—literature must make ample use of the immediate reality for its stuff to educate the people in the don'ts they must avoid and do's they must follow. Journalistic treatment of matter and propagandistic presentation which are negative charges against Bhattacharya here in the light of the present line of understanding his work appear to be virtues which the novelist consciously practises to do his fellow countrymen a real and definite good service. The characters in Bhattacharya's hands have a free and unfettered growth. The necessity to follow the social roles to play out, which various characters have been conceived is important as the social identity of individual characters develops on lines of the expectations which their roles conform to in various social situations. The acceptability of the characters is largely a case of the social expectations as these tend to be fulfilled or frustrated through various decisions and actions that these characters take.

The expectations in relation to a society and in case of a given individual are mostly roles-specific or duty-conforming and these notions happen to be culturally determined. The culture question in dealing with the formation, change or fixity of the social identities of the characters is hence very important in our study of literature. In context of post-colonial literature this culture question needs to be studied very carefully because a post-colonial society has at least two parallel running cultures the native culture of the colonized and the culture the colonialist has deliberately decided to bring into existence for certain planned effects through its "civilizing" projects and its educational establishments. Here it is important to remember how for its own use the British colonial might has variously labelled Indian culture to be that of a barbaric people. Gandhi in his understanding of the motive of the colonial maligning of the native Indian culture and his emphasis on the need to recognize the strengths of our own tradition and our past stresses on working towards a knit-into- one world-family project has worked out the very essential nature of our individual and collective identities in the post-colonial era in his recognition of the role of nonviolent character of the nations new world which needed to see the results of co-existence from out of a healthy and sustained dialogue and cooperation. The colonial civilizing mission as understood in the post-independence era in India and elsewhere in the ex-colonies has been seen as a biased project meant to establish the superiority of the colonial master's culture to the disadvantage and disregard of the native culture of the colonized Bhabani Bhattacharya in his *So Many Hungers*! has tried to restore the Indian traditional culture in lines suggested by Gandhi in which he agreed with the latter in spirit that non-violent character of the people and the nation holds the key to the prospects of life and prosperity in the post-colonial phase. Social identities accordingly have been conceived for characters with whom the novel *So Many Hungers*! has been peopled as a result of which the plot of the novel so powerfully emerges as eminently suited to deal with a post-colonial context.

The clash of social identities in *So Many Hungers*!

Bhattacharya in *So Many Hungers*! has moved from the world to India under the British rule to India's freedom movement to its impact in the Baruni village and again to the two families of Devesh Basu and Kajoli living in that village. From World War II, to India's partition and India's winning Independence, to rural India's dream of transformation the novel makes significant references from individual determination to collective cooperation in the project of fighting the oppressive forces of colonialism the discussion ranges across the pages of the novel. The children's education, the women's active participation in the struggle for India's freedom, the youth supporting the Gandhian method of non-violent resistance to the unjustified foreign-rule etc. are a few important aspects with which Bhattacharya very ably deals to lend his novel the grand sweep of ideas that a nation preparing to unchain itself from the foreign yoke very definitely needs. Parallel references to sufferings under the cruel and exploiting foreign rulers and to changes a happier time would bring on India getting freedom are meant in the context of the novel to suggest why the India after August 'will not be' the India of before. Clearly throughout the novelist has concentrated on how hope of a new society coming into birth is definitely taking shape with the unfolding events. The novelist alongside is stressing the changes in the individual ways of the people in the new society without which the achievement of independence would be of no use.

The change of heart principle of Gandhi in matters of handling the delicate job of equitable distribution of the nation's resources on lines of commendable social justice is a prescription that is well in line with Indian culture and Gandhian philosophy of non-violent social transformation. Such a well-advised approach follows the line of Gandhian, anti-colonial non-violent measures because a new society based on non-violence would see mutual respect of individual as well as collective needs of the people essentially as a thing of cooperation out of which everybody is to benefit while neither offending nor hurting any one's tender feelings. The trusteeship approach to management of the nation's accumulating fortunes as envisaged in the Gandhian scheme is to allow conscientious and moral custodianship over vast sums, which honesty and love as aiding factors would take care of when the grand dream of collective prosperity is to be addressed. In this new social character of a new India about which Gandhi's freedom thought were aligned there one could see how Gandhi was keen not only to free the land-mass geographically politically referred to as India but also to free the Indian people from the mental slavery to which the colonial systems of administration and education have conditioned the Indians. Amartya Sen, the Nobel laureate has in recent years talked about the powerful positive links between freedom and development. Gandhi probably was aware that prosperity of a newly free people depended on how they decided to use freedom and on how their character as a free people came to be gradually more and more clearly expressed. There in the Gandhian scheme of development administration was recognized as something undeniably very significant. Education in the scheme of Gandhi in the true Indian traditional sense was the means to freedom *(=sa vidya ya vimuktaye)*—political, social and economic. It was to pave the path clear to understanding, amity, cooperation depending on honesty of purpose, transparency of procedures of social transactions, and keen and sincere commitment to the cause of general well-being of all. It was to link the vyakti with the *viswa* along the principle of conscientious action in every sphere of mutual interaction.

This in sum was Gandhi's ideal free citizen in his much talked about *Ram-Rajya*, an individual of strong moral conscience and true free thinking with promptness of decision and bold and honest action.

Bhabani Bhattacharya in his *So Many Hungers*! has created Samarendra Basu in the mould of a colonized Indian who seeks his fortunes only in active support to and servile collaboration with the colonizer. He is depicted as one without any proper considerations of patriotism, fellow feeling and sacrifice. He is utterly selfish, highly corrupt, incorrigibly money-minded and a doggish follower of the plan of oppression and grand executor of such plans carved out by the colonialists. His double-dealing, his mammon-worship, his love of the life of money and power, his disrespect for women (=his lechery) etc. are important aspects that make Bhattacharya look upon him as the detestable degraded fellow that he is. In his portrayal in the novel and in the lack of reader's sympathy for him Bhattacharya suggests that such enemies of the country and the people are not going to be the fit citizens of the new India when freedom is achieved. In his position as a moneyed businessman, a social worker of standing (till his real self is not exposed) besides his links with the administration (which make him appreciate and work for proliferating ills and evils), Bhattacharya suggests that free India's businessmen, social workers and reformers and men in liaison with the government and administration should have a character different from Samarendra. The ilk's of Samarendra, by implication, are only to perpetuate serfdom under the base colonial masters. In the rejection of Samarendra, Bhattacharya rejects the way of development of the personality of Samarendra and that of his social identity. His rejection entails his thorough dismissal of the western colonialist culture, which is anti-human and inhuman in every conceivable way.

Rahoul is the son of Samarendra Basu and the grandson of Devesh Basu. He is the elder brother of Kunal who goes missing in Italy after his joining World War II as a soldier. He is a D.Sc. from Cambridge University and an astrophysicist in Calcutta University. He is a young man with clear nationalistic leanings. He is close to discovering the Death-ray, but his decision to join the people to fight for freedom makes him renounce prestige, power, position and pelf in reward of something remarkable. His doing this under his grandfather's Gandhian ideas is indicative of how love of freedom of the country and respect for the country in the youth had led them to do great sacrifices of their career and future in outward materialistic terms. He is inspired when Nehru's Gorakhpur Jail statements at his trial stir the country. He seeks the advice from his grandfather in Dehradun Central Jail and becomes an active worker in the Quit India Movement. His work at the Relief Centre where he feeds the destitutes of the Famine-1943 the very morning of his arrest shows his service-mindedness, his commitment to a career of social work and above all his voluntary participation in the struggle for freedom. At the prison gate he is joined by other prisoners in their singing Tagore's memorable lines—"The more they tighten the chains, the more the chains loosen." The novel closing virtually with Rahoul associating with all sections of men seeking voluntary imprisonment is assertion of Bhattacharya's characteristic Gandhian faith in the youth as he accepts others and is accepted by others in turn, making the fact of union hope inspiring as far as the struggle for India's freedom is concerned.

In Rahoul's character as a young scientist Bhattacharya appears to be suggesting that education and research degrees need to be properly soaked with a spirit of patriotism, nationalism and freedom and an obvious preparedness for dedicated social service with clear-cut emphasis on the collective goals of freedom, food and general happiness. Gandhian emphasis on education for freedom and for nationalism stands filtered out here in Rahoul's example. Rahoul is the Scientist who knows not to sell his freedom in his research on the Death-ray and it is important that Bhattacharya recommends his social role as a young scientist. This is against his father's desire—Samarendra Basu who is proud of his son Rahoul's D.Sc. degree and wants him to occupy the highest post of Technical Adviser in New-Delhi.

The social identity/recognition of Rahoul as a Scientist is much in conformity with his role he plays in the novel—as a committed nationalist and Gandhian servant of the people. Had he been a tool in the hands of the colonial rulers, his education would have been condemned as having produced in him a cultural-opposite from the Indian point of view—he should have been bound (=in bondage to colonial masters) and not a seeker of freedom. In his choice of the path of the freedom fighters, he could overcome the temptation that otherwise he might have been a prey to.

Devesh Basu, Samarendra's fathers and Rahoul and Kunal's grandfather, also the grandfather of Kajoli (whose mother was his adopted daughter), is portrayed in the novel as the Gandhi of the Baruni village. He lives a simple life, follows Gandhi's preaching, arouses the spirit of nationalism, patriotism, service, understanding and cooperation among the people, teacher, small children and his example accounts for his popularity as Devata. His adoption of Kajoli's family after her father and brother Kanu were sent to prison under charges of participating in the Civil Disobedience is an example of his rich generosity and large-heartedness. His example fails to move his son Samarendra, but his influence on Rahoul proves to be of definite significance. His arrest and imprisonment in Dehradun Jail are instances that flare up the sentiments of the masses and the people start courting voluntary arrest in great numbers. Bhattacharya in creating the character of Devata has invested carefully so that the social identity of Devesh Basu has become a powerful tool to work out the ends of Gandhian Satyagraha. His fast unto death at Dehradun Jail as a piece of news *is* able to change Kajoli's decision—she rejects the offer of the betel woman (Jackal-woman) and resolves not to be a prostitute, she instead decides to earn an humble and simple living as a newspaper hawker. Devata as a role model for volunteers of the Quit India Movement is a fit social worker and freedom activist and his social identity as a Gandhian worker earns him the respect and admiration of the common people cast in the mould of Gandhi and expected to inspire the masses for effective participation in the struggle for freedom, Devesh Basu is able to take Gandhi's message to the people and enlist their support and active co-operation in the Quit India Movement. His call to 'Be Strong, Be True and Be Deathless' sends out the inspiring message to get over weakness, give up falsehood and acquire longevity across eternity. The call carries his basic philosophy of life—to be strong, to be true and to be deathless i.e. to be strong enough so as to be true because by being strong as well as true can one acquire lasting reputation thereby truly defying death. In other words Devesh Basu saw in Truth the strength with which even Death could be overcome or approached without fear. His depiction as a *Satyagrahi Karmyogi and Nirbhik Mukti-Sangrami* is Bhattacharya's sincere tributes to Gandhi and Gandhians alike. As a staunch follower of Gandhi, Bhattacharya greatly recommends the role of Devesh Basu and supports his social identity.

In Kajoli's character Bhattacharya has drawn the portrait of suffering, sympathy and sacrifice. Kajoli is a victim of the 1943 Bengal Famine and a powerful representative of the starving and suffering people. We meet her as a girl of 16 whose father and elder brother Kanu are sent to jail for their participation in the Civil Disobedience Movement. Her mother is adopted as daughter by Devata who starts living with them, taking with them their simple food. She grows up in the atmosphere of thinking of freedom of India. Her husband Kishore's death leaves her a widow. When the Famine strikes, she sees the great sacrifice her mother makes by giving their family-cow Mangla to the one who would need her most. She is raped by the foreign soldier and on her return from the hospital after her abortion (she was five months pregnant by the time) and recovery she decides to become a prostitute and maintain her family consisting of her mother and younger brother. Her decision to sell newspaper and make a living shows her inherent goodness and her preference for a life of simplicity. Her begging from soldiers to help her fellow sufferers and victims of the Famine shows her concern for the helpless people who look upon her as sister and mother. Kajoli in Bhattacharya's hands has emerged as an Indian woman who knows the value and virtues of sacrifice while always being bold about decisions she must be taking to help others and to save her own simple life and dignity. The social identity of Kajoli as a poor and helpless girl and yet a helpful and service-minded girl shows her as strong, true and without any fear for sacrifice of life and career which in some sense is a death. In difficult situations she has been presented, but the unique merit of her character is that she does not know how to bend or bow low. Bhattacharya seems to be suggesting through his portrayal of Kajoli's character that neither poverty nor the pressure of the unfavourable circumstances in life should ever be given—to lead a woman to compromise with the dignity of being. Further, by being determined to follow a life of simplicity and full of genuine love, concern and sympathy for others while keeping prepared for adequate and just sacrifice, one—woman or man—should live a decent and successful life. The creation of Kajoli in full conformity with her social identity and role has proved to be a great artistic success on the part of Bhattacharya. In her character Bhattacharya has tried to bring up the Indian cultural values as against the Western values as are represented by lady Bare-Back.

Concluding Notes

So Many Hungers! is a post-colonial novel with an eye on the anti-colonial struggle for India's Independence from the British rule and with the other keenly focused on the post-colonial condition in which the Indian society would have to take steady decisions without which the meaning of freedom would be lost for all practical purposes. The novelist Bhabani Bhattacharya has created this great work of art with situations and characters which at one and the same stroke refer to the poor and simple masses living their lives at individual levels, to the village of Baruni and all the Indian villages for that matter which have been hit hard by the cruelty of the colonial rule, to the city of Calcutta where a culture of heartlessness has very definitely come to exist which needs to be properly corrected in Calcutta and in all metropolitan city centres that are coming into being in India because, without adequate concern, sympathy, fellow-feeling and sharing of sufferings and resources, it is impossible to conceive of a world of living human beings—the colonial culture of aloofness and alienation need to be properly corrected such that life in the post-colonial new order should be possible, to a war-free world where love and interest in others ensures a life of comfort for all. Thus

Bhattacharya has perfectly realized the nature of things that the post-colonial situation in India would confront. Accordingly, he has laid in the context of *So Many Hungers*! appropriate stress on the necessity of clean and effective leadership, corruption-free business houses which would know the service-spirit embedded in the job of social transaction, daring and freedom-loving men, women and young people who need to give their education and research to the task of sustaining and promoting the prospects of life and who would fight the forces of death in every way. Since colonial culture of corruption, exploitation, plunder, cruelty and lack of moral responsibility in every sphere has been behind the 1943 Bengal Famine becoming such killing and catastrophic, Bhattacharya has been categorical in his enlightened stress, that India 'after August' in order not to be the India 'of Before' would have to shun this base and inhuman alien culture of colonialism-imperialism.

Hence, the post-colonial world instead of carrying forward the savage culture of detested colonial violence need to adopt the enlightened post-colonial Gandhian/Indian culture of non-violence. As such, the global necessity in the post-colonial new order is definitely of co-operation, concern and consideration, and social identities in their shaping must be guided by all such new set of requirements based on love for all and cruelty towards none. *So Many Hungers*! is indeed a "Giant Step" by an Indian English novelist who has intelligently probed colonial question and insightfully established the application value of Gandhian ways for the practical life situations in the post-colonial world.

Writing in English, Bhattacharya has made the sweep of his appeal the widest that could be possible. Thus, towards the commitment of his art to be giving to tangible social purpose, the present novel is a resounding success. The novel asserts that the post-colonial world is to cater to really "so many hungers" together. Since the challenge posed in this is quite of an astounding order, the need to create appropriate social identities remains the biggest task in the post-colonial situation everywhere. *So Many Hungers*! through the clash of social identities has tried to show what is the need and how conscious efforts could answer it. If the choice is between the colonial violent culture and the post-colonial nonviolent culture, the world has to decide which way to go if peaceful co-existence for progress and prosperity is definitely to ensue.

REFERENCES

1. Bhabani Bhattacharya, *So Many Hungers!*, Bombay: Hind Kitab, 1947.
2. Hari Mohan Prasad, *Response:* Recent Revelations of Indian Fiction in English, Bareily: PBD, 1983.
3. K.C. Mishra, Bhabani *Bhattacharya's So Many Hungers*! as a Post-colonial Text, Paper presented at the Utkal University Ist world conference on Post-Colonialism and Annual convention of Indian Association for the Study of Contemporary Literatures (IASCL), 2003 held on 30-31 Jan., 2003 at Vanivihar, Bhubaneswar, Orissa.
4. K.K. Sharma, *Bhabani Bhattacharya: His Vision and Themes*, New Delhi: Abhinav, 1979.
5. Kh. Kunjo Singh, *The Fiction of Bhabani Bhattacharya*, New Delhi: Atlantic, 2002.
6. Leela Gandhi, *Post-Colonialism*, New Delhi: Oxford, 2002.
7. M.K. Naik, *Perspectives on Indian Fiction in English*, New Delhi: Abhinav, 1985.
8. M.K. Naik, *Aspects of Indian Writing in English*, New Delhi: Macmillan (Reprinted), 1999.
9. M.S. Nagrajan, N. Ekambaran and A. Natarajan (ed.), *Essays in Criticism on Indian Literature in English*, New Delhi: S. Chand, 1991.
10. Rama Jha, *Gandian Thought and Indo-Anglian Novelists*, New Delhi: Chanakya, 1985.
11. Ramesh K. Srivastava (ed.), *Colonial Consciousness in Black American, African and Indian Fiction in English*, Jalandhar: ABS, 1991.
12. Susan Sontag, *A Roland Barthes Reader*, London: Vintage, 1982.

2

Amitav Ghosh's *The Glass Palace*: A Post-colonial Novel

MANSING G. KADAM

The term 'post-colonial' is applied to the cultures affected by the imperial process or the agenda of western imperialists for cultural domination. It means 'after the beginning of colonialism', not necessarily 'after decolonization.' 'However, post-colonialism is a complex cultural process that represents the general mood of a particular period of history, as shown by ideas, beliefs or the spirit of the times. The post-colonial discourse offers different perspectives of colonialism. The rupture between colonialism and post-colonialism is an artificial one and nowadays post-colonialism has become a myth. The post-colonial identity of marginal groups, their exploitation and oppression, displacement, nostalgia, and the loss of language and culture are the predominant issues related to post-colonialism. The 'centre-periphery dichotomy,' resistance and subversion of the imperial centre, the colonizer and the colonized are some broad postulates related to post-colonial literature, which mainly consists of the Third World Literatures in English.

Harish Trivedi (1996: 244) refers to post-colonialism as another term of metropolitan imposition, whereas Makarand Paranjape (1996: 37) says, "real post-coloniality is not contained in the discourse of post-colonialism." But later on, he regards post-colonialism as one of the most "wanted" 'isms' in academic discourses (1998: 48). Bill Ashcroft, Gareth Griffiths and Helen Tiffin (1989: 2) use the term "to cover all the cultures affected by the imperial process from the moment of colonization to the present day. This is because there is a continuity of preoccupations throughout the historical process initiated by European aggression." Russell Jacoby (1995: 30) complains that the term 'post-colonial' has become "the latest catchall term to dazzle the academic mind." Some critics like Edward Said and Gayatri C. Spivak regard post-colonial writing as resistance to colonial hegemony. On the other hand, some like Homi K. Bhabha, Arun P. Mukherjee and Benita Parry oppose to their ideas and explore that there is no unitary quality to post-colonial writing. Post-colonial writing refers to literary creations of non-white minorities located in Britain, Canada and such other countries. These writers negate the binary of the oppressor and the oppressed or the subject and object positions and open new possibilities for culture contact. The term is largely used to refer to the body of writing known as 'Commonwealth' in which the colonial experience is the central link that defines and contains the life of the post-colonial subject. Colonialism, as we understood it, is an imposition of colonial forms on pre-colonial societies and post-colonialism is an ongoing process. It is a continuation of colonialism. The colonial encounter has been a seminal event in the history of both the West and the non-Western world, shaping culture, literature, politics, and history. The colonial ambivalence is comprised of materiality and spirituality, that is, the economy and the cultural identity.

During the last two decades of twentieth century the marginals or the peripheral cultures occupy the centre. In fact, the post-colonial literature writes back in order to compete the supremacy of the British literature, and its tastes and values. In today's global context, all cultures are mixed and no one culture can claim for its distinctiveness. Globalization is now on everybody's lips, but some crucial issues related to it are the globalization of human heart beyond the boundaries of the nations and the practice of cross-cultural and trans-civilizational dialogue.

The novel of colonial consciousness, as said by Om P. Juneja (1995: 24), "foregrounds that writing is a socially symbolic act; that the novelist of this genre nativizes the English language by subversion; that he either hybridizes a literary form or uses it with a dichromatic lens of a bicultural/multicultural perspective." Bakhtin also asserts that culture is the site of social struggle, which is located in language. Salman Rushdie, too, believes that cultural regeneration can be achieved through the desalination of language. In view of Ashcroft, Griffiths and Tiffin (1989: 83), the post-colonial world examines the legacy of imperial colonialism and the post-colonial novel becomes a major cultural instrument. They identify three common areas of all post-colonial writings as:

> The silencing and marginalizing of the post-colonial voice by the imperial centre; the abrogation of this imperial centre within the text: and the active appropriation of the language and culture of that centre.

Indian Writing in English reveals the dialectics of imperialism in its journey from the periphery to the centre and echoes a deep core of neocolonialism based on power politics. The stalwarts like Salman Rushdie, Khushwant Singh, Mukul Kesavan, Vikram Chandra, Shashi Tharoor, Amitav Ghosh and the like are writing in a post-colonial space, using novel as a means of cultural representation. These writers of the 1980s, as said by Jasbir Jain (2000: 32-33) "aimed at enhancing an Indian cultural identity, and projecting Indian cultural and historical heritage to enable an assertion of the Indian self."

The Indian Novel in English is treated as the 'Third World Novel' and according to Aijaz Ahmad (1994: 124), it refers to "representations of colonialism, nationhood, post-coloniality, the typology of rulers, their powers, corruptions, and so forth." He sees the novel engaged in post-colonial consciousness but the study of the thematic range indicates that the novel also attempts to universalize humanistic gesture, for human nature and social relationships are as important as the interplay of power and national relationships. Amitav Ghosh is one of the foremost Indian diasporic writers in modern Indian English writing who believes in what Ahmad has said. His reputation rests on *The Circle of Reason* (1986), *The Shadow Lines* (1988), *In An Antique Land* (1992), *The Calcutta*

Chromosome: A *Novel of Fevers, Delirium and Discovery* (1996), *The Glass Palace (2000),* the non-fiction *The Imam and the Indian* (2002) and *the travelogues Countdown* (1998) and *Dancing in Cambodia, At Large in Burma* (1998). As a post-colonial writer, he uses English as an Englishman, stays in America, and frequently visits his hometown Kolkata in India. He is the New York-based serious novelist and anthropologist, writing with a post-colonial consciousness. He is certain of his human and historical insights. He belongs to the nation that was once conquered and ruled by Imperial Britain. It is intended in this paper to read Ghosh's latest novel *The Glass Palace* in the post-colonial context, focusing on his vision of globalization, not only of economic, mercantile but also of culture and human gesture. He attempts to plumb the depths of human experience in this fictionalized historical narrative through the exploration of lives and concerns of different nationalities.

The Glass Palace won the 2001 Frankfurt e-book Award of fifty thousand dollars Grand Prize for Fiction. It was also named the Eurasia regional winner for the 2001 Commonwealth Writers Prize on March 12, 2001. But Ghosh withdrew it from the competition on account of his objections to the nomenclature "Commonwealth Literature," as it is related to a disputed aspect of the past. In a letter written to Sandra Vince on 18 March 2001, Ghosh writes, "As grouping of nations collected from the remains of the British Empire, the Commonwealth serves as an umbrella forum in global politics. As a literary or cultural grouping, however, it seems to me that "the Commonwealth" can only be a misnomer so long as it excludes the many languages that sustain the cultural and literary lives of these countries." This evinces his awareness of the past history of his own country and how past is to be remembered is at the core *The Glass Palace.* His writing in a post-colonial space combats the unequal power structures. As the post-colonial-postmodern writer, Ghosh "is one who sees," as said by Brinda Bose (2003: 15), *"history as that trajectory of events that causes dislocations, disjunctions, movements and migrations, eventually replacing solid markers with shadow lines, destabilizing our notions of the past in the reverberations of the present."*

In his earlier canonical novel, *The Shadow Lines,* Ghosh deals with the issues of identity vs. nationhood, self vs. nation, and the representation of history and concludes that all borders are imaginary constraints. He dismantles history, the frontiers of nationality, culture and language in *The Shadow Lines* and *In An Antique Land.* N. Bagchi (1993: 187) rightly observes, "Amitav Ghosh's *The Shadow Lines* is a manifestation of the desire to validate the post-colonial experience and to attempt a reconstruction of "public history." Salman Rushdie's *Midnight's Children* (1981) and Tharoor's *The Great Indian Novel* (1989) politicize and make fusion of personal and public history. *The Glass Palace* treats several issues that intersect on the terrain of a post-colonial nation-state through three generations and three nations over a period of two centuries. It renders the enmeshed histories of Burma, Malaysia and India in the British regime. Ghosh debunks the national, political and geographic boundaries and supports his own idea that nationalism is an imaginative construct. While looking at The *Glass Palace* through post-colonial lens, Jayita Sengupta (2002: 26) observes, "Ghosh's rendering of British colonialism and its aftermath in the three countries is an interplay of fact and fiction in an illusory place of imagination to create an awareness of the experiential reality of the post-colonial worlds." It offers us a picture of life in the former colonies of the Empire as if it is a multi-national cultural bazaar. As observed by Ranjita Basu (1997: 160), "*History is a brooding presence in Ghosh's books, almost a living entity able to shape the lives of his characters.*" The novel projects the political and cultural complexities through his concepts of nationalism, imperialism, and the subjugation of gender, class, and caste. He believes in transgression of the frontiers of nationality, and for him, nationalism seems to be an illusion and a force of violence and destruction. He has presented a unique rendition of history in fiction from the international perspective and writes imaginatively about the process of colonization in India, Burma and Malaya. In an interview with Tehelka.com

(7th August 2000), Ghosh says about his transformative experience:

> Writing this book has completely transformed me as a person and as a novelist. Very few novelists get that experience. It was not just the vastness of the material, or the hundreds of different voices, or that for me writing this book was unlike anything I, or other writers I know, had written before. It was what I saw and what I began to recognize while writing this...you know, it changed my understanding of history.

History, fiction and travelogue combine into a unified whole into The *Glass Palace* which is a novel of memory and movement. The historical and personal blend into a perfect harmony in it. Ghosh (2000: 62) himself says, *"It's coming together of the many themes of my earlier novels. Writing this novel was like fighting a war."* Furthermore, he says that he attempts in it *"to humanize history, to make it a part of the existential grammar of the living."* Like the spectacular seven-coloured rainbow, the novel is structured into seven parts displaying various shades of human personality of several nationalities like King Thebaw and his queen, Rajkumar and Dolly, Beni Prasad Dey and Uma, Saya John, Arjun, Dinu, and many more colonized victims. Here is an excerpt from the blurb:

> Through the intertwining stories of Dolly and Rajkumar, the history of the twentieth century is told across the three generations, spread over the interlined parts of the British Empire: Burma, with its conflicting undercurrents of discontent; Malaya, with its vast rubber plantations; and India, amid growing opposition to British rule. With World War II and the terrifying Japanese juggernaut, Rajkumar's universe is once again set adrift. ...his family makes a treacherous 1000-mile trek to India. The door to Burma closes behind them, and the glittering lights of an extraordinary civilization are finally extinguished.

The novel opens with the distant noise of the 'English cannon' outside the royal palace called the "Glass Palace" in Mandalay where a coal-black *kaala* Rajkumar, the eleven-year-old Indian orphan from Bengal, is serving, in Ma Cho's tea-stall. The Burmese King Thebaw and the pregnant Queen Supayalat, the royal prisoners, are deported into exile in Ratnagiri in Maharashtra and the palace itself is on the brink of defeat after the declaration of King Thebaw's "Royal Proclamation":

> His Majesty, who is watchful that the interest of our religion and our state shall not suffer, will himself march forth ... will efface these heretics and conquer and annex their country. To uphold the religion, to uphold the national honour, to uphold the country's interests will bring about threefold good—good of our religion, good of our master and good of ourselves and will gain for us the important result of placing us on the path to the celestial regions and to Nirvana (16).

And the war began on 14 November 1885 in which the Burmese army surrendered to the British, followed by the captivity and exile of the King. The Burmese King, once a colonizer, bewails the loss of kingdom and his present confinement in Outram House in Ratnagiri. The reference to the Indian Mutiny of 1857 is a fleeting glimpse of the subjugation of India in the past. The mutiny of 1857 was a landmark for the Indian psyche. It centres on the Ghadar party. India had tried to resist the colonial yoke but it was the moment of utter defeat for the nation. The Indian Imperial army had to surrender and the heads of several soldiers were cut off after the mutiny. During the First World War, there was a macabre of dance of death as described in *Countdown* after Pokharan II. Beni Prasad Dey, the new Collector of Ratnagiri, educated at Cambridge, believes in the smug notions of the Empire and the white man's burden and submits himself to the hegemony of the Empire. Ghosh reveals the imperialist presence in India through him. King Thebaw asks him, "Did you ever think that we would live to witness the day when an Eastern country would defeat a European power?" (107). When the Collector is reluctant to permit the princess to marry the Maharashtrian coachman Mohan Sawant, Queen Supalayat rebukes him:

> We have heard so many lectures from you and your colleagues on the subject of the barbarity of the Kings of Burma and the humanity of the Angrez; we were tyrants you said, enemies of freedom, murderers. English alone understand liberty, we were told; they do not put kings and princes to death; they rule through laws. If that is so, why has King Thebaw never been brought to trial? Is it a crime to defend your country against an invader? Would the English not do the same? (150).

The Collector is defeated in arguments as well as is a failure at domestic front. But this agent of colonizers meets his tragic death while rowing out in the sea and the King Thebaw spots Dey's drowning through his binoculars. Towards the end, King Thebaw dies of heart attack in exile, and the history of the last Burmese King is lost and forgotten with the passage of time. Life, death, success and failure come into full circle. Ira Pande (July 2000) says, "*What makes the tragedy of human life bearable is a graceful acceptance of the inevitability of pain and suffering.*"

In the middle part, Ghosh has incorporated too much history in the novel. He displays the role of the British Indian Army fighting against the Japanese in Malaysia during the Second World War. He handles the clash of loyalties via *Uma* Dey's nephew, Arjun Roy, his batman Kishan and Hardayal Singh in 1/1 Jat Light Infantry. Some students and the Congress leaders ask Arjun, "*From whom are you defending us? From ourselves? From other Indians? It's your masters from whom the country needs to be defended" (288)*. Indeed these and other remarks reveal the writer's indictment against the position of a colonized subject. Like Beni Prasad Dey, Arjun Roy was also proud of the Empire. He was proud of being recruited in the regiment that had received medals such as the Victoria Cross from the Somme, two Military Crosses for putting down the Arab rebellion in Mesopotamia. He writes to Manju, "*What makes me prouder still is the thought that Hardy and I are going to be the first Indian officers in the 1/1 Jats: it seems like such a huge responsibility—as though we're representing the whole of the country!" (262)*. He regards himself as the first modern Indian who actually lives with the westerners not weighed down by the past.

Ghosh in "The Anglophone Empire" (2003) says, "*I am Indian, and my history has been shaped as much by the institutions of this empire as a long tradition of struggle against them.*" Another theme that emerges as equally important is that of resistance to imperialism. Some of the Indians involved in the rebellion were erstwhile soldiers of the empire who had been seized by the nihilistic ideas. It is Hardayal Singh who makes Arjun conscious about Britishers' prejudice, distrust and suspicion about Indians and their notion of sovereignty. When their long-awaited mobilization orders came, Hardayal remembered the inscription in Chetwode Hall at the Military Academy in Dehradun and resisted to the idea of the country in these words:

> Where is this country? The fact is that you and I don't have a country—so where is this place whose safety, honour and welfare are to come first, always and every time? (330).

The central dilemma is the conflict in loyalty of the Indian National Army soldiers. The pamphlet signed by Amreek Singh says, "*Brothers, ask yourselves what you are fighting for and why you are here: do you really wish to sacrifice your lives for an Empire that has kept your country in slavery for two hundred years?*" (391). Arjun is torn between sympathy, revulsion, and fear. He faces a moral crisis and gets a setback. He is caught into two worlds and tells Dinu, "*We rebelled against an Empire that shaped everything in our lives.... We cannot destroy it without destroying ourselves*" (518). He faces a dilemma about joining the rebels in the Indian National Army while fighting for the British in Burma. Hardayal joins the Indian Independence League and fights for Japanese. Arjun, then, realizes that the Empire has been dead, as "*he knew this because he had felt it die within himself, where it had held its strongest dominion*" (441). Along with Hardy, he joins the Indian Independence League; becomes the voice of resistance against the British Empire and registers a protest against it. What characterizes his attitude is a curious blend of loyalty to the British and an awareness of the ills of subjection. He grapples with the question of India's subjugation. For him, the feeling of patriotism and loyalty to the Empire become antithetical to one another. Arjun felt for a while that hope, lay with the British but "finally protests the Empire to guard the interests of the natives." Towards the end, the loyalty conflict in Arjun is over, he dies and seeks his own identity in the signifying process of history.

Uma Dey's indignation about the Empire is due to its "racialism, rule through aggression and conquest" (294) and for being a model of the Empire for nations like Japan and Germany. After her husband's death, she goes on the Continental tour, yet the Indian nationalist cause gives her what Edward Said (1991: 12) terms an almost *"aggressive sense of nation, home, community and belonging."* She joins a non-violent movement against colonialism and goes to Mahatma Gandhi's Ashram at Wardha. Rajkumar's granddaughter Jaya in 1996 realized the role of Aung San Suu Kyi in establishing democracy in Burma or Myanmar as it is now called. Ghosh's observations on the politics of isolation and resurgence are, as Novy Kapadia (1999: 290) remarks, *"a sensitive insight into the post-colonial experiences and politics of isolation, violence and hatred."* Ghosh reveals the crises of shifting identities and blurred nationalities through the interaction of his characters. Rohini Mokashi Punekar (2003: 54) comments on repositioning borders:

> The puzzling nature of power between people and communities and nations, the constant flux in the positions of power seems to be the underlying thrust of the novel symbolized by the beautiful title *The Glass Palace* which suggests an unattainable shimmering beauty, fragility and exclusion all together.

Ghosh pinpoints the resistance to the dictatorial military rule in the post-colonial Burma through some student activists' arguments about the atrocities of dictators like Hitler and Mussolini in Dinu's photo studio called The Glass Palace in Rangoon. Besides power politics, the Indian diasporic experience in South East Asia is the focal point and Ghosh records its historical depth and its meaning in the novel. Several stories of expatriates and exiles mingle and jostle with the intersection of class, race, gender and religion in it. Rajkumar Raha who is infatuated with Dolly Sein, as beautiful as the Glass Palace itself, marries her and ventures into the rubber plantation industry as Saya John's partner. Rajkumar's lifestory is a story of struggle for survival in the colonial turmoil. As a colonized subject from Bengal, he becomes a colonizer in Burma by transporting indentured labourers from South India to other parts of the colonial world. Even, he has sexually exploited a woman worker on his plantations. Thus a former victim of the British Empire has become the victimizer. His post-colonial consciousness represents a conflict within his own self, a conflict through which he tries to step outside his colonial self, the history of the imperial phase and to approach his own past, history and reality from his present position. Rajkumar, Saya John and Matthew are engaged in the task of colonizing land and people for the sake of wealth. Rohini Mokashi Punekar (2003: 55) is right when she says that *"the line between the colonizers and colonized is blurred, even erased; colonization is seen as a continuous, ongoing process, and often reversible."* Rajkumar is the central character whose personal history is entwined with the colonial history in order to destroy and create new histories. He is projected as a prosperous teak and rubber merchant and his story of love, romance, war and Empire through three generations of his family takes place in many South Asian cities. But after the Second World War, his expanding economy collapsed, and he took shelter in Calcutta. He could no longer see himself as an Indian or Burmese, as his is a fractured or fragmented consciousness. To quote Meenakshi Mukherjee (2000: 6), *Human lives spill over national boundaries, refusing to stay contained in neat compartments. A person is remembered not as Burmese, Indian, Chinese, Malaya a or American.* She opines that the novel will remain memorable mainly for the most scathing critique of British colonialism, as the building called the 'Glass Palace' is heavily burdened with the images of loss and hope. The novel seems to be, in some sense, an elegy for the diasporic condition that is a product of history. Despite several cultures, the Indian immigrants and diasporic workers experience and yearn for global identities. All the characters confront the riddle of human existence.

The notion of unified identity implies 'unity in diversity'. An ideal writer like Ghosh believes in the co-relation of all cultures. As a cosmopolitan writer without any parochialism, he tries to explore neighbouring Asian countries in this novel where the West is a marginal presence. He discards European models and attempts to create his own. He maintains a balance between the memory of the past and the desire for a future by coming back to present. In his e-mail correspondence with Dipesh Chakrabarty who has a project of *Provincializing Europe (1998),* Ghosh (Dec. 14, 2000) writes:

> Two of my novels (*The Shadow Lines* and my most recent *The Glass Palace*) are centred on families. I know that for myself this is a way of displacing the 'nation'—I am sure that this is the case also with many Indian writers other than myself. In other words, I'd like to suggest that writing about families is one way of not writing about the nation (or other restrictively imagined collectivities). I think there is a long tradition of this, going back at least to Proust—and it is something that Jameso, Anderson (and even Bhabha) never seem to take into account.

About the epic dimension of the novel, Ghosh says to the reporter of The *Times of India* in an interview, *"It's just a family story, really, that triggered The Glass Palace, my father and my uncle, both were in Burma (now Myanmar). But then, the book ended up as something quite different. It showed me a way of living that really had a transforming impact."* Ghosh writes about families and nations to highlight the sense of dislocation. The novelist grasps the rise and fall of empires across the twentieth century and raises the question of national identity—cultural and political. Brinda Bose (2003: 30) aptly comments that The *Glass Palace "signals a dislocation in our understanding of the myth of our so-called community."* At the same time, Ghosh maps the rival geography of human heart. The human interest is predominant in this novel, under the spell of colonialism. The social chaos in Burma during the colonial days is one of its threads. Different strands of history of King Thebaw, Dolly and Rajkumar are woven dexterously in this saga of family matters. Rashmee Z. Ahmed (2001: 10) supports the argument against the imperial attitude in these words, "*The Glass Palace is nothing if not an indictment of imperial due process.*" It is a story of 'a people, a fortune, and a family and its fate,' in which Ghosh creates "a parallel, wholly fictional world" (Ghosh, 2000: 549), like Benedict Anderson's now widely used metaphor of the 'imagined communities'. Anderson (1983: 28) imagines the nation "*an imagined political community not uniquely produced by the constellation of certain objective social facts; rather the notion is thought out.*" He has discussed the idea of the 'nation' and the problematic of assigning a fixed historical space and character to nationhood, emphasizing the artificiality of national identity. Similarly, Eric Hobsbawm (1990: 143) upholds the idea that people should "identify themselves emotionally with 'their nation"' and then only nationalism gets validity. It means the idea of nation acquires an imaginative significance as it is *"the product of certain historical, regional and psychological conjunctions, and thus bound to vary across diverse communities of people"* (Moral, 2003: 140). From the post-colonial cultural perspectives, as observed by Homi Bhabha (1994: 139), the modern nation *"fills the void left in the uprooting of communities and kin, and turns that loss into the language of metaphor."* Bhabha emphasizes the point that nations are born of anti-imperialistic struggles and their identities are necessarily ambivalent. In the Indian context, the dispersal and scattering of people is the process of making of the nation. Rakhee Moral (2003: 143-44) rightly comments, *"The idea of the nation as metaphor of loss, and as being more symbolic of a unitariness than the physical entity which is society, finds elaborate figuration in the turbulence of cultural cross-overs and conflicting histories that makes up the central concern of Ghosh."* Ghosh believes in Ashis Nandy (1983: 2) who points out that colonialism *"represents a certain cultural baggage."* For him, the novel is an instrument of perception more like a lens than a mirror for the objective representation of reality. It seems that he is more interested in a sort of active moral engagement with human experience.

Ghosh describes the aspirations, defeats and disappointments of dislocated people in India, Burma, China, Malaysia and America such as King Thebaw, Queen Supayalat, Saya John, Rajkumar, Dolly, *Vma,* Alison, Dinu, Neel, Arjun, Hardayal, Kishan Singh, Jaya and Bongo. As said by Meenakshi Mukherjee (2000: 5-6), *"The story spans more than a century in the history of the subcontinent, people get involved in unexpected relationships across countries and culture, wars are fought, rebellions quelled, political and ethical issues are debated, fortunes are made and lost. The writer reports everything accurately, thoughtfully—his precision backed up by meticulous research."* Cultural hierarchies overlap in entwining of the high and low classes in spite of race, religion and class, in order to create new societies. The feminine consciousness in the novel recognizes the difference between a woman's vision and man's vision through Rajkumar-Dolly and Beni Prasad Dey and *Uma* relationships. Beni Prasad Dey's relations with *Uma* were just like the oppressor and the oppressed. For emotional relief, he needs consolation from *Uma* and not the wifely virtues. He felt that *"nothing was held in abeyance, to bargain for a woman's soul with the coin of kindness and patience" (153)*. It was *Uma's* subjection beyond decency, beyond her imagining. She could do nothing but to submit her. Rajkumar marries Dolly and has two sons, Neel and Dinu and Ilongo is Dinu's half-brother. He inhabits in the post-colonial space as a foreigner in Mandalay and is subjected to colonization. Neel marries *Uma's* niece, Manju in Calcutta and Dinu who loves Saya John's grand-daughter, Alison, marries a Burmese research scholar who wrote her dissertation on "The Glass Palace Chronicles." Dinu-Alison love affair, as shown by Rakhee Moral (2003: 150), is *"symbolic of exiles coming together, as it were, of families meeting out of a shared compulsion across disputed and dispossessed territories."* Saya John's son, Matthew marries Elsa and Alison is their daughter. These family ties come to full circle and the cultural differences are forgotten and the artificial borders are no more. However, at the economic front, after Matthew's death, a joint venture, to resist the capitalist structures and colonization is undertaken by Elsa, Alison and Ilongo in Malaysia, and at the political front, Dinu and his comrades in Rangoon have strange ideas of democracy. Ghosh refers to the imprisonment of Burmese political leader Aung San Suu Kyi. He also depicts Aung San Suu Kyi's struggle for democracy in Burma and its historical context in a travelogue *Dancing in Cambodia, At Large in Burma*. Dinu regards Kyi much greater than a politician as she succeeded in resisting the imperialist onslaught, the misrule and tyranny in Burma. He tells Jaya about the imperialists in Burma:

> They have no defence against her but to call her an imperialist...which is laughable...when in fact, it is they who invoke the old imperial laws and statutes to keep themselves in power. The truth is that they've lost and they know this...this is what makes them so desperate...the knowledge that soon they will have nowhere to hide...that it is just a matter of time before they are made to answer for all, that they have done (543).

For Dolly Sein, the past is recast in transformed patterns in Ratnagiri. Formerly, she was a slave in the erstwhile kingdom, loyal to the Burmese King Thebaw, Queen Supayalat and the princesses who were the real historical figures like Aung San Suu Kyi. She feels that the Burma she has left behind is lost to her forever and this displacement creates in her a crisis of identity. She confesses to Uma Dey:

> If I went to Burma now I would be a foreigner—they would call me a *kaala* like they do Indians—a trespasser, an outsider from across the sea. I'd find that very hard I think. I'd never be able to rid myself of the idea that I would have to leave again one day, just as I had to leave before (113).

As a colonized subject like Rajkumar, Dolly suffers from a sense of imaginary homeland in India. After spending twenty years in exile in India, she leaves for Burma with Rajkumar.

Ania Loomba in *Colonialis/Post-colonialism* (1998: 256-57) concludes:

> 'If post-colonial studies is to survive in any meaningful way, it needs to absorb itself far more deeply with the contemporary world, and with the local circumstances within which colonial institutions and ideas are being moulded into the disparate cultural and socio-economic practices which define our contemporary globality.'

Amitav Ghosh like Salman Rushdie is not an insider/outsider who talks about cultural displacement through cracked lenses; on the other hand, he is an insider. He makes us think about the relation of culture to economic and political structures in the present days of globalization. As a writer of the Indian diaspora, Ghosh wants to record its historical depth and its meaning in the world. Ahdaf Soueif (2000:5) writes, "*Ghosh is one of the most sympathetic post-colonial voices to be heard today. He looks at love and loyalty, and examines questions of Empire and responsibility, of tradition and modernity.*" Throughout the novel, the Empire expands and then retracts, fortunes are won and lost. Namrata Mahanta (2003: 54) opines, "*The novel sees Amitav Ghosh's recurrent concern with nationalism; boundaries and statehood transform into multi-leveled dilemmas.*" He presents multiple viewpoints of the dispersed people of different nationalities and makes a plea for internationalism in order to define our contemporary globality. He intends to show how the context of imperialism has changed in globalization. Like George Orwell and many other commentators, Ghosh believes that empires imprison their rulers as well as their subjects. In his hands, the novel becomes a cultural instrument for the hopes of social betterment. He negates the binary of the subject-object positions and attempts to universalize human relationships in the wake of globalization. In fact, it is his civilizing mission that is essential in the turbulent modern world.

REFERENCES

Ahmed, Rashmee Z. "Speaking in Tongues: Stones from within a Glass Place," *The Times of India*, April 12, 2001, p. 10.

Anderson, Benedict, *Imagined Communities: Reflections on the Origins and Spread of Nationalism*. London: Verso, 1991.

Aschroft, *et.al. The Empire Writes Back: Theory and Practice in Post-colonial Literatures*. New York: Routledge, 1989.

Bagachi, Nivedita, "The Process of Validation in Relation to materiality and Historical Reconstruction" in Amitav Ghosh's *The Shadow Lines. Modern Fiction Studies*, Vol. 39, No. 1, Spring 1993. pp. 187-202.

Basu, Ranjita, "The Novels of Amitav Ghosh" *London Magazine*, 37: 3&4, Aug./Sept. 1997. pp. 159-61.

Bhabha, Homi, *The location of Culture*. London: Routledge, 1994.

Bose, Brinda, (ed.) *Amitav Ghosh: Critical Perspectives*. Delhi: Pencraft, 2003.

Ghosh, Amitav, *The Anglophone Empire,* 4-7-2000.

Ghosh, Amitav, *The Circle of Reason*. London: Granta Books, 1986.

Ghosh, Amitav, *The Shadow Lines*. New Delhi: Ravi Dayal, 1988.

Ghosh, Amitav, *The Glass Palace*. New Delhi: Ravi Dayal, 2000.

Ghosh, Amitav, *In An Antique Land*. New Delhi: Ravi Dayal, 1992.

Ghosh, Amitav, *Dancing in Cambodia, At Large in Burma*. New Delhi: Ravi Dayal, 1998.

Ghosh, Amitav, *The Calcutta Chroitwsonw*. New Delhi: Ravi Dayal, 1999.

Ghosh, Amitav, *Countdown*. New Delhi: Ravi Dayal 1998.

Ghosh, Amitav. *The Imam and the Indian*. New Delhi: Ravi Dayal, 2002.

Hobsbawm, Eric, *Nations and Nationalism Since 1980*. Cambridge: Cambridge Univ. Press, 1990.

Jain, Jasbir, (ed.) "Post-coloniality, Literature and Politics," in *Contesting post-colonialisms*. Jaipur & New Delhi: Rawat Pub. 2000.

Jacoby, Russell, "Marginal Returns: The Trouble with the Post-colonial Theory," *Lingua Franca,* Sept./Oct., pp. 30-37.

Juneja, Om, *Post-Colonial Novel: Narratives of Colonial Consciousness*. New Delhi: Creative Books, 1995.

Kapadia, Novy, "The Politics of Isolation and Resurgence" in *Dancing in Cambodia, At Large in Burma," in The Novels of*

Amitav Ghosh, ed. R.K. Dhawan. New Delhi: Prestige, 1999. pp. 282-285.

Loomba, Ania, *Colonialis/Post-colonialism*. London: Routledge, 1998.

Mahanta, N.R. *History in Retrospect: Amitav Ghosh's The Glass Palace, Litcrit,* Vol. 29, No. 1, June 2003. pp. 46-54.

Moral, Rakhee, "In Time of the Breaking of Nations," *The Glass Palace* as Post-colonial Narrative, in *Amitav Ghosh: Critical Perspectives*. (ed.) Bose. Delhi: Pencraft, 2003.

Mukherjee, Meenakshi, "Of Love, War and Empire," in *Indian Review of Books,* 16 Oct. 2000.

Nandy, Ashis, *The Intimate Enemy: Loss and Recovery of Self Under Colonialism*. London: OUP, 1983.

Pande, Ira, Review of *The Glass Palace. Outlook,* India, July 2000.

Paranjape, Makarand, "Coping with Post-colonialism," *Interrogating Post-coloniahsm: Theory, Text and Context*. Ed. Harish Trivedi & Meenakshi Mukherjee, Shimala: ILAS, 1996.

Paranjape, Makarand, 'Theorising Post-colonial Difference: Culture, Nation, and Civilization.' *SPAN*. 47, October 1998.

Punekar, R. Mokashi, "Repositioning Borders: A Reading of *The Glass Palace*" Critical Practice, Vol. X, No. 1, Jan. 2003. pp. 52-58.

Rushdie, Salman, *Midnight's Children*. New York: Avon Books, 1980.

Said, Edward W., *The World, the Text and the Critic*. New Delhi: Vintage, 1991.

Sengupta, Jayita, "Ghosh's *The Glass Palace* through Post-colonial Lens," *The Quest*, Vol. 16, No. 1, June 2002, pp. 26-32.

Soueif, Ahdaf, Review of *The Glass Palace, Indian Review of Books,* Oct. 2000.

Tehelka.Com. Interview. 7th August 2000.

Tharoor, Shashi, *The Great Indian Novel*. New Delhi: Penguin Books, 1989.

Trivedi, Harish, "India and Post-colonial Discourse," *Interrogating Post-colonialism: Theory, Text and Context. 1996.*

3

Transcending Gender Parochialism in Modern Indian Feminist Fiction

SANJAY KUMAR

Feminism refers to the belief that woman should have the same social, legal, educational, religious and spiritual rights that a man in society enjoys. Emanating from the West, *feminism* is no longer an innovation even in our country with a staggering amount of literary output coming from a host of Indian women writers writing in English and raising the question of woman's emancipation in a patriarchal Indian society.

In the recent past, however, a shift in the settled feminist psyche, that has hitherto been to challenge man's attitude towards woman, has undergone a change as some of modern Indian feminist writers, like their counterparts across the world, are beginning to consider not the male but human existence and its absurdity to be the genesis of all the problems they encounter in their life.

The present paper ventures to establish how Indian feminist fiction in modern times has been attempting to break free from the circumscribing feministic vision and how the modern women fiction writers have been delineating their work in a universal and existential hue thereby transcending the parochial feministic perception.

Observed closely, it appears that the female writers writing in a spiritual squalor today believe that human beings stand alone in an incomprehensible world and confront meaninglessness in all human endeavours as the universe they inhabit, snubs them with its indifference.

In fact, confronting vacuum and void in a world that appears devoid of a meaning, like all other writers, the modern feminist writers too feel compelled to explore the intrigue that characterizes human life with all its inconsequentialities. In a world of unwholesome and fractured identities to some and these some are a large number today, and have a better perception as well, life is an arduous journey and to cope with the existential reality on everyday basis is a matter of greater concern than casting a censorious glance on their male counterpart. Indeed, the modern feminist writers are beginning to realize that all humans exist in a spiritual void and suffer from an insurmountable existential vacuum. In such a meaningless voyage, that we call life, no matter whatever be our sex, race, caste, creed, culture or nation, we are puppets who exist and perish at the whims of an invisible and inscrutable design above and beyond us. With this realization comes the feeling of commiseration not only for the exploited female but also for the exploiting male, as being a victim if a woman appears helpless and incapable, man too appears vulnerable in victimizing her. In an age of incertitude and given the psychological awareness, we are fully aware of the fact that any manifestation of strength is, in fact, a desperate attempt to masquerade our weakness of one sort or the other. Therefore, the women writers of today appear far closer to reality as they possess not a feministic but a comprehensive view of life.

One such unbiased realisation on the part of modern fiction writers can be observed in the remarks of Joyce Carol Oates who in an interview stated:

> I am very sympathetic with most of the aims of feminism, but cannot write feminist literature because it is too narrow, too limited. I am equally sympathetic with male characters as with females...an unfortunate situation, but one which I cannot help.[1]

In the Indian context, one such comprehensive vision, where the oppressed and the oppressor appear equally out of sorts, makes itself visible in Arundhati Roy's Booker winner novel *The God of Small Things*. For instance, though the feministic reaction of the author is obvious in her depiction of Pappachi who tyrannizes his wife and imposes his male superiority by beating her savagely, Arundhati, like all great authors, seeks to depict the action that eludes the apparent eye and reveals the unexpressed vulnerability of Pappachi. Though Pappachi looks callous, powerful and capable apparently, the author deftly perceives the nervous wreck that lurks behind the obviously vehement and violent person. Despite his obvious cruelty, the author concentrates on his vulnerability and loneliness as he is seen *sitting in his mahogany rocking chair all along rocking himself silently in the dark.*[2] The mood of alienation, violence and a crippled anger looms large as the author analyses Pappachi's disquieted and vulnerable psyche with poetic brilliance.

Another instance of a similar sort makes itself visible, albeit suggestively, when the author delineates her apathy towards Rahel, the female protagonist, and seems chary of colouring her agony in a feministic hue. In delineating Rahel, Arundhati does not portray the picture of a woman who has been victimized by the male dominated society around her. She unmistakably captures the mood of apathy and the matrimonial boredom as Rahel is shown to have "drifted into marriage like a passenger drifts towards an unoccupied chair in an airport lounge" (18).

Having established thus the purposelessness of such a relation, Arundhati portrays the effete matrimonial ambience against which the man and the woman attempt to orchestrate their harmony through a physical union. However, the vacuity and ennui, so inseparably a part of their mutual relations, comes to the fore even as the couple goads themselves into making love. Rahel's weary attempts to show some kind of involvement in her sexual union with Larry are betrayed as Larry feels "offended by her eyes" (19), for Rahel's eyes "behaved as though they belonged to someone else. Someone watching. Looking out of the window at the sea. At a boat in the river. Or a passer by in the mist" (19).

The above instance clearly demonstrates to us the basic intentions of the novelist in bringing up such a preposterous scene of physical union between Rahel and Larry. With an immaculate perception, Arundhati delves deep into the heart of the matter and captures the psyche of her characters focusing not on the obvious and apparent but the subliminal as trapped together in a cage like incarcerated birds, these characters respond to their deep-seated, haphazard and convoluted feelings of nostalgia, guilt, love, hostility and boredom. Thus, it is the unexpressed and perhaps the unsayable anxiety that Arundhati attempts to explore through such characters. Rahel, the woman here is not wronged; the novelist obviates all such gender prone interpretations, and evokes in us the feelings that are filled with existential void and emptiness. Emphasizing clearly on the rudderless drift in Rahel, Arundhati reveals that Rahel certainly lacked clarity, ambition, force and even purpose, as she walked into Larry's life as his bride. Her marriage therefore does not appear to be the realization of a well-cherished dream, but seems to have been resorted to because of lack of other options.

The distance the female novelist thus maintains from her female protagonist is truly remarkable and suggests a significant shift in the perception of modern Indo-Anglian women writers. As the creator detaches herself from her characters, what strikes the reader is the unique disjunction and the consequent objectivity that the novelist maintains throughout her work.

The scenario is none different in the arena of short-fiction too where Jumpa Lahiri has already made waves with her "timeless treatise"[3] which possibly is considered so because of, its sexless tone to some extent. Jhumpa's *Interpreter of Maladies*, the Pulitzer winner collection of short stories, clearly exhibits a similar shift from the settled feminine or feministic vision that hitherto characterized the writings of earlier Indian women writers.

In the first story of the collection *A Temporary Matter* itself the reader is taken to the realm of reality as it chooses to depict the disturbing years in the conjugal life of Shobha and Shukumar. The couple is expecting a baby but Shukumar has to go away for a conference. On his return he is shocked to receive the news of the birth of a stillborn baby to Shobha. The incident seems to have created a chasm between them and now they live under one roof but only as strangers and have become *experts at avoiding each other in their three-bedroom house.*[4] This alienation has affected both the husband and the wife. While Shobha has become slovenly and keeps the house in disarray, treating it only as a hotel, Shukumar nostalgically reminisces the romantic past he shared with Shobha. It is clear that both the male and the female are shown to have been tormented by the tragedy as well as the consequent emotional void that engulfs them.

The story ends on a probable note of optimism as the couple rediscovers passion for each other, thanks mainly to the regular blackouts, which render them unable to do anything else but sit in the candlelight and share and thus enable them to come close to each other. Ultimately, it is this outer darkness that results in their inner illumination and leads to an understanding between Shobha and Shukumar as they *"wept together for the things they now knew"* (22).

Throughout the story, Jhumpa nowhere obfuscates the fact that both Shobha and Shukumar are possibly the loners who are trying to bridge the existing void with the company of each other as in the words of Sumana Roy, *Shukumar and Shobha are exiles who are trying to locate space through time. It is only when the electric lights are off that the electricity of their closeness lights on them; their area of darkness is flooded by the flashlights of memory.*[5]

It is obvious then that the purpose of the author, in delineating the relationship of the couple is not to highlight the atrocities of a male against a female but to depict the journey of two outsiders who struggle to relate to each other in the course of their life. The whole story revolves round the concept of matrimonial boredom in which both the male as well as the female feel trapped and nowhere the suggestion comes from the author that it is the male who has engineered this emotional incarceration.

In her title story "*The Interpreter of Maladies*" too Jhumpa seems to be focused on depicting the emotional divide that characterizes the life of Mrs. and Mr. Das. In this story, we come across a penitent wife who feels contrite as she betrayed her husband eight years ago and suffers from the pangs of guilt and grief ever since. Though it has been insinuated that both Mr. and Mrs. Das are poles apart yoked together in a family that now looks effete and tepid emotionally, it is hardly possible to gather from the story the image of an exploited woman who has to experience guilt due to the tabooed archetypes prevalent in orthodox mindset.

Thus Jhumpa chooses to depict her females not essentially different from her male characters. They all behave like zombies who suffer from the decadence of relationship and fail to relate to each other. This failure is mutual and the female is as guilty and responsible as the male is for the resultant ennui and insulation. Her stories, thus, are commiserating and certainly not accusing in tone, style and dictum. Obviously the point of view of the author here is to depict the reality that is universal and cannot possibly be truly shown in a parochial feministic vein.

In Manju Kapur's *Difficult Daughters,* too, the crisis the woman protagonist Virmati faces appears to be existential rather than social. On the surface though, Virmati seems to represent the women of 1950's who, in a patriarchal society of that period were subjugated to man-made injustices and indignities. The daughter of an upper-middle class urban Arya Samaj Punjabi family in Amritsar, Virmati appears to be the woman who has to undergo all the tortures and torments of life just because she belongs to an inferior sex. It seems that through her, the author recapitulates how a woman is denied all the opportunities to realize her social freedom in a patriarchal set-up. Virmati, being a woman, is denied to pursue higher studies, choose a career and to find out a person of her own choice to marry. Thus she represents the bleak past of Indian women who were not given any voice to assert their rights. Viewed from this perspective, the novel appears to be a document of resentment wherein the subdued, snubbed and subjugated woman registers her protest and rebellion against the prevalent male chauvinism.

A deeper look into the character of Virmati however suggests that there is more in this work than simply meets the eye. In fact Virmati is a complex character who is divided within her self to such an extent that she is unable to make up her mind what to pursue and what to forswear in her life. In Virmati's complex demeanour, we come across a woman who is daunted by the choices before her and suffers excruciatingly because of her inability to prioritize her multifarious desires. Virmati's problems arise as she wishes to fulfill her desire that stem from disparate and to some extent, mutually contradictory emotions.

Viewed retrospectively, it appears that she respects, like any other traditional girl, family name, its grace and seems quite proud of her roots. Her success in shouldering the household affair as an adolescent however, fails to satisfy her other self wherein lies her quest to be educated and lead an emancipated life not in the traditionally rich Amritsar but in Lahore, *the Oxford of the East.*[6] Shakuntala, Virmati's cousin, who has gone to Lahore and has been leading an independent professional life, works as a great pull for Virmati. Mesmerized by her emphatic life-style and an uninhibited existence, Virmati cherishes herself reliving her cousin's life:

> Virmati, looking at her glamorous cousin, marveled at the change Lahore had wrought in her. She looked better than merely pretty. She looked vibrant and intelligent, as though she had a life of her own (16).

With the passage of time, this *cousin influence* on Virmati only grows and she begins to feel disillusioned with the surroundings around her. Shakuntala continues to lure her into a different, unknown world where the temptations like *we travel, entertain ourselves in the evenings, follow each other's work, read papers, attend seminars* (17), are pretty hard to resist. For Virmati, *her cousin's world, becomes the most vivid thing on the horizon* (17) *and it does not take long before she blurts out I want to be like you, Pehnji* (17).

Thus, in the initial stages of the novel itself, the author gives Virmati the disposition wherein a desire to be someone and somewhere else rises in her like a powerful wave in a turbulent sea every now and then. In Virmati's desires to flee the sordid reality around her we can observe a quintessential restlessness and a consequent tendency to escape the immediate present and seek resort in the imaginative greener pastures. Before however she is able to realize her dream of freedom and education, Virmati lets the passion of her body overwhelm her. Though on the face of it is Harish, her professor, who seems to have seduced her yet it appears a bit unlikely that the author wanted her to portray as a victim of Harish's lust. Candidly judged, she, too is attracted towards him as her mind is filled with his thoughts. When alone, Virmati is shown to be thinking of him.

> That he looked at her she knew. That he paid attention to her, she was aware. But to think of him—was impossible, given the gap between them (54).

It is interesting to observe that Virmati's struggle for emancipation from the ills of patriarchy begins almost simultaneously with her growing fascination for Harish and a fulfillment of her own physical desires, hitherto untended and ignored singularly. The suggestion of the author is quite tangible. Her protagonist has been given a curious blend of diverse emotions and desires. In fact, as Virmati embarks on a journey to liberate herself from the suffocating orthodoxies of a traditional society, the reader is baffled to see her embracing a similar imbroglio by agreeing to the erotic propositions of the professor.

Later in the novel her silent confession to Swarnlata aptly suggests how desperately she craves to be someone else, anyone else, except being herself:

> Not everybody is like you Swarna—I'm not though, I wish I were. But when Harish is here, I stop thinking of other things. And when he is not here, all I do is wait for him to come (140).

Her lurking sense of uncertainty and the consequent torpid

reaction suggest how, like a zombie, she listlessly resigns to a fate she considers too enormous and oppressive to conquer. Made to succumb to the professor's desires, this is how she recollects her emotions:

> She cried afterwards, but not much. He dried those tears while she thought he was right, she was meant to be his. What was the point in foolishly denying it on the basis of an outmoded morality? (125).

Virmati's conflicting emotions clearly manifest the bewildering mass of diverse emotions that sway her from one extreme to another. Flabbergasted at the violent force of her own disparate desires, she sinks into a bizarre obsession of grief and continues to struggle against the enormity of her own conflicting identities. Therefore, her desire for establishing self-identity is *a value charged, almost a charismatic term, with its secured achievement regarded as equivalent to personal salvation.*[7]

Manju Kapur nowhere obfuscates the fact that more than any worldly forces, it is the inner anxiety that plunges Virmati into a deep melancholic void. Virmati is troubled as she has to establish her identity in a set-up that is hostile to women's such endeavours. She, however, is tormented more by her restive and perplexed psyche that does not let her feel in harmony with the circumstances around her.

Viewed thus, all the desires of Virmati and the subsequent hunt for their fulfillment appear to be the manifestations of self delusions in her. Caught in a vicious and preposterous circle of having to choose from a universe she finds absurd and feels indignant about, Virmati's search for self-assertion remains elusive to her. It is ironical that even before Virmati commits herself to the task of her emancipation, she is certain of its futility; hence her inconsequential struggle to redefine her reality and a concurrent abject surrender to let it overwhelm her. Indignant at her own inadequacy, she visualizes her situation analogues to that of the Fool in King Lear, as she reflects in a mournful apathy:

> Now each of Harish's words echoed in her mind with an irony he had taught her to recognize in Shakespeare's texts.

> Tragic irony, comic irony, how he had lived to expand on them! What species was this? It lacked the epic proportions of tragedy, and the life- courtship—marriage theme of comedy. In either case she was the Fool, that much at least was certain (154).

Virmati's recurrent guilt, that runs throughout *Difficult Daughters* almost as a leit motif, suggests to the reader her self-loathing for whatever she has done and become. If Virmati is chagrined at her earlier enslavement in a tabooed, orthodox society, she is equally indignant and appears out of sorts with the world of her own dreams and choices. Observed closely, the world of free voice and an emancipated existence looks equally hollow and decadent to her. Manju Kapur brilliantly outlines the alienation of the protagonist while delving deep into her psyche and bringing to the fore the feelings of vacuum and aloofness raging in Vinnati:

> All the women had such strong opinions. Virmati was amazed at how large an area of life these women wanted to appropriate for themselves (144).

She finds it irrelevant for a woman to talk about: *Strikes, academic freedom, the war, peace, rural upliftment, mass consciousness, higher prices due to the war, the medium of instruction, the Congress Committee, the Muslim League, anti-imperialism, Independence Day movement, rally, speeches* (144). Thus, the world of her desires that tempted her initially appears to be hollow and meaningless. The irony in her life is complete as the novelist captures her feelings of isolation and loneliness:

> Virmati's head was swimming. They were talking a language she had yet to learn. She began to feel stifled. Her legs had gone to sleep. She shifted uncomfortably on her haunches, the cold from her feet seeping in her despite the heat of the bodies around her. She felt out of place, an outcast amongst all these women (144).

Exasperated by her own existential vacuity, she clings to the fossilized forms of comfort that alleviate the feelings of emptiness in her. Shorn of her erstwhile familial protection, she has none else but Harish and his love *or lust* for her to fall back on. Her feeble consolation that *She must be satisfied with that* (144), serves only to underline her own rootlessness.

With feelings of unrelenting restlessness, the feelings of guilt come to her with added force. Sitting in the company of other educated, modern woman, she feels like an *imposter*. As the feelings of guilt, humiliation and shame increase in her, Virmati runs out of all contrived consolations as she berates:

> I am in the position of being your secret wife, full of shame, wondering what people will say if they find out not being able to live in peace and study in peace and why? and why? Because I am an idiot (137).

With the aggravating feelings of loss, penance and pain in her, the whole edifice of her aspiration crumbles. She suffers the indignities of having to undergo the trauma of abortion before and familial opprobrium after her marriage to her already married professor husband. She loses her father and feels crushed to realize that *her father had died without forgiving her* (221). Gradually for her what remains behind is a sense of loss and wonder at the enormity of power, and indifference of the universe that encapsulates her. It is in this sense that Virmati's quest for self is a *spiritual odyssey of the modern man who has lost his social and spiritual moorings and who is anxious to seek his roots.*[8]

Thus, in creating Virmati, Manju Kapur has concretized the image of the female sequester who fails to cope with the reality of her own self. Essentially like a true outsider, she gropes in darkness and attempts to understand the purpose of her own course in life that to her seems to be a rudderless ship drifting aimlessly.

It is in this sense that the modern feminist fiction seems to have evolved considerably. To the modern feminist writers, it is the human life and its mystified ambience that is the truth to explore. Thus, they refuse to confine themselves in depicting the exploited, traumatized and troubled life of a woman who has been victimized by a man-made society. Obviously to modern feminist writers, it is not the predicament of just the woman but that of human beings, that serves as a happy hunting ground. That is why in the works of Jhumpa Lahiri, Arundhati Roy and Manju Kapur the women characters are depicted not only as women but also as human beings-complex and confused, and struggling to scrutinize and decode the unyielding mysteries of our existence. It is this existential and metaphysical anxiety that sufficiently distinguishes the characters like Shobha, Mrs. Das, Ammu and Virmati from the run-of-the-mill women characters seen in many other feminist writers.

It is through such characters and their existential void that the Modern Feminist Fiction Writers attempt to broaden the canvas of depiction as in dealing with the existential void, they have touched upon the basic human predicament, which is existential and not just social. Thus in the works of Arundhati Roy, Jhumpa Lahiri and Manju Kapur a subtle but sufficiently explicit manifestation of human dilemma of choice, struggle and survival provides to these writers an elevated pedestal from where they communicate the reality that transcends the parochial walls of gender.

REFERENCES

1. Jayce Carol Oates quoted in Sijoberg Lief, "In Interview with Joyce Carol *Oates," Contemporary Literature* XXII, 3 (Summer 1982): p. 273.
2. Arundhati Roy, *The God of Small Things,* Delhi: India Ink, p. 181.
3. Parmanand Jha, "Home one Abroad: Jhumpa Lahiri's *Interpreter of Maladies," The Indian Journal of English Studies,* Vol. XXXVIII (2000-2001), p. 116.
4. Jhumpa Lahiri, *The Interpreter of Maladies,* New Delhi: Harper Collins, India, 1999, p. 4. All the subsequent reference from the text, have been taken from the same edition of the text, hereafter cited, with page numbers within parentheses.
5. Manju Kapur, *Difficult Daughters,* New Delhi: Faber and Faber, 1998, p. 6 1. All the subsequent references for *Difficult Daughters* have been taken from the same edition of the novel, hereafter cited, within parentheses, with page numbers.

6. Sumana Roy, "Fusions of Horizons in Jhurnpa Lahiri's *Interpreter of Maladies,*" *Critical Practice,* Vol. VII No. I (January, 2000). p. 95.
7. Dennis H. Wrong, "Identity: Problem and Catch Word" *Voice of revelation, ed.* Nancy H. Deane Boston: Littlebrown, 1970, p. 77.
8. R.S. Pathak, *Modern Indian Novel in English,* New Delhi: Creative, 1999, p. 52.

4

The Nostalgic Note in their Flute—A Reading of Arundhati Roy and Jhumpa Lahiri

NANDINI SAHU

The critical attention that has been paid to the young Indian writers in the last two decades needs a critical inquiry. A re-reading of their staggering literary output adding tremendously to the tradition of the Indian literary scene—with special reference to Arundhati Roy and Jhumpa Lahiri—that is what is the essence of this paper. The intensity and the narrative technique, which both Roy and Lahiri use in their creative pursuits, are the matter of research and vital importance here.

In the post-colonial era, young Indian writers have succeeded in drawing the world attention with their psychoanalytical methods of characterization. Jhumpa Lahiri, Manju Kapur, Arundhati Roy, Gita Mehta, Sashi Tharoor, Pankaj Mishra, Rajkamal Jha, Geeta Hariharan, Amit Choudhury, Manila Suri, Anita Nair, David Davidhar, Radhika Jha have written masterpieces which can be termed as literature of encounter and synthesis both culturally and linguistically. The object of this study is to analyze how literature is a gateway for a meeting point of the world tradition through encounter of the cultures and an existential rediscovery. The semitic creativity is enhanced by a significant enrichment of the narrative in the hands of young experts like Arundhati Roy and Jhumpa Lahiri who employ their cultural, racial past as well as familial past as their recurring theme. The literature of exile is not peculiar to modern Indian, particularly the literature where recollection acts as a mode of redemption. So important is the past to both Lahiri and Roy that a consciousness of it colours their insistent preoccupation with living. Memory plays a vigorous, creative role in their writings, a preoccupation with their personal, familial past leads in the long run to a search for the racial roots.

Life is viewed as a nostalgic recollection through the eyes of sensitive, vulnerable and observant characters. These two writers do not write from the position of a distant observer, rather their writings reflect the perspective of someone between a paradisal past and a tormenting present. The oppressiveness of the present reality and the temporal time are the facts to accept here and now. The writers' efforts to bring out a meeting point for the past and the present has been intensified by their nostalgic representation of characterization. The dichotomy with which both these writers present the present existence is resulted by the aesthetic dilemma, which they perceive due to their nostalgic experience. In the context of the contemporary milieu, the lack of unity of being with the self is reinforced by the lack of unity of the past and the present, which is focused throughout. Their characters live in two worlds—one within and one without and the past keeps intruding into the present.

In the case of Arundhati Roy, she greatly concerns her writings with the necessity to regain her identity through language as a creative mode. Her lines contain open statements about her passage from alienation to the awareness of a sense of discovering the world and its values and roots. The knowledge of the world gives her the knowledge of herself. In *The God of Small Things* early euphoric adolescence of himself in the part of Estha works as a stepping stone towards his maturity. Rahel's unrestrained enthusiasm of everything around gives her a broad vision to narrate the picture gallery of life as a whole. Rahel, the persona whom of 31, "a viable diable age" is in a self-introspective mood crossing the border of youth on a way to maturity. Though her stance is detached and controlled, it is all the while infused with emotion. She recalls the years of mistakes they have committed, the years they have been deeply wronged, have been "more sinned against than sinning." In the process, self-delusion overtakes her, she gets distanced with her present self while evoking the moments of their past.

A sense of loss, non-fulfilment, of apparent failure, a desire for the oblivion, and a love for the small things, which, in fact, convey big things, find repeated occurrence in the novel. *The God of Small Things* is a story about love, death, lies and law, and hence the universal tale of love and tragedy.

Through it, Roy pictures a child's view of the adult world, a tragic world of the feudal Christians, a barbarian communist who wipes his armpits with his terelene shirt, and a few sentimental untouchables. Love, that is erotic and cross caste between a Paravan and Syrian Christian, and politics, an insight into the complicacy of Kerala, are the two mainstreams of the story.

Roy uses flash-back technique for the narrative, memory being the source of narration in most parts. Her characters are life-like, almost alive in each one of us. They are allegorical, sometimes they seem to be attributes rather than individuals. Baby Kochamma, stands for jealousy, inferiority complex, Ammu for suppressed desire and hurt pride, Rahel and Estha for curiosity and unbounded love, Chacko for affectedness, Pappachi for male-chauvinism, Mammachi for inner blindness of a woman. About this deep concern for humanity in the novel, Roy says, "My work is not an academic, sociological study of untouchability but a human story that springs from love for human beings and a close contact with what happens to them"(1). Rahel, the narrator, is sometimes a stranger, sometimes the observer and yet some other times she is the performer. She expresses herself in the language of generic human emotion with its inevitable commitment to images, symbols, allegory, repetition, fluidity of language and the tension between the intense experience and its verbalization.

Early memories of life are suddenly activated years later when once again the siblings meet at youth. The memories of trivial things of childhood reveal how childhood impressions years later add new meanings to those with an adult experience. Roy's thematic strategy is exactly the right one for a writer of her situation, who loves her characters dearly.

The familial memories she employs are more of human interest at large, prone to social plane speaking of the higher values of life and complex human situation. Her small memories create a masterpiece of moving psychological fiction. Rahel remembers, though the "Little Man" Estha had always thought that "anything might happen to anyone, so it's better to be prepared" (p. 118), yet he himself was never prepared for that anything in his life. Sophi Mol's funeral, the memory of her 'child sized', 'satin-lined', 'brass handled Shined' coffin, her go-go bag, yellow bellbottoms that made Rahel feel inferior, Baby Kochamma's expensive funeral saree, are haunting, picturesque. Other funny memories like the 'porket-munny' of children, their learning of pronunciation to impress Sophie, Kochamma's make up, K.N.M. Pillai's sister's rendering of the poem "Lochinvar" Ammu and Baba's pushing the children to each other like billiard balls, "Et Tu, Kochu Mariye" to the housemaid, incidents in the Abhilash Talkies bathroom, the Orangedrink Lemondrink man episode.

Rahel's sneezing a bead out of her nose, Ammu's "Lay Ter" Rahel's request to Mammachi to inherit her contact lenses after her death, children returned, and re-returned like library books' all these make one nearly laugh. But the underlying deep tragedy, mysterious like the Meenachal river speaks volumes of the deceptive simplicity of the novel. Nostalgia is the only motif throughout that plays a great role to arrange the present in a right order. Estha's story called "Little Ammu" that Rahel reads at thirty-one, Ammu's gifts of a pencil box and a comic book that reaches Estha when he is thirty-one after Ammu's lonely death leaving her death receipt No. Q. 498673, all these memories have big emotions to convey. Roy loves her characters, that is why they seem so lifelike. When the producers propose her for the picturization of the story, she would say, "It may sound silly, but I could not bear the idea of seeing actors play Eshta, Rahel, Velutha... it would kill me. I love them too much. I always will" (2).

Roy's tone gets satirical whenever she mentions the politics of contemporary Kerala. Comrade E.M.S. Namboodiripad is referred to as "Kerala's Mao Tse-Tung," about whom Roy satirises writing: "He broke the egg, but burnt the omelette" (281). Similarly comrade K.N.M. Pillai is an opportunist who pretends to forget the past and his role in Velutha's murder. Similarly the pickle factory 'Paradise pickles and preserves,' the jam, the jelly, the river Meenachal, all these bear bigger significance to the plot. The small things have made Arundhati Roy the winner of the Big Booker Prize. Observing life from all directions, blending the past, present and the future in the single thread of life, she makes the storyline timeless. Roy's concern is with memory and the way it establishes or falsifies the relationship in a challenging world. She is neither a nostalgic traditionalist nor an advocate of modernization, she is the product of both and her novel reflects a personality conscious of change, and also aware of memories, which form her inner self as the foundation. For her, past is a time before Fall, she can be viewed as a writer on cultural cross-roads.

Following the publication of three of her stories in the New Yorker in 1998, Jhumpa Lahiri's reputation was established among both critics and readers alike. When *Interpreter of Maladies* was released in 1999, it received a flurry of reviews. In an interview with Vibhuti Patel, Lahiri Commented on her first career progression from scholar to Pulitzer prize winner, saying "Its all been a surprise-getting an agent, an editor, a book contract—it was all so fast. I feel extraordinary gratitude and amazement. Writers need time, some money and a little encouragement. This book has given me just the right amount of all three" (3).

Jhumpa Lahiri concerns her writings with the consciousness of the need for regaining roots in the tradition of India and a rueful nostalgia towards that. Her quest for identity is a consciousness towards exile, the dynamic force working to bring about this quest is a point of active engagement between two cultures—Indian and Western. This collection is a 'confessional piece', speaking of the pattern of hope and disenchantment arising from the predicament of the writer placed between two traditions, neither of which she can wholly accept or renounce. Like all expatriates, it sounds as if the western culture forms a part of her intellectual and national make up whereas Indian culture is a part of her emotional make up. She writes about how the English culture produces disenchantment in the minds of the expatriate Indians, and how they find themselves crushed under the burden of alienation and rootlessness. There is a sense of loss of identify with their own culture, therefore the need for roots. There is an aesthetic continuum in her writing. The stories present the writer's intercontinental journey during which she gets herself accustomed to both the cultures-by her long stay abroad and regular trips to India during every summer. The realization that is dawned on her is about the possibility of affirming the identity of her Indian self. It seems that for Lahiri East is the symbol of intellectual alertness and West is of emotional poverty. An identification of herself with either one is a frustrating experience, the artistic self is at war with the collective consciousness of both. Her stories seem to attempt to bring meaning to the present by reassessing the past and by giving shape to the accumulated waste of experience of the character's past prior to the period of westernization. With every detail of the experiences of both first and second generation of Indian immigrants, the topics of the stories range from emotional struggles of love to immigrants battling a new world. The stories draw upon the racial past upon India, Indian cultural heritage, the topics of communication, relationships culture prove to be universal to the experiences of human beings. She is an interpreter of maladies of people "Who think in a way they can't fully express" (4). About her Indian past, she speaks to Rediff.com, "India is the place where my parents are from, a place I visited frequently for extended time and formed relationship with people and with my relatives and felt a tie over time even though it was a sort of parenthesis in my life to be there" (5). Her writings are scattered with the details of traditional Indian names, food, flavor and wardrobe giving shape to her stories. Her representation of Indian culture is inherently present without exaggeration. Even her characters belong to different ages, nationalities and religions. Lahiri's characters demonstrate the universality of real life experience. In a story 'Mrs. Sen's', an eleven year old boy in an American college town watches his baby sister Mrs. Sen with her eccentricities, from chopping vegetable with a blade curved like the prow of a Viking ship to applying a fresh streak of crushed vermilion to the parting of her hair with the head of a thumbtack while recollecting the life she reluctantly left behind in Calcutta. Lahiri manages to portray so well the confusion and despair a young Indian wife feels so far from home. Her anxiety for letters from her kith and kin from her motherland, hare blade from Indian, her Indian dishes—fish curry, family members. voice on the tape recorder during her farewell and many other things reflect the pathos of an expatriate Indian. In "This Blessed House" Sanjeev can barely stomach his young wife's glee at finding and displaying garish Christian objects—a typical Indian Hindu mentality. In "A Temporary Matter" the characters live with the memory of their lost love, and during the power failures, they remember India, Shobha's granny's house, where during such power failures each has to say something like a joke, a story, a little poem. This leads towards the confession game, and the catastrophe. "When Mr. Pirzada come to Dine" is an emotional story. Here, there is the flashback of Pakistan civil war and the partition, its history geography. Lilia's mother recollects her past in India during the Independence, the crisis, the power failures, the light of kerosene lamps, the pressures, the English tutors, the constant examinations, and facts secure about her daughter's life in the US. Still Lilia would never choose to distance herself from her roots, store her chocolates in her grandmother's sandalwood box, the only moment of a grandmother she had never know. The predominant tone of the story is nostalgia with Mr. Pirzada's memory of his wife and seven daughters living in Dacca. Ultimately, after Mr. Pirzada's departure, Lilia could realize "that is meant to miss someone who was so many miles and hours away, just as he had missed his wife and daughter for so many months"

(42). The title story "Interpreter of Maladies" deals with the racial past of Indians with a vivid description of the Sun Temple at Konark, and the confession of Mrs. Das about her past before Mr. Kapasi, the interpreter. In "A Real Durwan" for Boori Ma, the protagonist, the memory of her royal youth is the only source of remaining alive in her old age. She "Exaggerates her past at elaborate lengths and heights" (73). The story "Sexy" is about identity crisis. Dev is an expatriate Bengali boy. Miranda is born and brought up in the US. Dev talks to her about the Taj as "the everlasting monument to love" speaks of the Indian significance of her name Mira Goddess Kali, Indian food, Indian spices are mentioned all over the plot. "The Third and Final Continent" is a touchingly transparent story, it speaks of the protagonist's past with Mrs. Croft.

There is an ardor of empathy in the stories where she displays a steadfast curiosity about human behavior and a healthy respect for its mystery. She literally makes the readers share the character's tragedies, their nostalgic experiences. She does not point out the loss of their cultural identity directly, her characters seem to be relieved when they adjust to the new world and are regretful at the separation from their original culture. Indian food, spices, flavors is a talisman in the stories, a reassuring bit of the homeland to brood over. She doesn't filter life through the single, steady voice of a young satirist, instead she writes about Indian American experience from all angles in indelible, lifelike stores who cling to memory as a source of living, she herself being the interpreter of human maladies.

In her perception the journey of the Indian becomes a continuum reading the Indian landscape as a foreigner would read it. The characters look back to India satirically celebrating their freedom or asserting their biculturalism, look skeptically and wryly on their new homeland as outsiders, with a feeling of something being lost a sense of longing a loss that often comes with the life of an immigrant. She confesses to Elizabeth Farnsworth in an interview. "I think that, in part, it's a reflection of what I observed my parents experiencing and their friends, their circle of fellow Indian immigrant friends. It's also, in part, drawn from my own experiences and a sense of...loss from my parents that was so palpable all the time while I was growing up the sense of what my parents had sacrificed in moving to the US" (6). The character's ability to accommodate and absorb the other culture without losing the consciousness of being Indian marks the major concern of Lahiri. She pictures how life abroad is exciting, a bit absurd and often lonely.

Through Lahiri's stories, we learn bits and pieces about Indian life and how they fit into lives in America. In the title story, an Indian family from New Jersey who are every bit "ugly Americans" hire an old fashioned Indian guide Mr. Kapasi who knows nine languages. The dual theme of love and duty in the story emphasises on the word interpreter. Mr. Kapasi wants "to get to the heart of the matter" Getting to the heart of any matter is the best thing that Lahiri does through the themes, love, fidelity, tradition and alienation. In a conversation with Arun Aguiar, she talks about one of her Indian characters, Bibi Haldar, "...from going there and observing people. For that story I took as my subject a young woman whom I got to know over the course of a couple of visits... She lived in the same building as my aunt and uncle....I learnt from my aunt that she had some epileptic like disease." When asked about the reaction of the Indian readers to her stories, she says, "When I read for a predominantly Indian audience, there are more questions that are based on issues of identity and representation. That also happened in England last week. Some Indians will come up and say that a story reminded them of something very specific to their experience, (7). Prof. R.K. Kaul writes about her "Out of nine stories in this volume, at least six or seven have a touch of magic. The author has narrative skill which captures the reader's attention immediately. Unlike the other women writers, she is not interested in problems of gender, race or colonialism. Only the story 'A Real Durwan' arouses our awareness of the callousness towards a woman sweeper. Whether the setting is in Bengal or in the US, she creates a probable world where human relations are all that matter" (8).

"There is something to be said for exile," says R. Parthasarathy, "your learn roots are deep" (9). The illustration of this truth may be best found in the writings of Jhumpa Lahiri. In spite of the slightly ironic tone employed throughout her descriptions, the final impression is that of an obsession with and an admiration of Indian traditional culture. Arundhati Roy and Lahiri prove it wrong that a language a writer uses must be his or her own, and it must mean everything to him. There is a feeling of buoyancy for the language in their writing and they are comfortable with it despite their alien experiences with life. Even if there is any discomfort, it is purely intellectual. The use of private experiences, especially the inner world of memories and the continuities with the past can be seen on the basis of their writing. They are not attempts to intellectualize and make moral choices; their writings are a retrospective photoflash. Along with these intimate portrayals their vocabulary is touchingly Indian. The Indian phrases and syntactical patterns transplanted in the English milieu in their writings add a new flavour to the English idiom itself. Their writings convey the whole range of feelings—from the ecstasy of transcendence of emotions to the drugged mildless trance of passion, from the feeling of being cleansed by love and sex to the poignant bittersweet memories of the loved and lose, their flutes play the nostalgic note from their heart and intellect. In the writings of both Roy and Lahiri, the protagonists search for the symbols of collective past and their attempts to resensitise their sensibility through their communion with past, with heritage is obvious.

REFERENCES

Primary Sources

1. Arundhati Roy, *The God of Small Things*, India Ink, 1997.
2. Jhumpa Lahiri, *Interpreter of Maladies*, Harper Collins, 1999.

Secondary Sources

1. *Indian Express*, October 18, 1997, p. 1.

2. *Frontline*, Jan. 19, and interview with N. Ram, p. 17.
3. *Voices from the Gaps*, Deptt. of English, 207 Lind Hall, University of Minnesota, Minneapolis, 55455 I, p. 38.
4. *Ibid.*
5. *Ibid.*
6. *Ibid.*
7. *Ibid.*
8. R.K. Kaul, "Twinkling Interpretations of Bengali characters" *Indian Book Chronicle*, July, 2000, Vol. XXV, No. 7, p. 3.
9. R. Parthasaralty, "Exile" *Ten Twentieth Century Indian Poets*, Delhi, 1976, p. 75.

5

History in Shreds: A Reading of Shashi Tharoor's *Riot*

SATHYARAJ. V. AND JOE VARGHESE YELDHO

> History is a complex system of distinct and multiple elements, unable to be mastered by the powers of synthesis.
>
> —*Foucault*

Shashi Tharoor's *Riot* denounces history's reductive comprehension of multiple realties, as history's disciplinary sense tends to undermine a sense of extremely intricate social causation. In so doing, *Riot* as a document participates in the post-modern/colonial project of interrogating prioritized discursive narratives and historiographical hegemony. This stance binds the novel with the theoretical postulates of postmodern critics like Foucault, White, and Fukuyama who in different ways challenged the ontological, epistemological status of history and thus problematized the notions of history, historicity and historiography. The present paper takes this direction and attempts to place Tharoor's *Riot* in the matrix of historiography, history and literature to explicate the nature and function of the same.

Published in 2001, Tharoor's *Riot* is an interesting mixture of fact and fiction presented through various narrative modes. The plot revolves around the death of Priscilla Hart, an American doctoral student working for an NGO in Zalilgarh in Northern India. The book begins with a newspaper report informing us about the killing of a foreigner in India during a riot. The novel revisits the sight of the incident and reconstructs the circumstances surrounding the death. Along with the main thread of the story that revolves around the affair between Priscilla Hart and V. Lakshman, the Stephen's educated District Magistrate, the narrative also includes perspectives on the socio-cultural milieu and political traditions that influence and shape the environment of the Indian subcontinent.

The theme while focusing on the killing also involves a certain amount of background regarding the origins of communal discord and also the ideologies of the successive governments. The deliberations of the characters like Prof. Mohammed Sarwar, the History teacher of Delhi University and Ram Charan Gupta, the Hindu fanatic, help realize the thematic. The novel includes other characters like Rudyard Hart and Katherine Hart, the parents of the dead student who come to India in an effort to understand the reasons behind the murder. Randy Diggs, the New York journal reporter who wants to do a feature story on the dead person conducts his own investigation. Gurinder Singh, the Superintendent of Police and minor characters like Mr. Das and Kadambari add to the profile giving a chance for a more comprehensive picture of the personal aspects regarding the case to emerge.

There is an emphasis placed on the generic term "the novel" in the title page of the book. The contravention of the norms regarding the conventions of the genre could in fact give the entire work an appearance of an event or a case record, extracts from a diary or a monograph. The definitions of "the novel" as extended by Tharoor could also be taken to include the afterword and acknowledgement, which contributes to the background on the textual production. The factual detail lends an aura of credibility with reference to the ground realities of similar scenarios. Another interesting aspect of the book's production, which is of note, is the different covers adopted for release in the Western and Indian markets. While the Indian cover has an image of a deserted street, post-riot, the visual text on the American cover emphasizes certain stereotypical images associated with the Orient, with its image of a domed palace and Mughal tapestries.

Broadly speaking, *Riot* conflates personal events with political history by presenting a non-linear narrative and tampers with the notion of causality that is the basis of the historical documentation process. "The novel" is a complex admixture of journal and diary entries, interview transcripts, dialogic moments, personal notes, letters and news clippings. Furthermore, the textual divisions are the moments of reconstruction that attempt to detail the background behind the killing of Priscilla Hart. While official sources conclude the instance as related to the riots that took place in the town of Zalilgarh, the reader knows that a far more personal tragedy underlies the sequence of events that culminates in the killing.

The novel is an attempted reconstruction through a series of textual moments intended to throw light on the murder of the American student. In this process, the riot is not seen by the author as an isolated experience but an entire nation's history and socio-cultural ethos is brought to bear on the particular textual moment which examines the fundamental basis for the Hindu-Muslim communal divide and the reasons for the widely prevalent religious conflagrations in the subcontinent. The issue is complicated when the author offers divergent perspectives on history by people like Prof. Mohammed Sarwar and Ram Charan Gupta. Tharoor seems intent on creating probable and divisive subtexts by giving scope for counter views against the analysis of the individuals concerned. In the case of the History Professor opportunity is given to those so inclined to question his views based on his reading from a minority status. As a Hindu fanatic it is through his recourse to mythic and fabular elements and its perception as mainstream history, that the author subverts the operative notions of accepted history.

Tharoor, by simultaneously offering divisive and variant notions of the historical impetus, brings into sharp focus the limitations of historical knowledge that is at best seen as a creative discourse which "actively" survives with the nebulous notions of "truth" and "reality." In other words, *Riot* characterizes historical narratives as inventions/fictions "which have more in common with their counterparts in literature than they have with those in the sciences" (White, 60). Implied is the notion that history, like literary text, is a fictional construct that is open to interpretation and that 'writing' history inevitably involves the use of formal literary devices such as emplotment, tropes, narratives, intertextualities and diegesis. Besides these affinities, both history and fiction, to quote Hutcheon, "are cultural sign systems, [and] ideological constructions" (292). It is this "functional unity" between fiction and history (2) that underscores Ricoeur's observations in "On Interpretation"

The reconstruction of the past ... is the work of the imagination. The historian, too, by virtue of the links ... between history and narrative, shapes the plots that the documents may authorize or forbid but that they never contain themselves, history, in this sense, combines narrative coherence with conformity with the documents. This complex tie characterizes the status of history as interpretation (7).

In effect, *Riot* blurs the existing boundaries between fiction/fact, history/literature, universal/particular, aesthetics/ politics.

The limitation of the historical process is directly brought out in the implicit understanding that the circumstantial overview is never complete. To overcome such a limitation the author brings in various points of view to illumine the actual details behind the death. Such a critical stand provides an explorative possibility between the Muslim or Hindu fanatics or even the third option that is not made apparent. The only finality in the book is the resistance to closure, one does not know what set of circumstances conclusively led to the killing of this "idealist," one more statistic claimed by the frequent bouts of irrationality sweeping the populace.

The hostility and extreme behaviour characterizing those concerned is evident in Ali's outburst against the members of the HELP—US programme which neatly plays into Ram Charan Gupta's doomsday prophesying of a dominant Muslim majority. A lot of figures are tossed about to lend that much needed semblances of authenticity to the arguments. Demographics and related social and anthropological endeavors are implicated by the author in the process of cultural destabilization evident in the text. What this does is to negate notions of impeccability entertained by a vast public regarding statistics and archival documentation. The most cutting reminder of such an exercise would be the inability of the texts fact file to authentically document the murder of Priscilla Hart leading to a large degree of uncertainty regarding the case.

The text becomes conclusive proof of the inadequacy of the documentation process and the recorded facts. If at one level it throws open the question of causality with reference to a particular and personal history, then it also highlights in extension the inadequacies of the historical paradigms. The more fundamental question perhaps explored in the text is the question of what exactly constitutes history. As far as Hindu fanatics like Ram Charan Gupta are concerned they are clear in their view of Hindu myths and legends associated with texts like the Ramayana and the Mahabaratha as part of mainstream historical discourse.

> In Ayodhya there are many temples to Ram. But the most famous temple is not really a temple any more. It is the Ram Janmabhoomi, the birth place of Ram....In the olden days great temples stood there...a Muslim king, the Mughal emperor Babar, not an Indian, a foreigner from Central Asia he knocked it down. And in its place he built a big mosque, which was named after him the Babri Masjid (52).

A corrective is offered by historian Prof. Mohammed Sarwar who declares that *the whole point is that historians like myself, who haven't sold our souls to either side in this wretched ongoing communal argument have a duty to dig into the myths that divide and unite our people* (67). As the professor makes it apparent later on, his liberal secular ideology informs his notion of a near utopian *composite religiosity* (64). It is this notion of secularism as propagated by the successive Congress governments that is found to be at fault by both the Muslims (107) and the Hindutava brigade typified by Ram Charan Gupta (56). The problem posited is that a secular version of history is perceived to be complicit in the ideological movement of the majority community. The reductivism maintains an idealistic vision of State history that does not take into account traumatic community experiences caused as a consequence of communal discord.

The open debate in the text with regard to the veracity of facts surrounding the Ram temple in Ayodhya is emblematic of a deeper divide that goes beyond the veneer of acceptability that lies shrouded as a result of government institutionalization, in this case the Congress. While Ram Charan Gupta is vociferous in his evocation of the whole issue

> ...the spot with the best site on a hill, is occupied by a mosque? Do these secularists think that was an accident, or a simple coincidence? Or might it be, instead, that Babar, the Mughal invader, demolished the biggest, the best, the most important temple of the Hindus and replaced it with a mosque named for himself, just to rub the noses of the conquered in the rubble of their faith? (120).

Prof. Muhammed Sarwar clarifies later:

I know the Hindutava types believe that the temples of Ayodhya precede Babar and that he must have destroyed the biggest one because it was the best located. But the problem with this is that there's a lot of evidence for the opposite-for the building of temples in Ayodhya under Muslim rule, well after Babar built his Masjid (183).

But even he acknowledges that in the subcontinent and its history, religion and communal sensitivity has played a major role. In a way the professor undermines the sanctity of the historical process through the recognition of these limitation or rather religious constraints. While the professor would term the ideological underpinning of the Hindutva brigade as one that limits the process to an exercise in reinventing the past, people like Ram Charan Gupta would say that they are retrieving/recovering their heritage which has a truth value that is more than mere symbolism. In this way, *Riot* along with functioning as metaphor for historiographical flaws, also tactfully informs the postmodern notion of past as evanescent but everywhere inscribed. Thus, the novel dramatizes Hutcheon assumption that *...there are only truths in the plural, and never one Truth; and there is rarely falseness per se, just others' truths* (76).

The act of the riot would be an instance where personal and political spaces collapse in real terms. Tharoor, in the novel, shows how these spaces intersect constantly and examines the nature of an act that though impersonal at one level has immense bearing on subjective histories that frame personal angst. This situation is akin to what the narrator faces in Amitav Ghosh's *The Shadow Lines* where the riot becomes a personal marker or is a site of disjuncture that marks the point of departure from an alternate time/space continuum that helps the characters cope with the loss. But it loses its political significance, as it does not form a part of mainstream archives. The case in *Riot* is different, as the death of a foreigner has sparked sufficient international attention on an event that could be seen as mundane given the political scenario of the subcontinent. Thus it becomes a well-documented proceeding, given the involvement of the text itself.

The reductivism of the status of the subject into another impersonal signifier is countervailed by the author's conversion of the historical documentation process to a fictional enterprise. The a-chronological notations in the book can be seen as a process of filling in historiographical gaps or an "absence" in the domain of history. The unifying action that connects all the textual moments is the death of Priscilla Hart. The positioning of the newspaper articles towards the beginning and the end is also suggestive of the enterprise to recreate what transpired during that particular time frame. The ghostly presence of Priscilla Hart during the course of the book could be seen as an attempt to revisit the site of disjunction at a particular moment in time. The fictional framework emphasized by Tharoor simultaneously aids the reconceptualization of the historical framework and fits it into the unified time/space spectrum exposited by the conventions of the "genre" and the physical limits of the actual object of the book.

By fictionalizing a historical narrative the author distances himself from the requirement of the causality implicit in the genre of realistic fiction. The historical discourse would not be a unified mainstream progression as typically conceived, but would be one among various discourses open to interrogation. In short, there is a strategic attempt to realign historical methodologies/cartographies of histories through these voices/ narratives and the theoretical discourses they engender. This cerebral process estranges the political idealism of historical accounts and informs the epistemological limits of history. Such an interventionalist politics inhabits an interrogation of Hegelian causality and homogeneity of historical narratives to establish *schizophrenic disjunction* (Jameson 29) in historical knowledge.

The project of fictional narrativization also ends as a part of the archives within the rubric of the text, when Lakshman refers to the process of novel writing and quotes the instance of Tharoor's own book, The Great Indian *Novel I 've read about this chap who's just reinvented the Mahabharata as twentieth-century story-epic style, oral tradition, narrative digressions, the lot* (126). He goes on to detail the entire creative process arriving at a notion of truth that is the crux of the fictional historicization. To Priscilla's query regarding the reader's understanding of truth comes *the truth! The singular thing about truth my dear, is that you can only speak of it in the plural ... Truth is elusive, many sided...* (137).

The notion is given a truth that functions at various levels, it remains for the reader to be co-opted to the whole process. So we have the simultaneous interplay of fact and fiction throughout the work, while the references to official records (73) force the readers to undertake a deeper and more subtly nuanced reading presented by the book. The vignettes interspersed with the play of the universal/particular and fact/ fiction force the reader out of a complacent and passive response to the text and simultaneously enables the reader to rethink the generally accepted notions of the creative impulse, as tempered by the socio-political milieu.

The space of the text becomes a site of play for parallel/ alternative histories based on a series of reconstructive attempts by various characters. Through these polyvocality the text fills in a certain need by engaging with "the void" created by the prioritized history and also opens itself to the same criticism by the selection of specific recorded events to the exclusion of others. But it gets beyond this subversion by virtue of its creating a fictional narrative to fill in the gap with all that "fiction" implies. Thus, the text finally by the very nature of its content characterizes the production of history as another narrative and creative enterprise.

REFERENCES

Ghosh, Amitav, *The Shadow Lines*, New Delhi: Ravi Dayal, 1998.

Jameson, Frederic, *Postmodernism or Cultural Logic of Late Capitalism*, Durham: Duke University Press, 1991. p. 29.

Hutcheon, Linda, *The Pasttime of Past Time*: Fiction, History, Historiographic Metafiction, Genre. 20. Fall—Winter 1987. pp. 285-305.

Tharoor, Shashi, *Riot*. New Delhi: Viking, 2001.

White, Hyden, *The Historical Text As Literary Artifact*, in R.H. Canary and H. Kozicki (ed.), *The Writing of History*: Literary form and Historical Understanding—Wisconsin 1978. p. 60.

6

The Identity Crisis—An Immigrant Experience as Reflected in Jhumpa Lahiri's Novel *The Namesake*

SHUBHA MISHRA

A precarious balancing of two cultures, forging a path and forming a bridge are the tight rope walking, migrant Indian English writers do. The new generation of Americans, born of Indian immigrant parents are presented by this young and vibrant writer, Jhumpa Lahiri in both her books, in a very genuine and first hand manner. Her first novel, *The Namesake* published in 2003 and her collection of short stories, *Interpreter of Maladies*, published in 1999, which won the Pulitzer Prize for fiction in 2000, made her a literary celebrity overnight.

Born in London in 1967 and raised in Rhode Island, Jhumpa Lahiri has become a recognized and respected young writer. Her fiction transcends from mere ethnic to exoticism. She accomplishes this with subtle characterization, meaningful but never portentous details. She is like an artist who can capture likeness with two or three strokes, but keeps sketching until the face begins to breathe. The daughter of Bengali parents, her heritage and culture are influenced by India and the United States. This multicultural lifestyle, with perplexing experiences of these bicultural worlds is prominent in both her books. *Interpreter of Maladies* received a flurry of glowing reviews not only in India but also in the US. Following the publication of three of her short stories in The New Yorker in 1998, Lahiri's reputation was established among critics and readers alike. Composed of nine short stories, *Interpreter of*

Maladies details the experiences of both first and second-generation Indian immigrants.

In a recent review of her debut novel *The Namesake*, it was stated, "Lahiri mines the immigrant experience in a way superior to Bharti Mukherjee and others." Several critical interpretations will follow of this recently published novel. This paper makes a modest attempt to analyze the identity crisis, faced by the immigrants as portrayed in Lahiri's novel.

The Namesake revolves around the lives of the Gangulis. The novel begins with the protagonists Gogol Ganguli's father Ashoke. Ashoke is a graduate student in engineering, who returns to Calcutta for an arranged marriage with Ashima Bhadhuri. They portray the first-generation immigrants. All their lives, they, on one hand, try to preserve their "home cultures," and on the other hand they also try and groom heir children for the American way of life. The novel opens with Ashima who is about to deliver her first child, two months before the due date. The naming of the child revolves around Ashoke's past emotional memories and also the traditional ties to the family left behind in India. But still it is more than a book about a name. Though the importance of nomenclature to an alien society resonates throughout the novel, it begins in the year 1968 and finishes in 2000. Ashoke and Ashima have their first born, whom they are forced to name, because of hospital rules and fear of 'red tape.'

"For they learn in America, a baby cannot be released from the hospital without a birth certificate. And a birth certificate needs a name" (27). It is around Gogol, and around whose name most of the second part of the story revolves. They also have a daughter Sonia, who totally portrays the second generation of immigrant Americans and is least involved in family matters.

Ashima is the anchor for the first part of the novel, which presents the immigrant experience in a very genuine and first hand manner. Her attachment to her family in Calcutta gradually seems to loosen up, as her life begins to revolve around Gogol and his upbringing. Various experiences, which

Ashima has, during her delivery, are very lifelike and bring out many sharp contrasts between the two cultures. These experiences are presented in a first hand manner, as Lahiri herself was born of immigrant parents and she seems to understand the tiny bargains, this assimilation into a new culture has required. Ashima's experiences are also, not just filtered through the prism of set traditions but are projected in a lifelike manner. Ashima thinks:

> that Americans in spite of their public declaration of affection, in spite of their miniskirts and bikinis, in spite of their hand-holding on the street and lying on top of each other on Cambridge Common, prefer their privacy (3).

Through the power of names as markers of identity, the writer takes the reader through the life of Gogol Ganguli, a second-generation U.S. immigrant. He is born of Brahmin parents; caste however, does not play much of a role in their lives. For the second generation, Gogol and Sonia, caste ceases to be relevant, where the commonalities of class and ethnic interest cement bonds within the community. Throughout the book, Gogol's closest relationships are with mainstream American whites.

Lahiri's meticulous chronicling of Ashima and Ashoke's relocation is a prelude to Gogol's own cultural identity crisis. Gogol Ganguli's problem, as he sees it, is his being saddled with a 'daknam' (pet name) in the place of a 'bhalonam' (good name). Readers learn why he has been given this name well before Gogol does. During a major train accident Ashoke had been saved because the pages of a book of short stories by the Russian writer, Gogol fluttered in his hand, catching a rescuers eye. Ashoke names his son Gogol in gratefulness of surviving the train wreck.

Gogol himself hears this story, as a college student, reacts in a very different manner. At this point of time he is also feeling estranged from his family. But this realization of the background of his name is perhaps most important in the book and contributes to the building of the fragile bridge between the generations.

"...And suddenly this sound of his pet name, uttered by his father as he has been accustomed to hearing it all his life, means something completely new, bound up with catastrophe he has unwillingly embodied for years. Is that what you think of when you think of me ... do I remind you of that night?

'Not at all,' his father says eventually ....You remind me of everything that followed" (124).

The father has named the son Gogol in honor of the Russian writer, but at eighteen Gogol wants to become his own person and to change his name to Nikhil. When he makes his announcement, there is an uneasy silence at the dinner table. At last the father says, "In America anything is possible. Do as you wish." Gogol as if reinvents himself and frees himself from his parents' constraints. He embarks on his adult life as Nikhil and begins to have relationships with white American women, keeping his private life a secret from his parents.

In spite of becoming a part of the mainstream American life and its ways, the name Gogol still seems to haunt him. Gogol seems to have an invisible hold on Nikhil. Sonia, his sister insists on using his daknam, though she herself is already very much Americanized. In an interview given by the writer in New York Times magazine, it is quite clear the book, 'The Namesake' has biographical undertones. Lahiri's comments echo the sentiments of the young characters in her book. Many second-generation immigrants share her experience. Jhumpa Lahiri also admits that she never felt comfortable with her name. Her own name is a 'daknam', the importance of which will be obvious to any Bengali reader. She admits, "When I entered the American world as a child, I endlessly had to explain to people how to say my name and how to spell it and what it meant. I really felt like my name was causing people pain on some level. ..."

Jhumpa Lahiri's novel, not only speaks to immigrants but also to the original settlers on different levels. It is different from the exotic outpourings of Indian immigrant writings in English. *The Namesake* portrays people who need to make sense of their own destinies, in their own terms. Like her portrayal of Sonia, who adopts to the American lifestyle much more easily than Nikhil. She sees herself as wholly American, yet the remains committed to her Indian family. She acts as a catalyst which draws her mother into a more American lifestyle.

Lahiri's short stories and her novel recount the lives of Bengali immigrants and their American reared children (like the author herself) Presented in an understated plain style, Lahiri weaves together numerous narrative threads in the novel. Her ambitions crowd out the sublety, structural intricacies and thematic resonance that brought her first collection so much praise. The ordinariness of immigrant tales, which project cultural sacrifices, material gain, which was hard earned with perpetual adjustment, make *The Namesake* a fresh and worthy contribution to literature. Lahiri steers away providing easy answers, offering readers a complex look into the immigrant experience. Her handling of the complexities of immigrant experience is a simple but a very mature manner of a mature fiction writer.

REFERENCES

1. Review of *The Namesake* by Aditya Sinha. 'The Malady of Naming' in *Hindustan Times*, September 28, 2003.
2. Jhumpa Lahiri, 2003. *The Namesake*. Harper Collins Publications.
3. *Ibid.*
4. *Ibid.*
5. Jhumpa Lahiri Interview with Elizabeth Fransworth-May 20, 2003 <www.askjeevs.com>.
6. Mandira Sen 'Names and nicknames' (Book review) *The Women's Review of Books*, March 2004.
7. Jhumpa Lahiri 1999. *Interpreter of Maladies: Stories of Bengal: Boston and Beyond*. India: Harper Collins Publications.

7

Raj Kamal Jha's *If You are Afraid of Heights*: An Interpretation

KANHAIYAJEE JHA

Raj Kamal Jha shot into literary fame with the publication of his debut novel *The Blue Bedspread* (1999) which subsequently bagged the prestigious Commonwealth Prize for literature. His second novel *If You Are Afraid of Heights* (2003), though published after a considerable gap, continues to maintain the standard that Jha, as a novelist, has set for himself. The novel presents a haunting rendering of landscape and life of Kolkata, a typical Indian city undergoing fast change to cope with the pace of development. It focuses the common and often neglected class of individuals, struggling to come to terms with their hopes and despair.

Structurally, the novel is set in three parts, each part presenting a different tale. The chance meeting of Rima and Amir in a midnight road accident and consequently getting involved with each other, the travails of reporter Mala to uncover the incident of a girl child's rape and murder in a suburban town, the fears of a young girl shaken by suicides in her neighbourhood, are the central stories recounted in the three parts respectively. Eventhough placed independently the three tales are linked together in so far as these commonly constitute the body of the fictional world, the novelist aims to project. The stories themselves, as such, are not as important as the atmosphere evoked through them is. The narrative, while portraying the stress, tension and conflict of modern urban people, creates a milieu having aura of *something* calamitous and nightmarish. In fact, the sense of fear is the central motif, which runs through all the three parts of the novel. The title of the novel also suggests the sense of fear, which operates in various ways in the narrative. The novelist makes ample use of fantasy as a device to evoke the atmosphere and also to bring out the subconscious self of the characters.

Each part of the novel is preceded by a prologue, which brings a sort of continuity in otherwise independently shaped tales. In the First Prologue, like a snap shot, there appears the glimpse of a middle class family, consisting a girl child aged about eleven or twelve years and her parents. The father, a middle aged man, who is an employee of City Building Clearance Office, has just returned to his two bedroom flat. While washing *he can smell the city on his hands,*[1] the mother, a housewife is busy in setting dinner for her husband; but the child, standing on the balcony of the building is "crying" (1). The overall atmosphere is that of gloom and despair. The descriptions of the building and inside of the flat are also aimed to create this atmosphere. The building looks like a "crying face" and the windows are 'smudged and wrinkled.' The walls are old and streaking in several lines, looking like 'line of tears.' The mouth of the balcony is "rusted and misshapen," like the "stained teeth of someone very sad" (1). The omniscient narrator is riding on the back of a flying crow, his body raised so that the crow does not feel his weight. He takes a panoramic view of the city from the heights and also comes down to have a close look in the lives of the average inhabitants of the city.

The First Prologue introduces some key images of the novel *viz*; the crying child, the crow and the crowman, the sad house etc. These images are recurrently used as devices to bring the elements of compassion and fantasy in the narrative. The crying child is often shown in the novel with the mother, which further heightens the pitch of pathos. This key image assumes different shapes in different parts of the novel. For example, in Part One, Rima is haunted by the crying of child like a nightmarish dream. In Part Two the murdered child and Mala's memories of her own childhood find correlation with the image of the child. In Part Three, the narrator is herself a child and through her consciousness, the description of the macabre suicide epidemic and the situations arising in the aftermath of it is given. The image of the crow and the crowman serves two purposes. Firstly, it provides the narrator a bird's-eye view of the city and secondly, it becomes a device to introduce fantasy. This image, which finds elaborate treatment in Part One, is present in Part Three also as fantastic visions.

The First Prologue sets not only the atmosphere of the novel but also the pattern of the narrative to follow. There is a lack of sequence and linear movement in the narrative. In Part One, introducing the story of Rima and Amir, the narrator stresses the need to "pick up details strewn along the way. Often the obvious, sometimes the obscure. Like a power cut in the neighbourhood and Amir's kerosene lamp (12). This pattern of presence and absence applies to the other parts of the novel also. The prologue opens with the description of a picture:

> Look at the picture on the cover, there's a child, a girl in a red dress; there's a bird, a crow in a blue white sky. And then there are a few things you can not see (1).

So, the ground is prepared for the accommodation of several inexplicable elements in the narrative. The interplay of reality and fantasy is one of the frequently used aspects of such elements.

In Part One, the main characters Rima and Amir who "met in an accident, face to face," are not only individuals but also representatives of any man or woman in the city. Their story reveals how, out of all the men, women and children in this city, sixteen million at last count, it had to be Amir and Rima (12). Amir belongs to middle or lower middle class section of the city. He works as an extra Departmental Agent in the Post office and lives in a two room flat in an old building having 'sad' and gloomy look. Financially, he is a man of modest means (25) and even physically there is "everything medium" (29) about him. His neighbours know nothing either about his lineage or his marital status. In a city where people are generally keen to interfere in the affairs of others, Amir prides himself for being "able to keep to himself" (30).

Amir's middle class living condition is reflected in many ways. For example, his wardrobe has only 'two pairs of trousers,' a few shirts and 'a pair of shoes.' His toilet bowl is 'stained' and cockroaches crawl at night on the floor. The rent of the room is low which is the reason that "the pump that supplies water to his flat is switched off for most of the day and the light bulb in the staircase is rarely replaced" (26). He has to carry water buckets twice from Municipal hydrant store "in containers of all kinds" (27). He keeps his lamp ready to counter the intermittent power supply.

Amir's job is not a permanent one and so, five evenings a week, he teaches the daughter of Mr. A. Sarkar, his boss at the post office. This child is also between eleven or twelve years of age. Returning from his office "Most evenings, he takes the bus to Park Street, walks down right upto ... street where once a week he visits a prostitute. Then he boards a late-night tram that trundles into a sweeping arc around the Maidan" (31), giving view of the shimmering skyline of the city.

Part One starts with a brief synopsis of the story, given elaboration later. It is indicated how Rima is haunted by child cry which ultimately results in her mysterious disappearance. Then there is an introduction of Pàradise Park, another significant image used in the novel. It is "the tallest building in the city" (14), from the height of which one "could see the Bay of Bengal, which is at least five hundred miles away" (15). Rima lives in one of the apartments of this building, which becomes the centrestage of the story later. These introductory details are only preparatory to the central event of this part- the tram accident, which ushers the relationship between Rima and Amir. In between, there is the recording of the particular day's movement of Amir, split in four parts viz; the morning, the afternoon, the evening and the succeeding night of the accident. In the process the novelist also evokes the milieu of the city in which the story is placed.

In the morning, at Shimla Post Office, Amir writes "letters for those who can neither read or write" (33), the group consisting of people as varied as "handcart pushers, rickshaw-pullers carpenters-on-call, masons, maids, all sending a part of their monthly wage to their families back home, far away from the city" (35). Amir is quite conscious of the humanitarian aspect involved in his job, so, he maintains utmost honesty and cleanliness while dealing with the poor helpless people.

In the afternoon, at lunch hour, he watches a crowman making a public show:

> If you are afraid of heights, brothers and sisters, I have nothing to show you...but if you don't care how high you go...climb on to my crow's back and fly out of this city.
>
> Across and over, above and beyond. No pushing in buses, no shoving in trams, no saying sorry, no jumping puddles of pee, piles of shit. In short, my friends, no headache (41).

The usual rush in public transport services and the presence of filth in Kolkata are well reflected in the crowman's utterance. The flying crow promises a good view of the familiar landmarks of the city such as 'Chittaranjan Avenue,' 'Bowbazar,' 'The Indian Airlines Building,' 'Park Street,' 'Grand Hotel,' 'The New Bridge' (*The Vidyasagar Setu*), 'The Maidan' etc. The people are warned to be careful while flying past over 'Paradise Park,' the tallest building in the city, as one has to 'fly straight' there. The references like 'black tar of the road,' 'the white of the cars,' 'the yellow of the taxies,' the green of the Maidan' further add colour to the picture of the metropolis.

The title of the novel, explicitly mentioned recurrently in crowman's remarks, is suggestive of numerous kinds of fears one lives with, while being a part of the city life. In the metropolitan context 'the crow' is a vehicle of allurement to take one to the 'heights' of material success. But it is always difficult to maintain a hold at such a position. There is a suggestion, as the crowman says, "don't you worry, just make sure that when you're on top, your legs are firmly pressed against the bird's back, hard and tight" (41). This proposition is desirable but not always secured. Paradise Park also, in a similar way, symbolises point of desirable height one may wish to achieve materially. But Amir is unable to make his stay stable there.

In the evening, after teaching Mr. Sarkar's daughter, Amir walks through Park Street and reaches the flat of the prostitute. His relationship with her is not mere sensuality, even though, "he feels nothing special for her" (64). There is a desire in him to find some sort of substitute for the emotional solace, which he lacks in the absence of a family life. The prostitute even advises him to marry a suitable girl. Late in the night he boards a tram, which collides with another tram coming from opposite direction. Rima, the only other passenger, happens to be there and she brings severely injured Amir to her own apartment in Paradise Park. The newspaper report of the accident makes reflections on the outdated technology used by the Tramways Corporation.

The centrestage of the story now shifts to Paradise Park. Rima is "a woman of this city, born and raised here" (100). and she represents the higher strata of the society. Nothing is indicated about her profession or the source of livelihood, yet her living bears ample evidence of affluence. Living in the apartment of Rima, Amir discovers a new world. He feels the impact of the exposure to the new situation sometimes "stronger than that of the accident" (74). The glitter and the gleam of Rima's household appear to him "containing all the things in the world, both imagined and unimagined" (75).

Nursed affectionately by Rima and carefully treated by the attending doctor, Amir soon begins getting accustomed to the objects around him" (78), but he is well aware that he cannot stay in this apartment for long, although, for him the allurements are sufficient to immerse himself in a sort of blissful forgetfulness. Rana is aware of Amir's uneasiness to get back to his place. She emphatically asserts: "I'm not holding you back, you are free to go anytime you want to but why not stay here until you get better" (97), Amir has no choice left in the matter. Like the wounded bird which Rima one day brought in the cage, Amir feels "reciprocating her kindness in the trapped... way" (97).

The physical relationship develops between them soon on Rima's initiative and Amir becomes the passive player in numerous types of games that Rima fancies. Amir is well aware of "the lack of permanence about everything around him" (108) there and is impelled to "look at Rima in a whole new light". (108) He appears convinced "that lying ... wounded and hurt, he had filled her with overwhelming pity and there was no way he could repay her kindness except perhaps through gestures of gratitude, awkward and absurd. Like lying in bed with her, playing along, making up words for different parts of their bodies" (108). The closeness makes him aware of her true nature: "that she has holes in her heart she needs to fill everyday, be it with someone like him, a stranger hurt in an accident, or a crow with its beak sewn off, holes he can never even plumb the depths of" (109). One day Rima makes a request to go to Amir's place and the latter consents without suspecting that "it could be the beginning of the end" (109) of their accidental togetherness.

The use of fantasy is a significant aspect of the novel and it is present in the narrative in many ways. Fantasy, literally, means non-real, existing only in imagination or irrationally imagined etc. It is an important literary device used in novels, as Forster suggests for *divings into and dividings of personality.*[2] It may be "used at different levels—at the level of incident and imagination and also at a purely lingual level. It objectifies itself in various ways, as hallucination and nightmare, as wishful thinking and personal aspiration, and as a private world characterized by an obsession or a psychological fear or confined in some other ways "as hallucination and nightmare, as wishful thinking and personal aspiration, and as a private world characterized by an obsession or a psychological fear confined in some other ways.

The relationship between Rima and Amir is shrouded in a thick layer of mist in which the real and the fantastic often overlap. Initially in Paradise Park, Amir is haunted by the vision of the child and the mother whom he had seen as part of the crowd, watching the crowman. One night he sees them drowned and dead in the bottom of a jar. This fills him with a "vague sense of dread" (89). Rima is also a part of the dream, seen standing and smiling at his kitchen door. He feels as if she is "mocking at his fear" (92). The visions of the "bleeding sparrow" (92), the echo of crowman's voice, the flashes of the images of his flat and the glimpses of people he has interacted with, all seem to elude any coherent meaning to him. He is "only dimly aware that ... the sound of the child crying, the sound he could not hear, his dream and now Rima's decision to leave Paradise Park, take him home, are all in someway connected" (114).

In the case of Rima, it is the sound of 'child crying', which becomes a nightmarish experience to her. Even in her own apartment she has this hallucination. One day she asks Amir "Did you hear the child crying" (111) and the latter denies. Amir is unable to give a logical thought to the incidents like this. Together with Rima' in his flat, Amir has several terrible experiences. Rima walks in his flat even in the absence of light as if she is familiar to everything. (116) Amir finds everything in his flat, even after a long gap of time "as if someone moved in his house in his absence and lived exactly like him, moving out only moments ago" (116).

Amir tries to help Rima to adjust to the new surrounding such as, listening to the footsteps of the people walking in street, the noise coming from upstairs, movement of cockroaches in drain, the sight of the lamp burning, the power cuts etc. Rima, too, appears to be enjoying Amir's neighbourhood and is exhilarated to be a part of the crowd watching "a man swallowing a fish" (121). But these soon wane as Rima has repeated hallucinations of listening the sound of child crying. At first, she thinks it is her fancy but the sound becomes increasingly resonant. Amir has a casual response to it "there are a thousand and one reasons in this city for children to cry" (10). Rima is acutely tormented by her broken sleeps and hence, decides to find out 'who this child is' and 'why does it cry.' So one night she walks down in the street in search of the crying child. When Amir wakes up, he realizes that "Rima is gone, never to return, leaving nothing behind" (128). In the whole house there is nothing to show 'she was here.'

Amir makes efforts to come out of the miasma created in association with Rima but fails to do so. Haunted by sound of crying child himself, he has to leave everything on the forces beyond his control.

The sense of fear and disaster continues to dominate the narrative in Part Two also. The central incident in this part is the rape and murder of a girl child, aged about eleven or twelve years, whose body was found at the bottom of a canal in the small town. The canal is located on a narrow road that veers off the highway connecting the city.

Mala arrives in the town on a rainy morning of July and procures a copy of the post-mortem report after bribing the hospital attendant. The crude lingual presentation of the report in the text, giving details such as multiple abrasions of various sizes and shapes, bruising of sexual organs because of the rape etc, create nauseating effect. Similarly, the elaborate description of the post-mortem man and his work creates disgust in Mala. Unable to get the required help in her search either from the Police Officer or the RMO at the hospital, she visits the sight of the canal where the dead body of the girl was found and even meets the mother of the deceased.

The girl belonged to a middle class family and had the only piece of favourite 'red dress' in which she was found murdered. Mala is unable to find clues of the murder but in the course of unravelling the mystery she is herself haunted by frightful visions and dreams. Just before meeting the mother of the child she has the vision of a flying crow, with someone on its back' (170). In the room of the hotel, in which she stays for the night, the memories of her own childhood come to her in various shapes.

The flashes of memories, though, come to her in bits and pieces, yet together these build up a unified picture of her childhood and early youth. She is the only child of her middle class parents. Her mother, like the other mothers in the novel, is completely a housewife. Her father, a reporter is shown as a self-centred person, not much caring even for her. At his funeral, when she was only eleven or twelve years old, she was unable to realize the gravity of the situation. Her mother shoulders the responsibility of her upbringings. Mala is filled with the feeling of pity and remorse when her mother tries to convince her for marriage "I am getting very old now, I can die any day, I can't take care of you for ever, you need a man of your own" (226). There is a sense of insecurity in her as a child and it continues to dominate her personality even at present. The grotesque fantasies, which haunt her, have links in the psychological state of her mind.

In her room in the hotel, Mala has a phantasmagoric vision in which she sees her head grow beyond any imagined proportion. "Then, in her room-sized head, she sees a darkness; her eyelids part like curtains in a movie theatre on which scenes begin to play out in gigantic frames with neither shape nor colour" (208). She sees the tea stall owner putting a boy instead of sugar, in the kettle. Then she sees herself being post-mortemed by the post-mortem man. But the most prominent of all fantasies is the appearance of human shaped creature 'Alam.' He is a friendly figure and intends to help her. She feels as if "she has seen him, not once but several times" (219), present on several occasions in her life. She is led by him through her memory lanes in the past and then to see the things related to her present search. She has the glimpse of the dead body of the murdered child lying in water in the bottom of the canal. The loathsome sight drowns her in a pool of fear, pain and disgust.

On waking up, Mala realizes the futility of her efforts and at once decides to return home. There is sudden emergence of an intense sense of insecurity in her, not only for herself but also for her child, who is lying fast asleep in her apartment in the city, housed in a building having the look like a "crying façe" (240).

In Part Three of the novel, the protagonist is a girl child who is again eleven or twelve years of age. She is badly shaken by the suicide spree in her neighbourhood. In a city where "three hundred and fifty people, plus or minus thirty, kill themselves every year" (247-48), it is not unusual. Yet, the incidents hit the news headlines because "all these deaths happened in just one neighbourhood" (248). The mother of the child tries to allay the fears of her daughter by explaining "people kill themselves when they are very sad" (252). But the girl on the contrary feels her fears growing, for her house has the "looks like a crying face someone sad, someone very old" (252). She has fears for her parents as well as for herself. In her fantastic vision she is told, "you were crying because of the people dying in the neighbourhood and this has made you afraid that your father or your mother may kill themselves or may be even you ... standing on the balcony... often thought what would happen if you fell down to the street below" (255).

It is significant to note that there is a continuity as far as the images of the crying child and her parents are concerned, and they finally converge in the narrative of Part Three. The characters of the narrator child and her parents bear link to the three Prologues and the other parts of the novel and as such, gain progression in this part. In fact, the novelist has maintained the images of all girl children, mothers and fathers in the same frame, hence all the girls are aged between eleven or twelve years, all the mothers are thoroughly middle class housewives and the fathers are always preoccupied with ownselves. There are also many other identical marks in all of them.

In Part Three, the motive of fear has been delineated in the context of a middle class family showing signs of strain under the impact of suicide epidemic. In the process the visuals of the city life also emerge to provide backdrop to the narrative. A fantastic human shaped figure, who appears as a 'friend' to the narrator, is the channel through which the narrative progresses. He appears to assure the protagonist that she need not to be "afraid of the suicides any more" (256), because her "parents never once thought of doing the same" (256). He has come to find out the reason, as an answer to it may stop others from dying. He declares that he has 'pictures to show' and 'stories to tell' to explain everything. Actually, he followed the movements of her parents to prepare the details.

A series of pictures are shown to the narrator which bring the visuals of her parents and her own self, set in a pattern, to reflect their family life. The mother is generally confined to her home, busy in disposing off her domestic chores. The father, an employee of City Building Clearance Office is a man of moderate means. He is expecting "several gifts, a washing machine and a new television set" (271) to clear permission for the construction of Paradise Park. He is, at least, externally satisfied with his social status. He assures his wife that he has no reason to kill himself. The news about a girl "killed and raped in the small town" and the dream in which her daughter sees herself drowning in a glass of water, make the mother apprehensive of some unforeseen calamity. But the father is yet full of reassuring explanations. He advises his wife "don't believe everything you read in the newspapers" (286). As for the fears of his daughter, he says "she has nothing to be afraid of, both you and I are here" (287). He expresses his dislike for her crying. He also wishes to have "a new album" as "the gum has dried off the old one, many of the pictures are about to falloff" (287). It is suggestive of a fresh vision of life full of hope.

The novel, which has otherwise a sad and catastrophic colouring, ends with a positive note. The child asks the fantastic figure "Are my parents safe?" (240), the reply is confident and assuring that they are "very safe." The secret of their safety lies in their stoic attitude to take life as it is. This is reflected in the pictures shown to the girl and also in the conversation of her parents. Suddenly a crow is formed in the shadow and the fantastic man becomes small. He rides on the crow and waves a good-bye to the narrator. She feels tears rolling in her eyes but she does not let them out. She no longer wants "anyone to wake up to the sound of a child crying" (292). The sense of security returns to her and now, she is "not afraid of heights" (292).

The most significant aspect of the novel is the evocation of the milieu of Kolkata, both at macro and micro levels, underlining the stoic attitude of the people to keep life going even amidst odds. Amir puts himself back on his earlier track of life even after the nightmarish experience with Rima. Mala shifts her attention from someone dead to her child awaiting succour. The narrator child in Part Three is full of hope at last and she is able to overcome her fears. This spirit to sustain life is even more explicit in the case of the minor characters of the novel, representing different cross-sections of the city. The situation, generating numerous types of fear psychosis are always there, but the spirit of survival prevails upon them.

There are many post-modernist features in the novel, the detailed analysis of which requires a separate study. David Lodge has specified five narrative strategies often used in post-modern fiction—*Contradiction, Permutation, Discontinuity, Randomness and Excess.*[4] Many of these aspects are obvious enough in the narrative of the novel, both structurally and thematically. The central incident of Part Two is mentioned in Part One, but Part Two refers Paradise Park as a building yet to be built, which is contradictory. The identity of a character like Rima is vague and indeterminate. Similarly, it is difficult to establish the correlation between the sound of child cry and various girl children appearing as characters in different parts of the novel. The use of fantasy lends randomness both to the narration and the structure.

The brilliant uses of lyrical and often elliptical prose, in combination with other features, make *If You Are Afraid of Heights* a significant fictional product of recent times.

REFERENCES

1. Raj Kamal Jha, *If You Are Afraid of Heights* (London: Picador, 2003), p. 3.
2. E.M. Forster, *Aspects of the Novel* (1987); rpt. Harmondsworth: Penguin Books, 1964), p. 118.
3. Jasbsir Jain, "The Use of Fantasy in the Novels of Anita Desai" *Explorations in Modern Indo-English Fiction*, ed. R.K. Dhawan (New Delhi: Bahri Publications Pvt. Ltd. 1982) p. 227.
4. David Lodge, *The Modes of Modern Writing*: Metaphor, *Metonmy and the Typology of Modern Literature* (London: Arnold, 1977) p. 228.

8

Indian Sensibility in Arundhati Roy's *The God of Small Things*

UMED SINGH

By the time Arundhati Roy published her maiden novel *The God of Small Things* in 1997, Indian fiction in English had already gained roots and recognition at home and abroad. Now the novel retains an important place in Indian English Literature. The literary voyage of this genre began in 1864 with the publication of *Rajmohan's Wife* by Bankim Chandra Chatterjee. Since then, Indian Fiction in English has acquired universal acceptability and now it is read and reviewed by English-speaking world. Many novelists contributed to its growth and maturity. Some of these luminaries are: Romesh Chander Dutt, Rabindernath Tagore, Mulk Raj Anand, R.K. Narayan, Raja Rao, Bhabani Bhattacharya, Kamala Markandaya, B. Rajan, Khushawant Singh, Manohar Malgonkar, G.V. Desani, Nayantara Sehgal, Anita Desai, Arun Joshi, Salman Rushdie, Vikarm Seth and a host of other novelists who have been contributing to the further maturity of this literary genre.

In one single stroke through *The God of Small Things*, Roy further strengthens this tradition. The popularity of the novel can be gauged from the fact that it has sold about nine million copies the world over and has been translated into many languages. The Booker Prize to this novel in 1997 made the novelist and her work known throughout the world. The novel has been critically and continuously examined by critics, scholars and reviewers for its artistic beauty. The beauty and strength of her novel lies in the fact that it is unmistakably rooted in the native soil. She proclaims her artistic independence and gets inspiration and insight from her own milieu *i.e.*, Indian values, Indian culture and Indian Society with its beauty and ugliness. British and European literary traditions in tone and tenor don't inspire her. In fact, she assumes her identity by relating herself to Indian tradition and culture. In this context, the observation made by Judith Wright aptly applies to Arundhati Roy also: *Before one's country can become an accepted background against which the poet's and novelist's imagination can move unhindered, it must first be observed, understood, described as it were absorbed. The writer must be at peace with his landscape before he can confidently turn to its human figures*[1].

Roy is deeply rooted in her native and national culture and it is evident from her themes, style, landscape, images and of course, in her successful experimentation with English language. The novel raises many issues of universal relevance and its beauty lies in the fact that it can be interpreted from various angles. Though the novel deserves a comprehensive review, the aim and intent of the present paper is to show Roy's Indian sensibility as reflected in this novel.

First, the locale. Indian landscape has inspired not only the Indian English poets but the novelists also. Roy sets her novel in Ayemenem, a village in Kerala. The place is vividly described with its geography, demography, climate, customs, caste, conventions, flora, fauna, food habits, religious affiliations, occupations and professions people are engaged in. The novel begins with the depiction of geographical and climatic conditions of this place in the month of May:

> May in Ayemenen is hot, brooding month. The days are long and humid. The river shrinks.... dustgreen trees. Red bananas ripen. The nights are clear but suffused with sloth and sullen expectation.[2]

The regular phenomenon of the onset of south west monsoon, which provides much needed respite to the local inhabitants, is described with minute and minuscule details. "Brick walls turn moss green.... Boats ply in the bazaars. And small fish appear... on the highways."[3] The river Meenachal which falls into the nearest sea is also not very far off from the house of Pappachi, the head of a Syrian Christian family which figures centrally in the novel. *The Meenachal Greygreen. With fish in it. The sky and tree in it. And at night, the broken yellow moon in it.*[4] Ayemenem where much of the action of the novel takes place, is a little hill town nearly two hour drive from Cochin. Kottayam is another nearby town. The river and fishing is an integral part of the life of people living in the coastal areas. This is how the novelist describes the scene:

> The first third of the river was their (twins) friend. Before the Really Deep began. They knew the slippery stone steps (thirteen) before the slimy mud began.... They knew the smaller fish. The flat, foolish pallathi, the silverparal, the wily, whiskered koori, the sometimes karimeen.... Here they had learnt to fish.[5]

Like R.K. Narayana's Malgudi, the place with its people and vibrant culture comes live before the eyes of the readers.

Unity in diversity—the national characteristic—is the characteristic of this place also. The people belonging to different religions and ethnicity are living together. In Kerala and within it the place where the novel has been set, Hindus, Muslims and Christians are living together. Roy herself is a Syrian Christian. The people of her community are socially and educationally active and economically well off. They are also running schools in and around Kottayam. While living in India with people of different religions, they undergo cultural osmosis *i.e.* they influence and are influenced by customs and conventions of other racial, religious and ethnic groups. Like upper caste Hindus, they are caste conscious and practise untouchability. Though they become part of the national culture yet at the same time they maintain their cultural identity. Pappachi's family is a case in point. They are Indian but they never allow their cultural identity to get subsumed. This shows that Roy herself is part of Indian landscape and through her first hand experience with people and place, she evokes successfully a truly Indian locale in her novel.

Roy's Indianness can be seen in the portrayal of the realistic details about food habits and clothes and even hairstyles of her characters. The climate of a particular place determines the food habits and clothing. Her characters, both male and female, wear mundu, which is a comfortable wear in a place like Kerala, which has a hot and humid climate. Though the new generation under the influence of western culture, wears fashion clothes, mundu remains the traditional wear, worn even by the policemen. *She (Kalyani) was a lush, beautiful woman with golden brown skin and huge eyes. Her long... Her White mundu and kavani were crisp and ironed.*[6] To add authenticity to the novel Roy weaves small things into the texture of her novel. She describes the jewellery worn by Mammachi. *Her sari was starched and perfumed. Her diamond earnings shone in her ears like tiny chandeliers. Her ruby rings were loose.*[7] She also describes the manner in which Mammachi plaits her hair *A few years earlier, when her hair began to thin and silver, to give it body she wore her jet-bun pinned to her small, silver head. At, night a rubber band at the end.*[8] These details may be 'small but they are important in presenting the characters in a particular social and cultural context.

The people cultivate their food habits according to the crops grown in a particular area and are fond of food items made from banana, fish, rice, coconut etc. When Estha and Rahel go to Velutha's house, they are entertained with sweet smelling fish curry. It is a common practice in Kerala to offer coconut water to the guests. It shows Roy's familiarity with Indian ethos and culture.

Roy's Indian sensibility is reflected in the choice of her themes also. The novel is a powerful indictment of those ugly social forces which crush an innocent young man Velutha, who belongs to an untouchable class Paravan. The immediate cause of Velutha's death is police torture and subsequent custodial death for his alleged involvement in the abduction of children and the drowning of Sophie Mol in the river. But the in-depth study of the novel shows that Velutha is a victim of many ugly social forces.

His victimization and marginalisation begins the day when he was born in an untouchable caste. As he grows up into a young man, he does not seem to toe the line of his father, a typical untouchable who accepts the caste-based discrimination as the will of God. Velutha does not play serious attention to his father's advice regarding his conduct towards Touchables or high caste people. He has a sharp mind and because of *his carpentary skill.*[9] He can understand, maintain and handle machines very well. It induces a sense of self-respect in Velutha and he does not behave the way an untouchable 'should behave.'

> An unwarranted assurance. In the way he walked. The way he held his head. The quiet way he offered suggestions without being asked.... While these were qualities that were perfectly acceptable, perhaps even desirable in Touchables, Valley Paapen (father) thought that in a Paravan they could (and would, and indeed, should) be construed as insolence.[10]

His father fears for his son because he, being a socialized person, *recognizes the voice of oppressor even if he is not able to see his real face sometimes.*[11] Through his intelligence and technical skills, Velutha endears himself to the family members of Pappachi. The gulf between son and the father grows further and to escape his father's nagging and bickering, Velutha disappears from the village for a couple of months.

On his return, Velutha is re-employed as the factory carpenter and *in charge of general maintenance*[12] much to the dismay and disappointment of workers belonging to Upper Caste. Going by expediency, Mammachi offers him *less than a regular worker and more than what is paid to a paravan*[13] For his superior knowledge and superior position, Velutha is envied by the upper class workers in the factory. According to the other Touchable factory workers, Paravans *were not meant to be carpenters and prodigal paravan like Velutha was not meant to be rehired.*[14] Velutha annoys and infuriates his father by touching the household articles in Mammachi's house. His father does not like his son's intemperance and threatens to kill Velutha. It pleases and satisfies the inflated and perverted ego of Baby Kochamma. In *Annihilation of Caste,* B.R. Ambedkar vehemently decries this degrading practice: *I do not believe that we can build up a free society in India so long as there is a trace of this ill-treatment and suppression of one class by another.*[15] Mahatama Gandhi and B.R. Ambedkar waged a relentless battle against the practice of untouchability. Though the practice had been declared unlawful long back yet unfortunately this shameful and inhumane practice still persists. The malaise is so deep rooted in the psyche of Indian people that case bias surfaces with the slightest provocation even among the most educated and cultured sections of our society. In the novel, Paravans are hated by the upper class people because they emanate 'foul smell.'

It is believed that during his absence from the village Velutha became a political activist, an extreme leftist. He committed another crime by participating in the political demonstration staged by the Marxist Labour Union against the Govt. He is recognized by Rahel among the marchers.

Velutha commits another 'sin' perhaps unpardonable in Indian society. He is instinctively drawn towards Ammu, an estranged and an unloved daughter of Pappahi. (Since she had married against her parents' wishes she is an unwelcome guest in her parents house). They transgress the Love Laws and establish physical relationship with each other. They seek solace in each others' arms because they belong to the same 'class' *i.e.* marginalized and oppressed class. Vallay Pappen is shocked to learn that his Untouchable son has fallen in love with the woman of an Upper Class family. He brings this disturbing matter to the notice of Mammachi because of his loyalty to the family. Mammachi is terribly upset and spits venom on him.

> Suddenly the blind old woman... pushed Velley Pappen with all her strength... He was taken completely by surprise... She (Baby Kochamma) found Mammachi spitting into the rain, Thoo! Thoo! Thoo! Mammachi was shouting, Drunken dog! Drunken Paravan liar!

Velutha and Vellay Pappen are representative characters who show the degrading and discriminated life being lived by the people belonging to low castes. The lovers are severely punished. Velutha is warned and dismissed from the job. Henceforth, he will not be seen in and around Mammachi's estate. Baby Kochamma, for the sake of family honour, misreports and misinforms the police about Velutha' alleged involvement in the kidnapping of children and the subsequent death of Sophie Mol. Velutha is arrested, inhumanely tortured and beaten till he bled to death. Pillai, the local political, could have protected Velutha but he, like modern politicians, does not waste his patronage on the poor person like Velutha. In fact, many social forces contribute to the systematic victimization, which ultimately lead to his death. The novelist castigates the society which denies dignified and decent life to certain individuals because they are born in a 'low caste'. Though unprotected and unpatronised, Velutha tried to live a dignified life but he becomes the victim of collective hatred of his own class (his father for instance), workers belonging to Upper Caste, Mammachi and Baby Kochamma, and police which only protects those who are protected by unscrupulous politicians.

The case of police brutality and custodial deaths of innocent people are on rise. It is a disquieting phenomenon, which puts modern Indian society to shame. Velutha's custodial death also exposes the unholy and unwarranted nexus between police and politician. In a welfare state the police is supposed to protect the innocent and law abiding people but the police follows the dictates of the politician particularly those who are in power. Velutha's case is not an isolated example of police atrocities and highhandedness. It is a grim reality of Indian society. The police victimize the poor, the underprivileged and the marginalized sections of society. After Sophie's death, Ammu is summoned to the police station with her twins for further investigation of the case. The police inspector behaves in an indecent manner and taps Ammu's breasts repeatedly with his baton.

> He spoke the coarse Kottayam dialect of Malayalam. He stares at Ammu's breast as he spoke... the Kottayam police didn't take statement from Veshyas or their illegitimate children. *If I were you, he said, I'd go home quietly.*[4] *Then*

> *he tapped her breasts with his baton. Gently. Tap, tap. As though he was choosing mangoes from a basket... behind him a red and blue board said:*
>
> — Politeness
> — Obedience
> — Loyalty
> — Intelligence
> — Courtesy
> — Efficiency.[16]

How wide is the gap between words and deeds! The novel reflects the Indian society with its dehumanizing institutions dwarfing the human beings. The novelist is certainly raising the voice of protest against the ugly forces of society.

Roy also records her protest against Indian male-dominated society, which renders woman into a dependent and deprived being. Indian society is patriarchal one. Male dominance in every sphere of life has made women the most vulnerable section of our society. Society not only does grave injustice to them but also tries, through man-made institutions, to legitimatize their inferior and secondary status in the society. She is assigned relative positions through the process of continuous social and cultural conditioning. This process begins right from the day of her birth. This affects her whole being.

> She can not think of herself without man. And she is simply what man decrees. She appears essentially to the male as a sexual being. She is defined and differentiated with reference to man and not he with reference to her; she is the incidental, the inessential.[17]

Though gender inequities are neither culture specific nor country specific. The evil is as old as human civilization on the earth and it has travelled down from the primordial period to our times. It is ironic and pathetic to note that human civilization has evolved continuously ignoring the vital half of humanity *i.e.* women. Roy highlights the disturbing and disquieting feature of Indian society. Her protest against male dominated society and its degrading institutions is as strong as that of Simon De Beauvoir in France and Virginia Woolf in England.

The society, as Roy portrays in *The God of Small Things*, is very callous to those women who defy the established codes of social morality. If a woman dares to marry outside her community, religion or marries within her community but without her parents' consent, she is considered a rebel and her act brings 'disgrace' and 'dishonour' to the family. These women lose their respect and recognition first in the family and then in the society (society is in fact an extended metaphor of family). Ammu, Pappachi's daughter is not allowed to pursue her studies further 'due to commonly held views.' The patriarchal bias against women is evident from the fact that Chacko, Ammu's brother, could be sent to the Oxford for further studies. Pappachi insisted that a *college education was an unnecessary expense for a girl, so Ammu had no choice.. Since her father did not have enough money to raise a suitable dowry, no proposal came.. Ammu grew desperate.*[18]

In the want of care and concern, Ammu feels suffocated in her father's house and decides to go to Calcutta for temporary relief. In a chance meeting with a young man at the wedding reception, she loses her heart to him and marries him without informing her parents. To her dismay she found that the man whom she married was not an executive (as he claimed before marriage) but an uneducated and ordinary employee in the tea planation. He was an alcoholic also. Ammu feels distressed and disillusioned now. The husband and wife start drifting into opposite directions. His insensitivity and insincerity due to excessive drinking is evident from the fact that he was dead drunk and was sleeping in the hospital corridor while his wife was in labour pain. The situation further aggravates by his 'bouts of violence' which *began to include the children also.*[19] Then, she is deeply hurt because her husband is treating her as a commodity and asking her to accept an indecent proposal from Mr. Holick. She comes to the end of the tether and her disillusionment with her husband is complete. A pathetic description of her arrival at her parents' house:

> Ammu left husband and returned unwelcomed, to her parents in Ayemenen. To everything that she had fled from only a few years ago. Except that now she had two young

> children. And no more dreams. It was as though the window through which their father disappeared had been kept open for any one to walk in and be welcomed. For her self she knew that there would be no more chances. There was only Ayemenem now. A front verandan and a back verandah. A hot river and a pickle factory. And in the background, the constant, high whining mewl of local disapproval.[20]

Society does not give equal and adequate space to women. Ammu is a representative character who shows the plight of women in patriarchal society. She has defied the male made conventions so she has no 'Locus Standi' in the society. Like any other woman in Indian society Ammu, an estranged wife, lives a miserable life in her parents house. She is constantly subjected to taunts and harshness. According to Baby Kochamma, she (Ammu) has disqualified herself for a dignified life by marrying without her parents' consent. And to make the matter worse, she has been separated from her husband. This is how the novelist describes their plight:

> She subscribed wholeheartedly to the commonly held view that a married daughter had no position in her parents home. As for a *divorced* daughter—according to Babby Kochamma, she had no position anywhere at all. And as for a *divorced* daughter from a *love* marriage, well, words could not describe Baby Kochamma's outrage. As for a *divorced* daughter from a *intercommunity* love marriage Baby Kochamma chose to remain quiveringly slient on the subject.[21]

If any thing goes wrong in the house, the instant and immediate cause according to the family members, is always Ammu and her children. The wrath and neglect spills over to her innocent children also who are constantly made to feel uncomfortable and unwelcome in the house. Unloved and uncared, children feel elated in the company of Velutha. He loves them so they are very fond of him. Even Ammu, the Unmixable Mix, with deep void in her being, drifts towards Velutha, a young man of her own class, the oppressed class. Both are pushed on the margin with their space encroached upon. *He saw too that he was not necessarily the only giver of gifts. That she had gifts to give him too. Ammu saw what he saw. She looked away. He did too.*[22] In fact, they share a lot of common ground. Ammu's sexual relationship with God of small things is the last act of digression, which alienates her further from her family and society. In the name of family honour, Baby Kochamma recommends Ammu's expulsion from the house. Chacko, the patriarchal voice, shouts at his sister *get out of my house before I break every bone of your body*[23] Hapless Ammu leaves her parents house disgracefully only to die unattended and unlamented. The children also suffer. They are, left behind, unprotected, unloved and unconnected. The society, with its hypocrisy and double standards of morality, punishes the woman but the same digression on the part of man is always justified in the name of 'man's needs.' Separated from his wife Margret, Chacko has 'clandestine' 'sexual relationship with female factory workers' with the tacit approval of Mammachi and Baby Kochamma. It is very unfortunate that the character and conduct of a woman is judged from different and discriminating codes of morality. Patriarchal oppression is so severe that a woman victimizes her own class. Baby Kochamma's self suppression, frustration and her unnatural hatred for Ammu and her children is mainly due to the fact that her natural fine sensibilities have been systematically corroded in a male dominated society. Mammachi, who has been ill treated over the years by her husband, becomes an enemy of her own daughter. Such are the crippling effects of patriarchal ideology on women.

A woman is never allowed to grow as an independent and autonomous human being. She is always given a secondary and subservient place in the society. She is always considered as a weak and vulnerable creature that needs protection and patronage at every stage of her life. In the childhood she is protected by her parents; after her marriage protection is given by her husband and in the old age she is taken care of by her own children (sons). She is a relative creature who is always in need of support and sympathy. In the novel, Mammachi, now an old woman living with *scars of old beatings from the old marriage. Her brass vase scars.*[24] She is shown as a helpless woman who is beaten every night with a brass flower vase by her egoistical and domineering husband. It is only with Chacko's violent intervention that Pappachi stopped wife—beating operation. With this, the contact and communication between the husband and wife was snapped as if violence was the only way to communicate. Roy vividly describes the grim reality of Indian Society:

> Chacko strode into the room, caught Pappachi's vase-hand and twisted it around his back. I never want this to happen again, he told his father. Ever.... He never touched Mammachi again. But he never spoke to her either as long as he lived. When he needed anything he used Kochi Maria or Baby Kochamma as intermediaries.[25]

Wife-beating is a deplorable and dehumanizing practice of Indian society. Though Ammu marries a man of her own fancy but, as far as wife husband relationship is concerned, the same fate awaits her. She puts up with her husband's beastly behaviour but then he asks her to accept an indecent proposal of his employer. Ammu's silence on this proposal infuriates him: *Suddenly he lunged at her, grabbed her hair, punched her and then passed out from the effort.*[26]

Roy's Indian sensibility is further seen in the Indianisation of English language. She does not ape the standard English or the Babu English as used by the British writers. She does not imitate the Indian writers either. By evolving Indian idiom, which is best suited for the expression of Indian experience, Roy has accomplished the task, which was initiated by creative writers like Raja Rao and Mulk Raj Anand. In the preface to Kanthapura, in itself a creative piece of writing, Raja Rao expresses the problems of a suitable medium of expression being faced by Indian writers writing in English:

> The telling has not been easy. One has to convey in language that is not one's own the spirit that is one's own. We can not write like the English. We should not. We can write only as Indians. Our method of Expression, therefore, has to be dialect which will some day prove to be as distinctive and as colourful as the Irish or the American.[27]

Raja Rao overcomes the problem by evolving a suitable linguistic medium in which words are English but the organization is Indian. He uses the language effectively that the word becomes the perception. He uses breathtaking long sentence, sometimes page-long sentences and repetitions of names and words to experience wide range of experience. Mulk Raj Anand also contributes substantially to the evolution of Indian English. Besides his experiments with the dialogues of his characters, he also interpolates Hindi words in English. Meenakshi Mukherjee beautifully sums up their contribution in this regard:

> One important difference between the styles of Raja Rao and Anand is that Anand's experiments are limited to the dialogue of his characters; while Raja Rao's special effects permeate his entire style.[28]

Arundhati Roy further enriches Indian English in her own way: The text of *God of Small Things* is not amenable to western literary cannons. It subverts the basic edifice of Standard English, its syntax, morphology, phonology, grammar etc. Like G.V. Desani, she experiments with newer forms of expression according to the status and stature of her characters. In G.V. Desani's *All About Hatterr*, Hatterr is a half educated Anglo Malayan orphan and G.V. Desani uses a peculiar kind of English which is natural to a queer person like H. Hatterr. Roy's English startles an ordinary reader because she uses that variety of English, which adequately expresses the physical, mental and emotional responses of her characters placed in different situations and circumstances. She takes liberties with the language in the manner of a child who has not yet mastered the language. In the course of the narrative we come across sentences, which are made of single word or sometimes of two words. For instance:

1. Squashed dogs that ate the squashed frog-shaped stains in the universe. Feather, Mango, Spil (*GOST*, p. 82).
2. From the sea Queen florist Chacko had brought two red roses which he had held carefully. Fatly. Fondly (*GOST*, p. 137).

3. Gentle half-monsoons... they are as old as Ammu was when she died. Thirty-one. Not young (*GOST*, p. 3).

Roy uses capital letters even in the middle of sentences to express exactly what she wants her characters to express:

1. The Found Smiles watched Fondly. Little Girls Playing. Sweet. One beach-coloured. One loved One Loved a Little Less (*GOST*, p. 186).
2. A hot twin and a cold one. He and she we and Us (*GOST*, p. 122).
3. The God of Loss? The God of Small Things? The God of Goose Bumps and Sudden Smiles? (*GOST*, p. 217).

Sometimes the space between the words is obliterated to convey symbolically the encroachment of woman's space by man. The Compound words, phrases, expression are broken altered and some times twisted and disfigured to convey the sense of dislocation experienced by the characters.

1. Goodnight (*GOST*, p. 115).
2. Shutup.
3. Locas Stand 1.
4. Lay. Ter (later) (*GOST*, p. 146).
5. Whatisit? What happened and for a furrywhirring and a sariflapping (*GOST*, p. 6).

Her preoccupation with Indian experience and her experimentation with English language is seen in the evocative imagery and metaphor employed by the novelists.

1. Rahel's new teeth were waiting under her gums, like words in a pen.
2. Her head was too large for her body. She looked like a bottled foetus that had escaped from its jar of formaldehyde in a Biology lab and shriveled and thickened with age (*GOST*, p. 170).
3. She wore a long, printed skirt that reached all the way down to her ankles and a short, waist-length white blouse with darts that made rooms for future breasts (*GOST*, pp. 270-71).

Besides these linguistic experiments and innovations, Roy makes use of italics, parenthesis, abbreviations and sometimes words are underlined to give emphasis to a particular expression. Even mathematical signs are used in the course of the narrative.

> When the twins asked what cuff-links were for—to link cuff together, Ammu told them they were thrilled by this morsel of logic in what had so far seemed an illogical language. Cuff+link = cuff link. This to them, rivelled the precision and logic of mathematics. Cuff-link gave them an inordinate (if exaggerated) satisfaction, and a real affection for the English language.[29]

This is Arundhati Roy's queer experiment with English language, which makes it more flexible and more pliable to express the wide range of experience of characters living in a pluralistic and multi-cultural society of India.

The God of Small Things reverberates with a feel of Indian life and ethos. The very India life is brought live on the pages by evoking economical, religious, cultural, social, political, geographical atmosphere of the country. *The idiom that she employs perfectly matches with the themes she is concerned with. In her experimentation with the medium of expression, she does not imitate any Indian writer writing in English. She need not imitate because her style is Indian and it is genuine and individual rather than merely correct and competent.*[30]

REFERENCES

1. Quoted by Devindra Kohli, "Landscape and Poetry", The *Journal of Commonwealth Literature*, Vol. xiii No. 3, April, 1979, p. 54.
2. Arundhati Roy, *The God of Small Things*, (New Delhi: Penguin Books 1997), p. 1.
3. *Ibid.*, p. 1.
4. *Ibid.*, p. 203.
5. *Ibid.*
6. *Ibid.*, p. 270.
7. *Ibid.*, p. 79.
8. *Ibid.*, p. 166.

9. *Ibid.*, p. 75.
10. *Ibid.*, p. 76.
11. B.R. Ambedkar, *Annihilation of Caste*, Dalit Classic Series – 1 (New Delhi: Blumoon Books) p. 3.
12. A. Roy, *op. cit.* p. 77.
13. *Ibid.* p. 77.
14. B.R. Ambedkar, *op. cit.* p. 30.
15. A. Roy, *op. cit.* p. 256.
16. *Ibid.*, p. 8.
17. R. Seldon (ed.), *The Theory of Criticism: From Plato to the Present*, (London: Longman, 1998) p. 534.
18. A. Roy, *op. cit.* p. 38.
19. *Ibid.*, p. 42.
20. *Ibid.*
21. *Ibid.*, p. 45-6.
22. *Ibid.*, p. 177.
23. *Ibid.*, p. 225.
24. *Ibid.*, p. 166.
25. *Ibid.*, p. 48.
26. *Ibid.*, p. 42.
27. Raja Rao, *Kanthapura*, (Bombay: O.U.P., 1938).
28. Meenakshi Mukherjee, *Twice Born Fiction*, (London: Heinemann Educational Books Ltd., 1971) p. 186.
29. *Ibid.*, p. 51.
30. Meenakshi Mukherjee, *op. cit.* p. 201.

Note: Some references to this novel are indicated by the abbreviation *GOST*.

9

Resurrection of Self: A Study of Anita Nair's *Ladies Coupe*

BINOD MISHRA

Indian writing in English today has come to occupy a respectable position and the credit for it goes to a good number of women writers, whose pens have spilt much ink in bringing to light the various aspects left untouched and ignored by their male counterparts. Widely considered as feministic writers, these deities describe not only their family fluids and their inferior status but they also depict the sores in their souls and their agonies as individuals. They portray their characters as human beings who also feel a longing for their own space and their worth as individuals who not only sob when denied their due, but also shed tears to purge themselves of their deeds and misdeeds. Anita Nair joined the literary horizon much later before her compatriots had talked much about the heat and dust and of their subdued voices in the city and village by the sea often confined in custody to offer small remedies. Her ventures have produced some good works and in a little span of her career she has gained an international reputation. With *Satyr of the Subway*; a collection of short stories, as her first publication, she has made news with two novels, *A Better Man* (2000) and *Ladies Coupe* (2001). Her poetic sparks have also been realized with *Malabar Mind* (2002) and she has also edited a collection of writings on Kerala. Her latest release, *Puffin Book of World Myth and Legends,* which makes readers realize Nair's concern for all classes and groups of people. Anita Nair, like the veteran Anita Desai started writing at the age of seven or eight and both of them began doing so in their moments of emotional outbursts. Middle class family stories being their forte, both of them are not primarily obsessed with women's woes. Desai's novels depict the mental conflicts coiling their heroines whereas Nair makes her characters suffer and enables them to come out of it. Desai's heroines sulk, sob and submerge themselves in their calamity but for Nair's characters, their sufferings become their strength and weapon to fight out their predicaments. This becomes a matter of debate and as Anita Nair, herself reacts when Ladies Coupe is being argued as an important work of feminism by well known publications:

> Firstly, I don't like these broad categories and classifications. It is lazy journalism to use such generalizations. Only first book (*A Better Man*) was described as erotic. I don't think it was. Also there were so many aspects to the book and just classifying it as erotic literature was so superficial. In the same way, I was surprised when Ladies Coupe was described as feminist—another literary generalization. Also, I am not happy with the term feminism "—Well, firstly it is outdated. Secondly the word feminism implies a straining to be equal, a desperation almost, to get equal with men, while what is important is to know that you are equal and exercise that equality to experience that equality knowing it is yours, naturally."[1]

The present paper, is an attempt to explore the notion that Anita Nair's *Ladies Coupe* is free from male—female dichotomy and it is more a story of ladies who as human beings want to realize what they really require. An honest understanding of their choices and their fulfillment by dint of 'enough strength to stand on their own without a mandatory elephant thrown in' alone can bring success.

The story of the novel *Ladies Coupe* is set in a railway compartment specially meant for ladies. Six ladies travelling in the coupe narrate their stories and share their secrets lying deep in their hearts. All of them by turn bare their bosom and they feel embittered and emboldened, dyspeptic and eupeptic. The train journey, though through various tunnels and wild vegetation, unfolds a backward journey, which the ladies undertake in their lives. Their backward journey helps them understand the major bruises and injuries experienced by them in the course of their life. The ascents and descents which they have witnessed in their capacities as daughter, sister, beloved, wife and mother make them realize how isolated they stand amid the crowd where they are the part and not the whole. The vivid realizations of their roles separate them from their real selves. The societal presences and their individual pulls seem to tear them apart where they come across aleatory forces deciding the coarse of their action. Their agitated minds and their longing bodies need heaven's rain, which can not only wash their confusions but also soothe them. The realization of their self, lying ignored and uncared shouts to burst forth and when such realization dawns upon them, they feel empowered. This recovery is like a redemption and it enables them to defy everything which is not their own. In their conflict between their bodies and souls, the body finally wins since it's the body and bodily desires that dictate the soul.

The central character in the novel *Ladies Coupe* is Akhila who listens patiently to the ups and downs of her co-passengers' life and starts thinking of her own life devoid of meaning at the age of forty-five, an age by which many of her coevals settle. Akhila's responsibilities include upkeeping the house and discharging her duties to the satisfaction of everyone. She loses her father in the prime of her life and being the eldest child of the parents, shoulders the responsibility. Getting a job in the income tax department on compassionate grounds, she not only becomes the man of the house but also loses her individual choices. She guides her brothers in their studies and career and also arranges their marriages. The house is in order but the members have forgotten about Akhila's emotion and her emotional needs. Akhila handles all cumbersome responsibilities dexterously and she's allowed a bigger identity. Not called by her name, she gets the treatment of Akka, the elder sister. Even her mother used to call her Ammadi. Akhila feels at a war with her emotions. The upsurge in her inner chamber tries to awaken her. She suffers an identity crisis. The readers are touched to the core when Akhila gets berserk and asks herself,

> So who was Akhilandeswari? Did she exist at all? If she did, what was her identity? Did her heart skip a beat when she saw a mango tree studded with blossoms? Did the feel of rain on her bare skin send a line of goose bumps down her spine? Did she sing? Did she dream? Did she weep for no reason?[2]

Akhila has a volley of questions whose answers she tries to find from her co-passengers who had seen more life and had experienced the basic realities of living with husband, baby, home and mother–in–law. Akhila's circumstances enable her to think that woman could live by herself and that marriage was unimportant. She wonders how her co-passengers, despite their settled lives were living lives on margin. Most of them had a vacuum in their lives, stories to tell and had innumerable cries. Akhila is curious to know about the experiences of being married and if there was any danger in living alone. Janaki, one of the co-passengers, opposed to Akhila's ideas considers the basic purpose of a woman's life to get married. Janaki, though satisfied with her life hints at the dissatisfaction which all human beings have at a certain age. Woman, according to Janaki is a subordinate self and as her horizon expands, her sole satisfaction lies in being with the male counterpart. Janaki's assertions fail to assure Akhila. What Janaki says appears to be obsolete in today's changing times:

> I am a woman who has always been looked after. First there was my father and my brothers; then my husband; when my husband is gone, there will be my son waiting to take off from where his father left off. Women like me end up being fragile; our men treat us like princesses.[3]

Janaki believed that a woman's role was to keep the family intact and reach out to every member. But she finds herself at a certain age a victim of all sorts of taunts and derisions when she comes to help her son's wife Jaya, admitted for the Caesarean. Unable to bear insults, she decides to go home and live her life with her husband.

Margaret Shanthi also has a woeful ballad on her tongue. A gold medallist in Chemistry, she is drawn towards Ebenezer Paulraj who persuades Margaret, too, to become a teacher like him. Their love culminates in a hasty marriage and it literally becomes a deathbed for Margaret. Ebe's poetic leanings and his romantic swearings stunt when their consummation results in Margaret's pregnancy. He turns indifferent and stands in way against Margaret's natural right to become mother. His love seems to be based on the foundations of selfishness. Without understanding the impact of abortion he convinces her to do so. Ebe, the teacher defies even the dictates of religion and considers the killing of the foetus as 'a tumour that has to be removed'. He wants to kill the soul to preserve the body. This unsetlles Margaret and she is full of shock and shame, guilt and conflict before toeing Ebe's line. She hears a faint voice:

> Your hands shaped and made me. Will you now turn and destroy me?... You created my inmost being; you knit me together in your womb.... My frame was not hidden from you when I was made in that secret place. When I was woven together in the depths of the earth, your eyes saw my unformed body.[4]

Margaret couldn't conceive again for a long time. Bound by traditional fetters and social mores she considered her husband right only to evade divorce, a stigma those days. Her vulnerability put her in a state of indecision and she put the yoke. But her injured self longed for revenge. As time passed, Margaret fattened Ebe by her culinary skills. Margaret's connivance & her ignorance of Ebe brought the couple together. Ebe now needed Margaret and they bore a daughter. Margaret had her revenge and her knowledge of chemicals had an advantage over Ebe's admiration for poetry:

> Love beckons with a rare bouquet. Love demands you drink of it and then love burns the tongue, the senses; love blinds. Love maddens. Love separates reason from thought. Love kills. Love is methyl alcohol pretending to be ethyl alcohol.[5]

Akhila may not seem to be convinced with what the women in *Ladies Coupe* think about life but she establishes a common concatenation in their stories, and that is to 'make some sense of their own existence by talking about it to anyone who will listen.' Akhila finds that 'anyone' amiss in her life and her train of thought drives her to past life which she couldn't give a name, an opportunity which she got and lost because of the conflict between her emotions and her reasonings. Akhila had experienced a sensation by an unknown touch *albeit* by chance. This had created a sensation in her and she longed for such chances. She had allowed the unknown hand to meander around her navel. Her sensational experiences came to halt one day when the bus conductor realized this vagrant play and advised her to take an earlier bus. Ashamed, she decides to take the morning train.

The invisible touch creates waves in Akhila and for the time being she becomes oblivious to the identity of the person. It's for the first time that she realizes what it's to be sensitive and in her mind's eye she looks back. Her backward journey enables her to curse herself for missing such intimate sensations. The touch not only creates ripples but also augments her longing for such experiences. Blinded by this physical desire she rides the same bus every morning to reassure and enliven her dormant longings. Her age and status pose no threat to this pleasure, though from some one unknown.

> She knew that she was behaving like no self-respectable woman would. But there was a gratification for her as well. She felt desired. She felt as if she had a hunger. Akhila felt like a woman.[6]

Akhila never imagined that she would meet someone younger and smarter who'd propose her. They met like co-passengers, enjoyed some good moments and separated. Their acquaintances convert into a longing and Akhila, the aged one hides her propensity towards Hari. Her camouflaged camaraderie tempts her to go to Mahabalipuram with Hari. She is full of anger and feels her right at stake when her mother wants Akhila to seek her brother's permission. Her Ammadi status inhibits all her mellow feelings she wished and wanted to cherish with Hari. Akhila burns and boils but doesn't tell Amma because,

> in Amma's world, men married women younger than themselves. Women never offered their bodies to men before their union was sanctified by marriage. Women never went away with their men who were not their husbands. Women never knew what it was to desire.[7]

Akhila obliges Hari and spends a contented night in a seaside resort. Soon after, she realizes and becomes aware of what others say. Her guilty conscience haunts her and she feels it as a conundrum the union between a young man and an older woman. She decides to tell Hari the truth that the years between them could not be bridged. Neither society nor time would approve of such an unusual bonding. Akhila is every inch a realist and she feels burdened with these crumbs of regret. She discharged her responsibilities well and her brothers and sister too had their lives running smoothly. Akhila clung to her lost chord when her sister, Padma heaved, caressed and cuddled with her husband in the adjacent room. Akhila is torn and dejected and is also full of self-pity. Her crippling longing for Hari bisects her into two halves—to be or not to be. Two halves of Akhila seem never to make a whole. The novelist describes Akhila's condition with tear-soaked eyes.

> What she resented was being thrust into the middle of all this change, this expanding of horizon, while her life continued in its sedate, dull, spinsterish, constant way. No highs. No lows. Just seamless travel from day to day.[8]

Akhila feels emboldended with Prabha Devi's story. She considered Prabha Devi to be one of the most confident and contented persons she had met. Married to Jagdish, the son of a prosperous diamond merchant, Prabha Devi had all sorts of comforts at her beck and call. Jagdish allowed her freedom to wear and live life the way she wanted. Her admirable looks attracted others,' attention also. But she wanted to be treated as an individual and not as somebody's wife. When a friend of Jagdeesh, Pramod didn't take Prabha seriously she began practicing her wiles. It was only later that she realized, she had ignited the man in Pramod, who decided to take liberties with her when he found an opportunity. He wanted to make Prabha realize what she expected of him by sending sweet smiles and lustrous looks. And the moment when Pramod tries to wander and wade through her body, Prabha stops him by hurling abuses and insulting remarks. The way Prabha pulls her wrists out of Pramod's grasp and slaps him on the cheek shows how women can guard their fort to preserve their sanctity. But this incident filled her with shame and she turned inwards blaming her for all that happened. She reminisces about what her mother had hoped she would be:

> With eyes forever downcast and busy hands; embroidering, picking, birthing babies, preserving order and bliss in the confines of her home and all the while chanting to herself: this is who I ought to be, this is the way to be happy.[9]

Realization dawns upon her and she becomes aware that the old and traditional sayings are not mere idioms but they're statements soaked in reality. Life is not an experiment or a theorem but an accepted fact.

Prabha Devi decided to deaden her desires and negate her dreams of being the woman she wanted. Jagdish, too, became upset to see the calm and composed woman, the bubbling beautiful Prabha had converted into. Life for Prabha seemed to lose meaning and deprived of rhythm. But she wanted to live to float, to submerge in the subtleties of her bodily hungers that at time made her yearn for more life. She perhaps had forgotten that repressed desires and emotions are more dangerous. She regained her sensations when she joined swimming classes. Water renewed her desires and she longed for a flowering of senses. The novelist describes Prabha's renewed concupiscence in the following lines:

> But she discovered that desire spawns desire; fulfilment begets fulment. A kiss for a kiss. A caress for a caress. What one gives comes back manifold.[10]

Repression in tradition bound countries like India often results in acute suffering for sensitive individuals and women, according to M. Rajeshwar, *happen to be the worst sufferers as the social norms and moral codes have been so framed as to be particularly disadvantageous to them.*[11] Prabha comes out of this vicious vortex with the help of her will power. One needs to understand the gaps and also what these gaps require. If gaps are ignored, they widen to such an extent that no bridge can link them. We need to explore the cause and find their remedy. The sparks of life emanate from a strong will, the will to experience and enliven the rough and tumble of life and extract delight out of them.

Prabha's story moves Akhila and she tries to reassess and reevaluate herself. Akhila had sacrificed all her aspirations for the welfare of her family members who could never think she too had a woman in her. She is in a swivet over the attitude of her family members. Her sister, Padma's animus towards her is well known. Akhila's sizzling desires get some relief to think of her past, which comprised her isolation, undivided though. We find her wriggles in the given lines.

> Sometimes Akhila thought what she hated most was not having an identity of her own. She was always an extension of someone else's identity—Chandra's daughter; Narayan's Akka; Priya's aunt; Murthy's sister-in-law... Akhila wished for once someone would see her as a whole being.[12]

Her only worry that nobody could understand the waves undergoing within her makes her cry at times. She is touched to the core when her brother Narayan shows his concern about her decision of living alone. Akhila silences everyone by her decision and expresses her metaphysical anguish, saying: *Nobody's daughter Nobody's sister. Nobody's wife. Nobody's mother.*[13] The vibrations in Akhila's inner sanctum bring a moment of universal pity for women in general and Akhila in particular. She finds herself totally ignored, alienated and unattached. Her realization that everyone around her had their axe to grind and that nobody ever dared to think about her animal spirits, frightens her siblings Prabha Devi's experiences inspire Akhila and she thinks if she too could learn to move on with the tide of life rather than be cast on its banks. If Prabha's struggle created in Akhila a desire to live, Marikolanthu's travail strengthens and fortifies her.

Marikolanthu, the sixth passenger in the coupe motivates Akhila and tells her:

> Women are strong. Women can do everything as well as men. Women can do much more but a woman has to seek that vein of strength in herself, it does not show itself naturally.[14]

Marikolanthu's life resembles Akhila's with various ups and downs. She, too, had to depend on others for her livelihood. Her helplessness becomes a blessing in disguise for Chettiar Kottai, a family of high repute. Mari continues her parents' tradition of working in Kottai and comes closer to Sujata, the wife of Sridhar, Chettar's second son. Sujata obliges Mari with her cast off dresses and they become one for each other. Appointed to look after their son Mari feels an obligation to be sent to Vellore where she serves as a housemaid. Sujata's aunt had a tenant—two lady doctors who taught Mari not only decent manners but also offered to help her find a job in the hospital. But she had something unexpected waiting for her. In one of her visits to Chettiar household, she was eyed upon by Murugesan who perforce made a physical relation with Mari. This incident had a very destablising effect on her. Full of shame and hurt she tried to clean herself of that contract. But nothing happened. The sin weighed on her soul and the rotundity of her belly signalled all that she never wanted. Her mother, too, felt nauseous and none from the Chettiar family came to their help. The fear of obloquy forces them to think of other escape routes than have the pregnancy aborted. But all efforts fritter and the unwanted child is born, much to the delight of Periamma and more to the despair of Mari. The child is reared by Periamma as a relative's offspring.

Mari's tragic tale has another twist in it. Sujata, bored with her husband's hobnobbing with other women hates to be with him in bed yet she offers her carbunclar body to Sridhar only to stop him from flaunting others. Ironically, she longs for a passionate union, which Mari provides her with. The collusion of their bodies satiates their thwarted dreams and unfulfilled desires. Marikolanthu has become a true assistant to Sujata and to cherish their covert association she feels no qualms even when Sridhar enters her body. She pleases both at the cost of her own abuses. She finds the stains on her soul and scratches on her body. Her vivid realization makes her sensible:

> Neither of them loved me. But they needed me. Those who can't have love have to settle for need. What is love if not a need disguised? [15]

She understands her need when she is thrown out of Chettiar Kottai. She decides to undergo an operation to remove the growth developed out of her confluence with Sirdhar. She mortgages her son, Muthu in Murugesan's looms in return for five thousand rupees. She feels Murugesan's sin avenged by selling him his own son. But things take a sudden turn when Murugesan dies and his funeral takes place. His body does not burn completely and the relatives call Muthu to take care of the corpse. Muthu loads the logs and the body burns.

Mari watches everything from a distance and is full of remorse for her son, who without his fault had been forced to bear the brunt. Her hate for Murugesan is burnt with his ashes and she feels ashamed to have used her own son. The desire to own Muthu and cling him to her bosom purges her of all wounds and screams. She is transformed like the ancient mariner and the woman mellows the mother in her. What she says is not paranoia but a parable:

> All I wanted was a measure of happiness. All I wanted to be was Muthu's mother.
>
> For so long now, I had been content to remain a sister to the real thing. Surrogate housewife. Surrogate mother, surrogate lover. But now I wanted more. I wanted to be the real thing.[16]

The stories of her co-passengers generate in Akhila a desire for life, a life she wanted to live on her own. She too, like her compatriots, should respect her womanly feelings and start her life afresh. Living alone in a sea-resort at Kanyakumari gives her ample time to re-evaluate and re-assess her desires. Discovering a woman within her she decides to cast aside all that the world would say. She doesn't forbid the boy in his twenties when he tries to flirt her. What makes it more significant is that she takes his hand in her's and invites him to her room. Realizing the fact that the biddings of the body are blind to the identity of the individual, she neither tells him anything about her nor is interested in his credentials. Instead, she allows him to rave and graze over her body with the windows open and lights on. Akhila has of late understood the language of the real being lost in the grammar of becoming. The energies that she had, appear to unite in a catacomb of sensations and she determines to renew her bond. She decides to end her bondage and begin life anew. The yearning to connect the lines of communication she had swapped symbolizes her recovery.

Thus, we find that the characters of Anita Nair's novels undertake the journey of suppression and oppression in their lives. But they are not weak, as they don't tumble in a rough weather. They believe in the cruel hands of time yet they cling to hope and vicissitudes not denying the fact that they have to unearth their real power, their worth. Men and women are inseparable and the bond between them is not only a right but also a ritual. Most of the women characters, despite their misuse by society, preserve their real selves, the key to their salvation. The fact that all readers witness is that the ignorance of our self esteem is an insult to our identity and also that body is the ladder to the soul and without ladder one cannot reach the zenith. Janaki prefers to be with her husband than with her son and daughter-in-law. Margaret Shanthi regains her lost ground by making Ebe retreat to her. Prabha Devi recovers from depression and longs to float in the river of Jagdeesh' grasp. Mari wants to forget everything to claim her son. And Akhila, too, in whom everyone's stories swish-swash, refurbishes and with a sphinx like quality emerges to live life afresh.

Most of the characters in *Ladies Coupe*, thus, seem to find the ray of happiness only when they become aware. This awareness is created only when one looks at one's own self. This witnessing of one's self can make us stress-free. The awakening in almost all the characters, including Akhila, is similar to what Anjali Misra states:

> Awareness that we suffer from stress. Awareness that this stress is caused by the fact that we become the situations that take place around us. Awareness that this habit can be changed...we, in actuality, are not the situation or the feeling or the thought, but are only witnessing them.[17]

Akhila not only has witnessed everything but has also given a serious look at her soul. Her decision to break that long silence and her desire to think of Hari suggests Anita Nair's commitment as a novelist that the understanding in life does not mean regretting lapses rather it also implies restructuring and resurrecting. The determination to scupper her scourge and live life her way is awareness, rather a sort of purgation from purblindness she suffered long. *Ladies Coupe,* as a whole, is the story of resurrection, the resurrection of self.

REFERENCES

1. Anita Nair in conversation with Aruna Chandraraju, *The Hindu*, December 5, 2004.
2. Anita Nair, *Ladies Coupe.* New Delhi: Penguin Books. 2001. p. 84.
3. *Ibid.*, pp. 22-23.
4. *Ibid.*, p. 107.
5. *Ibid.*, p. 111.
6. *Ibid.*, p. 140.
7. *Ibid.*, p. 151.
8. *Ibid.*, p. 165
9. *Ibid.*, p. 184.
10. *Ibid.*. p. 195.
11. M. Rajeshwar in *Preface to Indian Women Novelists and Psychoanalysts.* Delhi: Atlantic Publishers and Distributors. 1998.
12. Anita Nair, *Ladies Coupe. New* Delhi: Penguin Books. 2001, pp. 200-01.
13. *Ibid.*, p. 207
14. *Ibid.*, p. 210
15. *Ibid.*, p. 262.
16. *Ibid.*, p. 268.
17. Anjali Misra, *Be A witness: Look At Your True Self* in http://spirituality.indiatimes.com. TOI, 11 March, 2005.

10

Diaphanous Exposé of Human Values in Jhumpa Lahiri's *Interpreter of Maladies*

DEVIKA

Jhumpa Lahiri, the recipient of the much sought-after Pulitzer award for her pioneering venture of a collection of short stories entitled *Interpreter of Maladies,* is named by the *New Yorker* as "one of the 20 best writers under the age of 20" (www.saja.org).[1] She may be considered a writer of Indian diaspora but her work reverberates the gloss of Indian ethos, values and beliefs. Her stay in America has not corroded her Indian sensibility because her adherence to Indian roots is deep and profound; as a writer Jhumpa is very candid in her confession regarding her visit to her native country:

> I went to Calcutta neither as a tourist nor as a former resident—a valuable position. I think as a writer. I learned to observe things as an outsider and yet I also knew that as different as Calcutta is from Rhodes Island, I belonged there in some fundamental ways. I didn't seem to belong in the United States (Lavina Melwani: 2000).[2]

Like Edgar Allan Poe, Jhumpa adheres to the fineries of a short story to heighten the effect to the apogee. She strives to achieve total effect through the process of brevity, perspicuity, and verity of experience. There is no hyperbole in Amy Tan's accolade treasured at the back cover of the text, "Jhumpa Lahiri is the kind of writer who makes you want to grab the next person you see and say, 'Read this!' She's a dazzling storyteller with a distinctive voice, an eye for nuance, an ear for irony. She is one of the finest short story writers I've read"

(Lahiri: 1999).[3] Jhumpa has not only won accolades from a restricted number of critics but she has also tickled the imagination of a great number of critics. Indubitably, Charles Taylor, another critic, is all praise for her achievement, "Lahiri doesn't write jeremiads about the loss of cultural identity; her characters are both relieved when they adjust to their new world and regretful at the separation from their original culture" (www.salon.com):[4]

Jhumpa doesn't want to present a set point of view that is entirely personal, instead she just observes things and tries to digest it from different perspectives so that she can keep herself in the background and let her characters speak for themselves. Her merit as an author can be easily gauged by the fact that the title story of the collection *Interpreter of Maladies* has been selected for the O'Henry Award as well as the Best American short story. It's not only the doctor that serves as the interpreter of maladies; in fact, Jhumpa herself acts as an interpreter for her readers. She allows them to have vicarious pleasure and get rid of something morbid in their attitude and passion.

The first story of the book *A Temporary Matter* silhouettes the stillness in the life of Shukumar and Shoba in Boston. The story is about the loss of their baby at the time of birth, an event that slits the bond between the two. After life starts stagnating for both of them, one day they get to know that there will be no electricity for five days. Here, at this stage, Jhumpa implements psychological approach to bring them together and share the poignancy of the irreparable loss. She has darkened everything surrounding them so that they can grope into their inside darkness, which they invariably do and move towards the light of realization. Their relationship has altered to such an extent that they have become 'experts at avoiding each other in their three-bedroom house' (4) (Lahiri: 1999).[5] Then, they whimsically initiate a game of telling insignificant secrets that they have shared with none. Very quickly, this game gets momentum and they start feeling the warmth of their relationship. Confessions lead to familiarity and intimacy. Darkness starts engulfing the sprawled shadows of grief and indifference, "Something happened when the house was dark. They were able to talk to each other again" (19). Love surges unhindered when it is fettered free of chains. They again feel united when Shukumar reveals to her that he has been with her at the time of the arrival of their baby and he has held the dead baby boy close to his heart and only that has helped him bear the loss. Shobha feels relieved to know that he has been with her though he has never revealed it to her unless necessitated by the blackout. The feelings of care and concern give her the courage to face life with a balanced view. Jhumpa leaves the end open because it is not certain whether the stillness is temporary or the patch up is temporary in their relationship. She does not conclude on the note of certainty. She allows space for her readers' imagination.

Life always does not turn out to be perplexingly subtle, as in her story *When Mr. Pirzada Came to Dine* Jhumpa presents the picture of life from the eyes of an innocent girl of ten years. Life is unfolded through the innocuous sensibility of hers. For the little girl the arrival of Mr. Pirzada is of utmost interest because she finds it strange that a man visits their house and keeps talking about his seven daughters and wife. Not only he, his parents also share his concern. She feels flabbergasted to know that Mr. Pirzada is not of their country but some other country though she fails to understand the situation because such a great affinity exists between her parents and their guest "as if they were a single person, sharing a single meal, a single body, and a single silence, and a single fear" (41). He always brings sweets for Lilia that the little girl cherishes with great delight. The story is unique because the emphasis is not on differences between the cultures but on tolerance and bond. The ever-present danger of lurking death in Mr. Pirzada's life is hinted at by the way he always dresses: "in preparation to endure with dignity whatever news assailed him, perhaps even to attend funeral at a moment's notice" (31). After certain time Mr. Pirzada returns to his country and sends the new year greeting with the news of the safety of his seven daughters, wife and house much to the relief of Lilia and her parents.

Cultural clash gets reflected very easily in the title story where Mr. and Mrs. Das show quite a relaxed and casual attitude towards their children. They act unlike Indian parents because they keep reminding each other what one has done at a particular period of time and now it's the turn of the other one to do the job. The usual spark that binds husband and wife gets dim by insidious silence in their relationship. Mrs. Das, a lady with vague interest in life, remains engaged with something else. Even their taxi driver, Mr. Kapasi notices it on the very first day and her casualness nurtures a feeling of an affair in the fluttering heart of Mr. Kapasi. On the contrary, the cause of her interest in Mr. Kapasi is entirely different because when he tells about his job as an interpreter of maladies at a clinic, she wishes to get rid of the ailment that has made her lose interest in her life. When Mr. Kapasi manages to be alone with her, she asks for the remedy for her malady, which keeps haunting her and taking the spark out of her life. To the utter shock of Mr. Kapasi, she reveals that one of their sons is not the child of her husband but one of his friends.

Jhumpa's proclivity not to dwell too much on idealistic situations allows her to test her characters against the tide of normal routine of affairs. That makes her characters more real and true to life with which the readers may feel associated. All the three characters in this story and the remaining characters of other stories are not caught in unusual situations that are outside the gambit of her readers' imagination. Her characters fluctuate from the characters of upper class to the characters of lower class but that does not diminish the worth of her contents. Her talent garbs all her stories with ingenuous touches to make them universal and special at the same time. No wonder, critics have lavishly praised her for her endeavour. To put it in Kipen's words dealing with "Interpreting Indian Culture with Stories" in *San Francisco Chronicle*, "Lahiri writes about the Indian American experience from all angles in indelible, lifelike stories that are completely predictable—but only in retrospect" (David Kipen: 1999).[6]

A Real Durban deals with an old lady who has no relatives and possessions but the memories of past to cherish. The lady is shown telling about her luxurious past but there is nothing to confirm it and the writer does not feel the need for this because her emphasis is not on her past but on her present and future. This is a story of deprivation where all the people lack something and desire for something more. Boori Ma does not want anything because she has tasted life in its best form as she keeps telling of the delicacies tasted by her. Here the lady is shown as a resistance shield between the residents of the colony and the outside world. She lives in her past and when the need arises on her part to seek the help from those whom she has served they are nowhere to think of her. Instead, she is accused of a theft and thrown out of the colony to make it safe from her unfair means.

In fact, the story is thus suggestive of the broader outlook with which Jhumpa manages to bring forth dark recesses of human heart and mind. Further, the story of Boori Ma shows the wide compass of Jhumpa because in this story there is no place for cultural clash. Feelings have always been at the center of stories and except for only two stories (*A Real Durban* and *The Treatment of Bibi Haldar*) where economic scarcity primarily dominates the scene. In the very first story the focus is not on cultural clash but on the emotional one. Shobha feels like moving outside her role as a wife because there she gets no satisfaction as a mother. Only when she gets to know that her husband has been there at the time of the birth of their baby, she is able to forgive him and the emotional clash gets resolved.

Jhumpa's other story *Sexy* revolves around a lady named Miranda who gets entangled in an affair with an Indian only to realize the worthlessness of a relation that is not socially approved and accepted. The concept of love is purely physical for her; that's why she does not hesitate to glide into a relationship that has no future. Physical satisfaction starts giving way to the realization that acceptance of body is altogether different from the acceptance of relationship. Initially she feels elated when her paramour Dev calls her sexy, "It was the first time a man had called her sexy, and when she closed her eyes she could still feel his whisper drifting through her body, under her skin" (93). Her mirage gets blurred when she has to look after the child of her roommate's cousin. The child becomes the vehicle that makes her realize the hollowness of her affair that would eventually result into nothing but pain and isolation. The child, like her lover, calls her sexy after forcing her to put on a glamorous silver cocktail dress. Her confusion requires an explanation and the explanation shatters her flimsy cobweb of illusions. The boy tells her that to him sexy "means loving someone you don't know" (107). The dawn of realization makes her decide the course of her drifted life and she prefers to opt out of an already dead relationship.

Jhumpa shows that realization is neither Indian nor American; anyone may feel enlightened at any stage of life. Here, the Indian male Dev never realizes the sin he has committed against his wife but the burden of guilt gets too heavy for Miranda, a foreigner and she decides to shed the sycophancy to breathe easily. She does not want to be a home-breaker and graciously exists from the scene to let peace prevail in the lives of others. Dev gets into this relationship in the absence of his wife and even after her return, keeps coming to Miranda to satisfy his libido. The thought of guilt or betrayal hardly crosses his mind. Even when Miranda stops seeing him, it does not affect his routine much because she has never been a part of life but of a hunger that has not been gratified.

The concept of alienation appears to be the focus of attention in Jhumpa's other story *Mrs. Sen* where the author makes her readers feel the pangs of rootless existence. The lady resides in the U.S.A. but lives in India, which the little boy Eliot finds very weird because he can't imagine this sort of disorientation and isolation. There she is deprived of the valuable ties with the members of her society. She gets tremendous opportunities to learn things that are of no importance to her because she fails to get the warmth required by her. Similarly the misery of being alone is too poignant to bear. To get rid of the loneliness she takes up the job of baby-sitting. Her bond with the boy Eliot is that of a mother. She gives him food to eat though it's not the part of her job and when she is busy doing something she keeps talking to him to make him feel important. His own mother, on the other hand, shows no such affection towards her son; after the dinner is over she leaves the left over work for Eliot to finish.

In this story *Mrs. Sen* the cultural gap between Indian and American mother is very beautifully highlighted. Though the emphasis is not purely on the differences yet as the story unfolds, further disparities get revealed effortlessly. Mrs. Sen takes proper care of the child not because it is the part of her job but because she feels like doing so. This type of affection is seen not only on the part of Mrs. Sen, Eliot also reciprocates her love and affection. He feels close to her because he finds her lonely and uncared for. His mother is concerned about the safety of her boy but does not have the time to give her child the emotional support that every child requires. She is very formal and not very warm to the hospitality of Mrs. Sen whereas Eliot gets the comfort of motherhood in her company only.

The story simply glides, as there is no place for conscious effort to make it a work of art. The ease and care is quite meticulously incorporated by the Pulitzer winner writer; nowhere the idea of forced presentation of facts spoils the worth of any of her stories. Mrs. Sen does not reveal her liking and disliking because she has to give an account of her life but the outlet of her deep buried and unfulfilled desires presents her character in lucid and elaborate terms. Here, Jhumpa Lahiri adopts the trusted technique of Robert Browning, who does not say anything for his characters but allows them to speak about themselves in unrestricted terms to reveal their characters to the readers. The famous characters of the Duke and Duchess in *My Last Duchess* get revealed by the long and rambling speech of the Duke. Similarly when Mrs. Sen shares her feeling with the child she tells about herself in no ambiguous terms:

> Send pictures, they write. 'Send pictures of your new life.' What picture can I send? she sat, exhausted, on the edge of the bed, where there was now barely room for her. "They think I live the life of a queen, Eliot." She looked around the blank walls of the room. "They think I press buttons and the house is clean. They think I live in a palace (125).

The title of her yet another story *This Blessed House* is deceptive because blessed houses are those where husbands and wives live an ecstatic life of care and affection. In this story the house is blessed because there are lots of scattered pieces of Christian things like a white porcelain effigy of Christ, a wooden cross key chain, a small plastic dome containing a miniature Nativity scene, a painting of clean shaven Jesus, and a 'plaster Virgin Mary' statue. Discovery of these items by the wife becomes the cause of uneasiness for her husband because instead of caring for her husband's needs and likings she keeps herself busy with these items while the husband keeps craving for the attention and love of his wife. Sanjeev, the husband feels parched and feels unable to show any sign of appreciation for these works of art because satisfaction in wedded life is the base of all secondary pleasures. Twinkle, the wife sidetracks her husband in her hunt for treasured icons and the gap stretches itself with great ease. It becomes apparent from his disliking for things because his wife likes them:

> He did hate it. He hated its immensity, and its flawless, polished surface, and its undeniable value. He hated that it was in his house, and that he owned it. Unlike the other things they'd found, this contained dignity, solemnity, beauty even. But to his surprise these qualities made him hate it all the more. Most of all he hated it because he knew that Twinkle loved it (157).

Like earlier writers, Jhumpa Lahiri does not blame males for the upheavals in the lives of others. In almost all her stories there is no distinction between males and females as per the traditional norms of superiority and inferiority. Twinkle is given full freedom to pursue her way of life but then Jhumpa seems to convey that males and females are complementary to each other and when this balance gets distorted, ample place gets reserved for unhealthy issues. Twinkle finds food preparation a burden and is not comfortable with her kitchen duties. Nowhere do the readers get the idea that she is detested or rejected because of this. In fact, Jhumpa displays an admirable detachment from her characters and allows them to do things according to their tastes:

> She bought preroasted chickens from the supermarket and served them with potato salad.... Indian food, she complained, was a bother; she detested chopping garlic, and peeling ginger, and could not operate a blender, and it was Sanjeev who, on weekends, seasoned mustard oil with cinnamon sticks and cloves in order to produce a proper curry (143-144).

Not only Sanjeev but Shukumar also cooks food for his wife when she is away from home because he stays at home. So Jhumpa has forced her male and female characters to move out of the traditional set-up where roles are more or less reserved for both the sexes. She shows her male characters making adjustments if circumstances demand it. However, it hardly implies that she wishes women to remain away from kitchen and expects men to serve females. In stories like *Mrs. Sen*, it's Mrs. Sen who does this chopping, grinding and slicing and where Mr. Sen is of no use to her. In *When Mr. Pirzada Came to Dine* it's Lilia's mother who prepares food for all. The idea that comes to fore after the perusal of this collection of stories is that there is no peculiar distinction between males and females. Males and females have certain duties to carry out and both have to do the work irrespective of their sex.

The Treatment of Bibi Haldar is a unique story in the sense that this type of illness has rarely been diagnosed and the treatment suggested is equally unique. But the treatment works in this story because it represents the need of every woman to have a home, husband and her own kids. The story is very engrossing because the reader is always kept on his toes and keeps guessing about what's going to happen next. Unlike the neighbours of Boori Ma, here in this story there are neighbours who help the poor girl start living afresh when her cousin and his wife disappear from the scene. It's the neighbours who help in delivery as well as selling the goods and establishing her. They tell her the practical tips of raising a newborn child. And the strange part is that her illness gets cured automatically after she is blessed with a baby. The father of the child remains a mystery and nowhere the need for father is felt.

Here the emphasis on money is laid to show that it may affect the relations. Bibi has helped her cousin in his trade and as a result, "For her services, Bibi received no income but was given meals, provisions, and sufficient meters of cotton.... At night she slept on a folding camp cot in the cousin's place downwards" (159). One thing gets clear from this treatment that she is treated as the member of the family; but when their turn comes to marry her off, they start making all sorts of excuses. Forced by neighbours they give an advertisement in a newspaper that is too bold to fetch any matches: "GIRL, UNSTABLE, HEIGHT 152 CENTIMETRES, SEEKS HUSBAND" (165). With such an advertisement when nobody turns up Haldar and his wife feel free to say that this sort of girl is not likely to be get married "Now do you see that she is unfit to marry? Now do you see no man of sane mind would touch her?" (166).

When the pressure mounts on them, stealthily they leave the scene never to return. Not only that Haldar and his wife become mean enough to hold Bibi responsible for the illness of their newborn baby. Keeping in touch with the mentality of the people of this class, they consider her unlucky for their family. Jhumpa does not remain untouched by these beliefs that spoil the congenial atmosphere of the society. However, she gives not a distorted but a true picture of the lower stratum of society where atrocities like these are not uncommon. In this story the clash is not between two cultures but between what one gets and deserves. Bibi gets this treatment because there is no sufficient money and because both Haldar and his wife consider her a burden who wields power to make others ill as she has nothing in her life to cling to and the happiness of others get affected by her presence.

The traditional male-female tussle is missing in the work of Jhumpa and the cross-cultural uneasiness is given proper place in her stories because she places her characters in an alien setting with nostalgic memories teeming inside them. One such good example is the last story of the collection named *The Third and Final Continent*. This is the story of a young man who leaves for England to educate and establish himself.

Some years later he gets married and moves to America because he gets a job there. He goes alone to establish himself first so that later he can call his wife there. Circumstances force him to become a tenant of Mrs. Croft, a lady of 104 years, who like all other Americans, is very proud of the achievement of the landing of Americans on the moon. The lady is very proud of her country and prefers sticking to the traditions of her country. When her middle-aged daughter comes to see her and is in the kitchen with the narrator who is of the age of her son, the lady does not like the idea of remaining a woman alone with a male.

The old lady loves adherence to the values and when the wife of the narrator comes to this unknown city and he brings her to meet the old lady, she scrutinizes her carefully and seems pleased with her because she finds that the young lady is very much in touch with her roots:

> I wanted somehow to explain this to Mrs. Croft, who was still scrutinizing Mala from top to toe with what seemed to be placid disdain. I wondered if Mrs. Croft had ever seen a woman in a sari, with a dot painted on her forehead and bracelets stacked on her wrists. I wondered what she would object to. I wondered if she could see the red dye still vivid on Mala's feet, all but obscured by the bottom edge of her sari. At last Mrs. Croft declared, with the equal measure of disbelief and delight I knew well: "She is a perfect lady!" (195).

Her approval makes him delighted because she makes him feel proud of his wife. She becomes the joining bridge between the two souls who don't know each other well and are tied by the sanctimonious bond of marriage. Her approval lessens "the distance between Mala and me" (196) and they start exploring their life.

What Jhumpa probably means to explore through her work is the fact that the distinction between human beings is man made. The narrator of the last story feels drawn towards the old lady because she fills the vacuum in his life. She takes care of him emotionally and when he is at the crucial stage of his life, she helps him realize the importance of it. When he learns of her death he feels the blow of loss. The human bond that has tied them gets affected and he feels bad about her death. Not only that, Jhumpa makes her characters very humble and down to earth as well. Her characters bespeak the glory of common life, "I know that my achievement is quite ordinary. I am not the only man to seek his fortune far from home, and certainly I am not the first.... As ordinary as it all appears, there are times when it is beyond my imagination" (198). That's how the narrator of the last story narrates his experience on three continents.

When an attempt is made to classify her stories of Bengal, Boston and beyond, critics fail miserably because her stories are tinged with universal appeal at once falling in the category of specific and general nature. *A Temporary Matter* deals with the problem of an Indian couple but had it been the case all over the world. All women have felt the same way because the loss of a baby is an irreparable loss for a mother. Similarly, if a wife or a husband gets immersed into something very much and the needs of the husband or the wife take a back seat, then frustration is likely to be there in the relationship. In *Mrs. Sen* Mr. Sen has no time for his wife and her needs and that results in frustration and in *This Blessed House* Twinkle bothers a fig about the care and attention her husband needs from her and likewise the gap widens between the two engulfing the bliss of their life.

As one ventures to compare *A Temporary Matter* with *Mrs. Sen* the thing that comes to the fore is that Jhumpa writes for both males and females. In 'Mrs. Sen' the story has been narrated from the point of view of a woman who lives in an alien land among strangers. Her husband provides her all the physical comforts but he has no time to spare for his wife and this kills the spirit of their married life. Mrs. Sen starts losing control over things. She considers herself a misfit there because her husband is not by her side. It is the case with Sanjeev also, after getting married he expects that he will get the undiluted attention of his wife but things start falling apart when Twinkle gets submerged into her new adventure of finding hidden sacred things. Her concern for her husband and his needs take a back seat resulting in a coldness creeping in their relationship.

In the last story of the collection, Jhumpa presents the same problem of adjustment in the married life. Here, she shows that by taking proper care of the needs of each other, life can be led easily and blissfully. They are married but don't know each other well. When both make proper efforts on their part, it turns out to be a happy married life wherein their togetherness leaves no scope for isolation, disorientation and dejection. Their relationship has given them the power to face the world, "But I remind myself that he has a father who is still living, a mother who is happy and strong" (197). Had the lady been treated like Mrs. Sen, she would have been neither happy nor strong. Similarly had the wife not taken proper care of the needs of her husband, he also would have been dragging the burden of his life.

This is not to deny the vacuum that is very much there in the hearts of her characters because most of her characters are uprooted from their roots. They are still struggling to settle down on a land that they feel is alien to them. The characters are not strong enough to give a tough fight to the hostile circumstances, instead they fall an easy victim to the circumstances because the distance from their roots has made them vulnerable. The most pitiable condition is that of Boori Ma who has no option but to serve the people in Calcutta who have lived a life of luxury in her *home* in East Pakistan. She suffers tremendously at the hands of others because she has nothing to cling to except the memories of her past.

To show the vacuum in the lives of these characters, Jhumpa has taken the help of names. It's a modern practice to deprive the characters of names for they lead an insignificant life. Even the novelists are following this practice of nameless characters. In the last story of the collection the narrator-protagonist is bestowed with no name because the need is not felt as he represents all Indians trying to make fortune in a land that is alien to them. Again, he stands as a husband who is to start his life with his wife and when started properly, there is no place for conflicts. Similarly, there is no first name for Mrs. Sen because she is nothing except the wife of Mr. Sen. She does not live for herself but for her husband otherwise her heart rests in India where she has left behind her real self.

Then we have characters who have no surname. Shobha and Shukumar have no surnames because they have neither roots nor any hereditary inheritance. They are solitary beings left adrift and only after they cling to each other, they find life easy and bearable. The past may not be there but present is there to help them. The characters like Boori Ma and Bibi Haldar have no names of their own and they get to be known by what others call them. They have individual identity; they live as a part of the society and it's society that decides their fate; they may neglect them or force them to lead a life of utter misery as happens with Boori Ma and they may give support to the weakling and help him or her live with dignity as they do with Bibi Haldar.

In Jhumpa's stories, society depicted is neither good nor bad. The characters are shown entangled into a struggle over which they have no control. Sometimes some unforeseen forces work in favour or against somebody. Stars favour Bibi Haldar and fail Boori Ma though both have been the victims of circumstances. Similarly Mira leads a happy and contented life, Twinkle leads a carefree life and Mrs. Sen leads a suffocated life because of no fault of hers, Mrs. Das leads a life of guilt because circumstances had forced her to be unfaithful to her husband in a fit of passion and Miranda after leading a life of sin comes to her senses and determines to lead her life afresh. The characters are neither good nor bad in these stories; only circumstances guided by some mystifying forces direct their lives.

How Twinkle dwarfs the personality of her husband gets reflected from the way she shortens his name from Sanjeev to Sanj. Her real name Tanima is brushed aside and the adherence to her name Twinkle shows her negligence for the original self of the person. She is like an ignorant child who remains happily immersed in her own world. She refuses to grow up and take the responsibilities of her married life. In another story, the name of the little girl is changed to Lilia to give it the colour of the place where they reside. Interestingly her parents are not at all named. They just remain her parents and host to Mr. Pirzada. Similarly Mr. Pirzada has named all her daughters with names beginning with alphabet 'A' giving the impression that he considers them some sort of commodity.

Names are given preference even by some other writers and Arundhati Roy is one among them. She shows that Estha and Rahel have no surnames in *The God of Small Things* because they have no solid past or the love of father and family to support them. Hence they have no surnames. Ammu also thinks adopting the surname of her father again but fails to come to a conclusion because neither her father nor her husband has given her a past to which she could relate. Even Toni Morrison is one among them; in one of her novels *Song of Solomon* she names her character as Milkman Dead because he is emotionally and psychologically dead as he receives the love and affection of his father not in the least and gets his mother's love in abundance to the point of satiation. Jhumpa also cashes on this practice of revealing the nature of her characters and that too quite meticulously.

There is no scope for mystery, intrigue, plots, and counterplots in Jhumpa's stories. All her stories are told in such a way that they seem like sashaying effortlessly. Even when the situation is delicate, the narrative counterbalances the tension and the reader is not overburdened by the intrigues. In accordance with the proverb 'still waters run deep' her stories appear very calm at the superficial level but when the reader goes inside, the real essence gets reflected. Thus, when observed closely, Jhumpa's stories are deceptively simple. Essentially a writer of human emotions, she abstains from delving deep into social or political issues. She does not raise issues of apartheid, loss of life, political upheavals, etc. and whenever she uses them, they are in the background and only enhance the effect of her narration. Her stories are of common problems that a person of any religion and stature may relate to in any corner of the world irrespective of being a male or a female. The author has brought to the fore difference between males and females as human beings. Both of them look at life from their respective outlooks and both have different ways of leading the lives and both have different roles to play. It's neither the superiority of males nor the inferiority of females that attracts her; what demands her attention are the strengths and weaknesses of both males and females as human beings.

To reprise, Jhumpa has created ripples in the field of short fiction because of her universal elegance and poise that has helped her bridge the chasm between males and females. She writes not merely about Bengal and Boston, she dares to look even beyond. She spins her yarns to highlight the void of trust and faith in relations that has made the relation hollow. This void, lack of roots, problems of adjustment in foreign land and married life, indifference towards the sensitive feelings of others, self centered life, proclivity for independent lives, race for economic liberation, etc. form the core of her stories. This writer of great sensitivity has taken uncanny care not to write in such a way that it produces negative effect on anyone. This wonderful writer of Indian origin has done India proud by following the footsteps of gigantic writers like Edgar Allen Poe, Hemmingway, Guy De Maupassant only to name a few. She has contributed her mite by plunging into the pale of writing.

REFERENCES

1. http://www.saja.org/lahiri.html, p. 1.
2. Lavina Melwani, "Interpreting Exile," *The Hindustan Times Magazine*, April 23, 2000, p. 1.
3. Lahiri, Jhumpa. *Interpreter of Maladies*. New Delhi: Harper Collins Publishers, 1999.
4. Taylor, Charles, "Interpreter of Maladies," http://www.salon.com /books/review/1999/07/27/lahiri.
5. Lahiri, Jhumpa. *Interpreter of Maladies*. New Delhi: HarperCollins Publishers, 1999, 4. All the quotes from this book are from the same edition cited here.
6. Kipen, David, "Interpreting Indian Culture with Stories." *San Francisco Chronicle*, 24 June, 1999.

11

The Insurgent Female Psyche in Manju Kapur's *A Married Woman*: A Socio-Ethical Study

ASHOK KUMAR

With the coming of women's liberation and feminism, the move is towards the insurgence of women in the face of the efforts of man to curb her freedom. To think that the impact of these movements has caused a radical change in the insights of women would be a conceptual error. Certainly there has been a shift in values and women have started acknowledging themselves the co-equals of man. Though the high hopes of Feminism have been washed away in the present social milieu, the relationship between man and woman becomes one of structured interdependence. But still the woman has to work for her liberation without resigning herself to her destiny. Gender equality still remains a myth. Man has always escaped unscathed, even when the sin is committed together. The autogenous impression of man about woman is that she is the 'second sex,' but this submission by woman comes only as an emitted response because society has groomed her to act dependent.

The finite dimension of the relationship between man and woman has been prescribed by man and not by woman. Her limits have been imposed on her by man who is ruled by the mastery-motive. She accepts it because of biosocial reasons. Very often this acceptance is not congruent with the reality that lies underneath. Modern women prefer to exercise their choices and break away from their traumatic experiences. A study of the man-woman relationship as narrated in the modern literature of the East and the West shows a disruption and the breakdown in the conventional expectations of female behavior. Women are now portrayed as more assertive, more liberated in their view, and more articulate in their expression than the women of the past. Instead of downgrading the elements of suffering at the hands of her lover or husband or man, she has started asserting her substantive identity in action, not in words. Whether it is Devi of Githa Hariharan's *The Thousand Faces of Night*, or Sita of Shashi Deshpande's *The Dark Holds no Terrors*, or Lucy of J.M. Coetzee's *Disgrace*, or Chantal of Milan Kundera's *Identity*, women have established a coherent class structure—one of assertion of identity and defiance of male supremacy, and protest at being subordinated by man.

It is the male ego that has given the woman an inferior status through the ages. Man has relegated her to a second-class citizen and when she could no longer endure the suppression, has revolted, her revolt ravaging like a tempest. A group of Indian women novelists in their in betweenness, hybridity of thought and multi-cultural, mult-lingual and multi-religious social dimensions have contextualised the women problem in general and middle-class and upper-class women in particular. While the gynocritics think that too many women in too many countries speak the same language of silence, some Indian women novelists like Githa Hariharan, Shashi Deshpande, Arundhati Roy and Manju Kapur have tried with sincerity and honesty to deal with the physical, psychological and emotional stress syndrome of women.

Manju Kapur's novel *A Married Women* is a work of investigative reporting on the most controversial and political issue of the demolition of Babri Masjid and a woman's obsession with love and lesbianism. The novel is a kind of narrative on a woman's incompatible marriage and resultant frustration and contemporary political turmoil in its historical context. In the novel, Kapur has taken writing as a protest, a way of mapping from the point of a woman's experience. Kapur negotiates different issues emerging out of a social-political upheaval in India. As a writer of new generation in an atmosphere of the nation's socio-political flux, Kapur has recorded the truth in her novels. With zeal to change the Indian male perception, she describes the traumas of her female protagonists from which they suffer, and perish for their triumph. She is shocked at the growth of fundamentalism and the rise of religious zealots to uplift and elevate the country by a crusade and establish paranoia by presenting evil as a historical necessity. R.K. Dhawan, a critic of repute rightly focuses the historical trauma snapped and enlarged by the camera of the creative eyes:

> A number of novels were written on the theme of partition, the destruction it brought and the plight of the refugees. They faithfully recorded the reign of the violence that characterized the period and provided a sad, telling commentary on the breakdown of human values. A strain of despair and disillusionment is predominant in these novels.[1]

Kapur has described politics of genocide as an important fabric in India's unique experience of democracy. She is sincere and naïve as a sociologist in exploring the bizarre paradox of rationality that underlines a sentiment of antipathy sheltered under political support and social approval. She resonates with her feminine assertion, hatred for violence, blood, death and ill feeling in the name of God and religion, and her feminine assertions remain untouched by history, politics and human interpretations.

Manju Kapur's *A Married Woman* is basically a novel for women at large. Astha, the protagonist, a young woman brought up in Delhi, is a typical middle-class lady. She succumbs to her parents finding her husband in a traditionally arranged manner. Within the bounds of marriage, she discovers a latent sexuality that is driven by love and passion and her desire is to assert her individualism. This theme of lesbianism is innovative in Indian fiction, though some writers including Shobhaa De and Namita Gokhale have earlier handled it.

In this novel basically there is an emphasis on three issues—reinterpretation of history, political ideologies and feminist views in the present context. The pointed reference to life and delicate dealing with political activities of the time are presented with the historical backdrop of Babri Masjid-Ram Janambhoomi episode. This gives the story a tangible shape with the articulation of emotional issues, communal hatred and women concerns. While the political backdrop is controversial and not conductive for the secularists, the demolition of Babri Masjid adds substance to the novel. The main ideas conceived in the novel are based on family life, sexual relationship, gender discrimination, socio-political upheaval and the desire for peaceful co-existence. The purpose of the novelist seems to be uni-dimensional with the idea of love what can really drive a woman into such a relationship.

Kapur has remained very candid and truthful in presenting the women and the challenges they face in their personal, professional, religious and socio-political levels.

Taking into account the complexity of life, different histories, cultures and different structures of values, the woman's question, despite basic solidarity, needs to be tackled in relation to the socio-cultural situation. The impact of patriarchy on the Indian society varies...and therefore...stream of feminism grounded in reality.[2]

Kapur desires to prove through her woman protagonist that, "A woman should be aware, self-controlled, strong-willed, self-reliant and rational, having faith in the inner strength of womanhood. A meaningful change can be brought only from within by being free in the deeper psychic sense."[3] She apprehends the approach of an apocalyptic social climate with the rise of the fundamentalists and fanatics in nation's spurious politics that takes religion to be ultra-patriotic. *A Married Woman* has sophisticated plot.[4] Its story of love is honest, set at a time of political and religious upheaval and is narrated with sympathy and intelligence for any one who has known life's responsibilities. It is a sincere confession of a woman about her personality cult in the personal allegory of a bad marriage.

Astha, the sensitive daughter of an enlightened father and orthodox mother has grown in a middle-class educated family in South Delhi and becomes a housewife, teacher, painter, and a lesbian in her status of a married woman. She fights for her self-assertions. Unlike many unmarried girls she had her infatuations of adolescent love for Bunty, a boy of another colony and for Rohan who left for overseas for a better career. But her real story of love and marriage started with Hemant, the son of a successful government official in Delhi. Soon after marriage Astha gets disillusioned about human nature in general and politics of the country in particular. Sharing her feelings "we should struggle with her, agonize together with her about her choices, and weep with her once she's made them."[5]

Astha's family affairs are also not so good and nothing is right with her. As a married woman she becomes an enduring wife and sacrificing mother. Her temperamental incompatibility with her corporate thinking husband compels her to play the role of mother and father for her children.[6] This denies her self-fulfillment and leads to the collapse of the institution of marriage. Discontentment leads her to defiance and restlessness. Her anxiety, discomfort, loneliness and isolation don't encourage her to give voice to her unhappiness over her troubled relationship, rather it prompts her to develop the feelings of guilt, negativity and lack of self-esteem in facing the challenges of her life. Astha understands a married woman's place in the family to be that of an unpaid servant or a slave and the thought of divorce brings social and economic death in her Indian status. She realizes for herself that, "A willing body at night, a willing pair of hands and feet in the day and an obedient mouth" (231), are the essential prerequisites of a married woman. She contemplates marriage a terrible decision as it puts her in a lot to enjoy bouts of rage, pain and indecision.

Being torn between her duty and responsibility, faith and fact, history and contemporaneity, public ethos and personal ethics, Astha thinks, "tired women cannot make good wives" (154), and struggles for an emotional freedom from the scourge of the nation. She develops psychosomatic symptoms of stress and depression balancing between existing and living.

Being marginalized by the affluence of her family, vicious social atmosphere, sheer hysteria of communalism and quarrel of two communities for God over a small thing, she is disillusioned in the empirical study of man's nature and his framing of social values.

Astha likes to have a break from dependence on others and proceeds on the path of full human status that poses a threat to Hemant and his male superiority. Although she finds herself trapped between the pressures of the modern developing society and shackles of ancient biases she sets out on her quest for a more meaningful life in her lesbian relationship. She canonizes and commemorates her insulted feminine sensibility raising the male tantrum to socially transform a society.

Understanding the socio-political realities of the country and the position of women in it, she becomes attracted towards Pipeelika, a Muslim's wife and a professor's daughter and as one who has "lost everything and had nothing more to lose" (184). Both of them fulfill female bonding in passionate, and intense fantasies of lovemaking with their overwhelmed body. Astha gloats herself in flirting by just feeling lesbianism as a component of larger human urge, as pleasure is an important element in sexual activity. In her shattered family life she prefers this as an antidote to masochism offering homage to her conventional morality.

If Astha becomes the victim of male passion, Pipeelika becomes the victim of communal riot and for the mistakes in history. In their feminine habit they forget their personal anguish and agony in dedication, thinking that their identities as individuals are threatened under the guises of mother, wife and daughter and they become a property, and the purity of their bodies come at a premium. While the lesbian attempts drag Pipeelika to the world of forgetfulness, Astha takes a sweet revenge on her husband. In this act of vengeance, unnatural sex, little excitement, little impatience and much imagination, she has a big jerk in her mind and this cripples her married life. Astha is Kapur's New Woman, "conscious, introspective, educated, wants to carve a life for herself, to some extent she even conveys a personal vision of womanhood by violating current social codes."[7]

The greatest strength of the novel lies in its rich social context that expresses the author's concern for a girl who, uprooted from the familiar environment of her childhood, girlhood and youth, leaves behind the most formative part of her life, and moulds herself anew in a completely strange environment, with a completely new set of rules and regards it as the only permanent fact of her existence.

Astha completely gets dejected with the male ego allowing the nation bleed with violence, murder and damage to other's faith in the name of religion and God. Ram Janambhoomi and Babri Masjid issue, ever the most controversial in Indian history, has been over politicized. It has greatly damaged the secular fabric of India. On 6th December 1992 the Babri Masjid was demolished with the rise of an aggressive Hindutva that made the Hindus a martial race. Thus, in rewriting of history and Hindutva, Ayodhya has become the epicenter of a political earthquake. She is shocked at the facts of history being twisted and the people being not so much careful of Rama's principles are worried about the exact spot of his birthplace. She believes that Ram is a sacred name and has his sacred place in myth, history, tradition and belief of Indians. Astha believes that:

> The Hindu religion...is wide, is deep, capable of endless interpretations. Anybody can get anything they want from it, ritual, and stories, thoughts that sustain (85).

While thinking about the script Astha has to write for Aijaz, she is unable to convince herself:

> The amount of blood, hate, and passion for ownership, these words evoked bathed each stone with a corrosive mixture, slashing through the surface so that it was no longer an old mosque. It was a temple, a birthplace, a monument to past glory, anything but a disused nesting place for bats. Despite all this it had endured for over four hundred years (108).

In the conspiring and hypocritical attempts, the facts have been distorted and faith has been tortured in the hands of the politics of the past and the present. Yet faith is sacrosanct and it needs political will to be protected. Astha realizes how the power seekers and politicians on both sides (Hindus & Muslims) have used religion quite blatantly in the name of secularism. While the holy men exhort a semitised Hindutva under the banner of saffron shade and trident, the Nehruvian secularists appeal for a higher and more enlightened Hindutva. They fail to realize secularism as the legalized sibling of humanism that neither dishonors God nor corrupts mankind. As Kapur's secularist intellectual, Astha understands the public sentiment, popular belief and political interpretations in her rebellious self and ejects her venom at the barefoot pilgrims moving towards Ayodhya like warriors. She thinks that intolerance is the real enemy to India's multi-cultural and multi-religious society, which needs political correctness and ethical orientation.

In their complex relationship Astha and Aijaz have their ideological love for man, religion and society. Aijaz and Pipeelika have their secular love and Astha and Pipeelika have their lesbian affair. Kapur has made a thorough sociological study in the Astha-Aijaz-Pipeelika relationship. Astha and Pipeelika are impressed with the community as they are good friends, partners and human beings in spite of oblique references—"four wives, large families, instant divorce, inter-community marriages, the religion of babies from such unions" (132), dating from Babur's time to the present day. While Astha's miniatures contain socio-political matters of the time with an ethical touch, Aijaz has a radical view with his ready impact on society through his theatre-activities. This leads him to be a martyr to the cause for his "working for everybody's good" (139).

Almost all the female characters of Kapur are educated, aspiring individuals cased within the confines of a conservative society. Their education leads them to independent thinking for which their family and society become intolerant of them. They struggle between tradition and modernity and develop the awareness of the New Woman, who has a voice of her own. Marriage, the social institution, traps and curbs their spirit by binding them to the responsibility of a home. In her novel, Kapur has exhibited the new facets of the married women. Her new women, Astha and Pipeelika are disillusioned in life with their suspicions of male integrity, and their awareness of male frailty. Astha was completely disillusioned by her discovery of a condom in her husband's travel suitcase in his business mission. In their sundry experiences both had found their husbands as "embryonic Othellos" (221). Unconsciously they were in search of a safe, warm and loved place after their shattered conjugal lives. This made them to be close in their emotional intimacy. Pipee as a lesbian lover and Astha as a lesbian beloved are passionately in love with each other.

In her writing Manju Kapur has emphasized on the issues in the context of patriarchy, inter-religious marriage, family bond, male-female bond, co-existence of past and present in the socio-political facts. She has narrated her woman protagonist as a victim of biology, gender, domestic violence and circumstances. She is serious in regard to the communal violence and disintegration of human values in the social trauma and political upheaval of the 1990. *A Married woman* is more like reportage; Ram Janambhoomi-Babri Masjid issue is presented in a realistic, imaginative reconstruction. She expresses her serious concern for the political zealots declaration that religion is above politics, nation and the court. Kapur, similar to Austen, Tolstoy, on the other hand, thinks that, "There is a man within every woman and a woman in every man when manhood is questioned and womanhood is fragmented."[8] By knowing the causes of problems of women in and out of the family, Kapur has emphasized on the causes of Astha's restlessness, and her search for identity. All the adversaries of Astha are her acquisitiveness, the code of dharma and the philosophy of quietism.

Kapur has revealed her main emphasis for women with zeal, enthusiasm and seems like Anita Desai, Bharti Murkharjee and Shashi Deshpande to suggest that a married woman's work is not as a housekeeper and child-bearer but to do something more. Through Astha, Kapur offers a frontal challenge to patriarchal thought, social organization and control mechanism by her inner potential as an individual and her desire to attain personal recognition.[9] In the gynocentric struggle for liberation and fulfillment, Astha struggles for the togetherness of the family as a unit. Neither as a flag waver nor as a patriot, she is fully aware that venality, brutality and hypocrisy are imprinted on the leaden soul of every fanatic Indian, Indian democracy has become a holy cow in socio-political crisis and the benefits it yields are used and abused at will by a diluted politics.

The age-old themes of marriage and politics are coupled with lesbian relationship, in the narrative making Kapur the first Indian English novelist to highlight women's desire for homosexuality. Dealing with religion, politics and social values Kapur feels India as socially cosmopolitan, politically egalitarian and religiously sectarian. Thus, *A Married Woman* proves to the rules of lesbianism and gay theories, and it is by exploring a hidden aspect of a woman's passionate life as defined by comfort levels without societal sanctions.

REFERENCES

1. R.K. Dawan, (ed.), *50 Years of Indian Writing*, (New Delhi: IAES, 1999), p. 14.
2. Seema Malik, "Crossing Patriarchal Threshold: Glimpses of the Incipient New Woman in Manju Kapur's *Difficult Daughters*," *Indian Writing in English*, ed. Rajul Bhargawa (Jaipur: Rawat, 2002), p. 171.
3. Chamal Nahal, "Feminism in English Fiction: Forms and Variations," *Feminism and Recent Fiction in English*, ed. Sushila Singh, (New Delhi: Prestige, 999), p. 17.
4. M.K. Naik and Shyamala A. Narayan, *Indian English Literature 1980-2000: A Critical Survey*, (New Delhi: Pencraft International, 2001), p. 100.
5. Padmini Mongia, "Finding Oneself, More or Less," *The Hindu Literary Review*, (May 4, 2003), p. 3.
6. Manju Kapur, *A Married Woman*, (New Delhi: India Ink, 2002), p. 189.
7. Seema Malik, p. 171.

8. Bhagabat Nayak, "Feminine Assertion in Manju Kapur's A Married Woman", *The Indian Journal of English Studies*, R.K. Dhawan, ed., (New Delhi: IAES, 2003-2004, Vol. 41), p. 137.
9. Sushila Singh, "Recent Trends in Feminist Thought," *Indian Women Novelists*, R.K. Dhawan, ed. (New Delhi: Prestige, 1991), Set I, p. 65.

12

Bed as Battlefield: A Study of Shobha De's *Starry Nights*

S.S. KANADE

Shobha De!...the tsunami in modern Indian English novel, has earned frequent credits of 'vamp writer', 'porn queen' and 'Desi Jackie Collins' with hostile reviews. She has been hailed as a supreme champion of a new novel due to subtle antagonism of gender discrimination by her novel *modus operandi.* She pens from the bottom of her heart with wholehearted appreciation and revolutionary ethos about the sexual relations of brave new world. She keeps a weather eye on the flair of instinctive sexual life and reflects it in her bestsellers. On that accounts she triumphs to originate various bestsellers.

The present paper knits together divergent views on sex in the present social milieu. In fact, it endeavours to analyze and scrutinize Shobha De's treatment of sex in terms of bed as battlefield in Starry *Nights*, giving sharp focus on her most celebrated character Aasha Rani.

It is a naked truth that, sex is the republic of letters of De. If truth be told, sex has got much currency in our times. She proclaims "...Sex is no longer the most dreaded and despised three-letter word in India, is enough cause to celebrate."[1] She subscribes to sex as bed, which is a battlefield. She throws light on the sexual act of bed with a prismatic vision. She is cognizant of it and believes that, it cannot be neglected; it is a principal constituent of man-woman relationship. For that reason, she has been acclaimed and has achieved worldwide recognition.

As a matter of fact, in the modern world bed has been transformed into a battlefield. It is a battle of philosophies as well as of human bodies. It becomes an affair of pleasant and unpleasant moments. Consequently it is a sort of sexual odyssey in search of the Himalayan height of all sensual gratification by the dreamy way of pleasure and pain. De exposes horrendous hypocrisy, self-seeing meanness and double standards of male by the act on bed through the eyes of Aasha Rani, "Sweet- heart of Millions" (14).

> She is called "the sex," by which is meant that she appears essentially to the male as a sexual being. For him she is sex-absolute—sex, no less...she is the incidental, the inessential as opposed to the essential. He is the Subject, he is the Absolute—she is the Other.[2]

The 'Other' spearheads the desired direction towards battlefield. She is cognizant of biosocial reasons, eventhough she bends over backwards for female potential.

The novel proposes a narrative about Aasha, an emerging actress, who is struggling to establish herself in the Bombay film industry, the jungle of sex hunters. She puts into service her bed as battlefield to survive in the labyrinth.

> Like a gangster. An attractive gangster. She wondered what he'd be like in bed. Funny, she always wondered that about any man she saw. Any. He didn't have to be good-looking and she didn't have to be attracted to him. He just had to be a man, that's all, and Aasha Rani's X-ray eyes would instantly undress him and get him into bed with her. What would he do to her? Or she to him? (90-91).

It becomes her inescapable perspective on sex. In fact, it is the modern way of modern world, where sex, and human relationship run smoothly hand in hand. It will be seen that the novel is the quintessential manifestation of personal ideals of De. Therefore, I have called the novel 'Bed as Battlefield,' because she has projected various sexual acts on bed with the conscious intention of battle.

Aasha commences her bone-breaking journey from Kishenbhai, a financer of films, with the warming of his bed on the conscious direction of Amma. She showers sexual love and gifts him as mental handicap of her physical beauty. Kishenbhai utters, "That will destroy me, and it might destroy you" (6). But later it comes to truth. He produces a film as the receipt of her pleasant company on bed. He utilizes to exploit her. She challenges, "All of you are just the same, but wait, I will show you. I will do to men what they try to do to me. I will screw you all-beat you at your own game!"(8). She performs the modern splendid sport by the high-tech way. She compromises on temporary adjustments with the permanent feelings, to teach unforgettable lesson on the bed by the battle. In view of the fact that, she is conscious of that, it is a long life· battle against various skilful combatants.

Amma's ever-increasing greed of money knocks the door of Sheth Amirchand, a Member of Parliament. Shethji's servant is rather punctual in woman's physical checkup, to get ready for battle. He scorns, "All you women are the same-screw a thousand men, get your womb filled by one of them and then come..." (59-60). Aasha's sexual encounter with Shethji is extremely curious. "Her head was full of colours and sounds. Her senses had been heightened to an extent that she experienced no pain..." (61). She succeeds to please Shethji. She deliberately adopts the whole system. Even Shethji kindly permits her to sleep with anybody. De brings out the sexual compromises on the part of women.

Aasha is impressed on "civlized divorce" (83) of Suhas and Suhaila, where they warm bed to each other. She exerts to warm the bed of Suhas. But his inability to perform makes him bad-tempered. Next she victimizes Abhijit, son of Amrish Mehra. She warms the bed of Jojo to survive in film industry. She monitors regarding Jojo,

> He treated sex like a casual sport. His bed manners were awful. And he did nothing for her ego as a woman. He made it clear, he was there to use her as and when he felt like it (185).

De treats sex as a healthy act; obviously she expects the same from her male counterpart. She puts forward woman is as equally essential, as wonderfully powerful as her male counterpart on bed. She forcefully emphasizes that woman can be more violent even than man on bed.

Gopalakrishanan, a terrorist succeeds to identify "pressure spots" (197) on the beautiful body of Aasha. He offers her a relaxing treatment, that she has never experienced such physical hunger and passionate intensity. She feels, he is a perfect sweet combatant. She feels, "his hot tongue on her-probing, searching, stabbing and withdrawing...." (198). De is exceedingly bold in her lucid description with the exposing of act on bed without the slightest hesitation. In fact, her women characters are transparently free and absolutely frank about bed.

At last, her father-in-law, who compliments her as a sexy woman, teases Aasha. He remarks, "I'm sure you need a really hot-blooded man in your bed" (204). Actually, De forces to determine on... "Everything is decided by the bed. On the bed" (50) and sex is "the bedrock of all relationships."[3] According to her, sex is vital for human beings as a driving force in life. It enables to create as well as destroy the human beings obviously it is constructive as well as destructive energy. But she is down-to-earth and practical in her 'take-it-or leave-it' approach.

Aasha is in cloud cuckoo land to wed Akshay Arora, a leading actor. However, she weds Jay, who moves heaven and earth to offer heart-rending encouragement. Jay is quite straight from the shoulder and big-hearted in his convictions. Both bring into the world a child, Sasha. Subsequently Aasha doesn't put her mind at rest with Jay. She is suspicious about Sudha and nanny, whether they have possessed her bed. She supposes undisputed validity of Appa's eternal truism.

> Men are cruel. Very cruel. There is no justice in this world And no equality between men and women. Don't believe that a marriage alters that balance. Sometimes it only makes it worse. Power lies with the purse—remember that. Whoever controls that, controls the relationship (193).

De doesn't feel content with the unbreakable bond between husband and wife. She directly hits the concept of marriage, which is truly universal. Actually marriage offers sex within the limitation. It seems her natural inclination towards the free sex and lesbianism. Her women characters are stubborn and hungry on bed. She tables various types of sex. They offer everlasting impression of never-ending exercises. In fact, these are the exercises of healthy mind and healthy body, but she utilizes violently.

De's basic concern with bed as battlefield is just a part of her gender concern because her deep investigations regarding sexual relation evinces her newer and deeper insight into the human soul. Aasha undergoes never-to-be-forgotten thrill of the female flesh from the Thai girls. It is the heavenly gift of Badshah.

> It was an experience, so sensuous, so arousing, so complete, that it was weeks before she could forget the feel of two, smooth, soft, oiled, practically breastless bodies on either side of her, touching, licking, stroking every naked inch, making her skin tingle and come alive in a way she couldn't have imagined possible (66).

She experiences "the greatest orgasms of her life" (66). The same multi-sensory experience she is entertained by Linda, the reporter of *Showbiz*. She puts out her mind for everything. She moans with sensual gratification. Linda evinces that she can perform like a *purusha.* Of course she insists, "THIS is love, understand? This is love-making, not what those bastards do to our bodies" (80). She exposes new skylines for Aasha. The lesbian relationship does not subscribe to bed as battlefield. For De, heterosexual relationship puts forward as masculine superiority. Perhaps she thinks to herself from many sexual descriptions,

> Everything that might concern the interplay of innumerable pleasures, sensations, and thoughts, which through the body and the soul had some affinity with sex.[4]

She subscribes to extensive investigation of sexual relationships that appear to a great extent unresearched even in the modern world, when chicken and egg problems have been investigated and resolved.

Aasha is besotted with Akshay. Shortly, she has earned the fame as a family destroyer. She creates the occasional misunderstandings between Akshay and Malini. Malini is repelled by sex with Akshay, who derives heavenly pleasure from the watching of Swedish blue films especially of more sado-masochistic variety.

> She knew Akshay often masturbated in bed, and even that put her off. What was he-some kind of insatiable monster? Could he think of nothing but sex? The bed would shake rhythmically and she'd lie awake in the dark hating the man next to her, thinking, 'Why does he do this?... (43).

She has a strong aversion to the acts on bed and everything associated with it. She feels emotional repugnance towards his breath. She clashes with Aasha with a serious allegation that she is utilizing her bed. At last she screams at the very idea of free sex and engages Aasha,

> SEX! That is all you have–SEX! That is what women like you use. Cheap bitches–part your legs and let any man in. Sex, sex, sex, dirty, filthy sex! Perverts. You must be a pervert. What do you do to him-hah? Suck his cock? Or suffocate him with your breasts? He will get tired of you, like he has of all the others (49).

She curses Aasha, that she will never be happy in her life. For her the bed becomes battlefield.

Malini shares her marital troubles with Rita with a deep rooted conviction that, "Men are all the same-animals..." (50). Rita conveys," Men like variety" (50) and verbalizes with enforcing authority.

> The only way to make a marriage work is through sex-and most women hate that too. But the day a man feels that his woman has lost interest in sex, and therefore in him, the relationship is finished and he starts looking elsewhere (50).

That being so the bed is converted into battlefield. The relationship between Akshay and Malini is purely robotic and shallow, without any sensual feeling of warm attachment and deep affection.

Aasha tries to destroy the families of her bed partners. It discloses that, she deliberately and forcefully warms the bed to satisfy her body as well as to scorn others. Her relationships are confined to physical sex without any beginning or an end. No one does understand what type of feminism is exercising in the novel, where one woman possesses other women's bed.

Every character in the novel is conscious of bed as battlefield. Time after time, Amma pronounces that Aasha is free to warm bed with anyone and anytime. Even Linda wishes at the interview, "Hire me. If you don't like my writing then fire me" (76). Kishenbhai is also perfectly sensible of 'bed.' Hence, he advises Sudha, "Stay away from men. I will be with you all the time. Speak to nobody. Trust no one. Whatever you want will be given to you by me and me alone" (147). Surprisingly Shonali, a call-girl of London advises Aasha to pay attention on being peerless beautiful and holds the view that men find them "relaxing, charming and desirable" (213). Owing to the fact that lustrous beauty is like a sexual fire, which stimulates the body on the bed. All these matters substantiate that, De's women put into service their bed in the specific circumstances due to struggle for existence.

Evidently it gives the impression of being that De throws on the scrap heap the concept of virginity. Her women characters make public that they wish to entertain the life like men. It is interesting to note that Aasha keeps her sexual relationships with married men rather than a single man. Even though she has knowledge that married men can't offer full justice to her. Eventually, De shows beyond doubt that, the Indian men are "high on ego. Low on performance."[5] They are mostly narrow minded, utterly ruthless and highly insensitive. Aasha has earned many bed partners but fails to win real one. In reality, she deals her bed as battlefield in the world of sex-hunters. To warm bed turns into the routine affair of her life. At the end she is trapped in her own labyrinth.

De is a spokesperson of new morality and for her, "Writing is pure sex."[6] She appreciates sex for herself very candidly and frankly. She forces us to envisage female as neither 'weaker sex' nor 'second sex'. She succeeds to draw our attention where sex is like fast food in the modern world. Time and again, readers wonder, whether this is the land of Sita, Savitri and Gandhari or the land of temples of Khajuraho. She succeeds to break open her bold stance on sex.

I feel inclined to sum up the paper with the view of Freud:

> The great question that has never been answered and which I have not been able to answer, despite my thirty years of research into the feminine soul is 'what does a woman want?[7]

It goes without saying; I have the same opinion. In fact, De practises bed as battlefield to survive in the modern world. Accordingly Aasha is the significant victor of several bed partners but loser of her life partner. Unquestionably it is her graphical study on bed, for bed, by the battlefield. Bed and battlefield are the grim realities of human existence.

NOTE

De Shobha, *Starry Nights*, New Delhi: Penguin Books, 1992.

(All the subsequent references to this paper are from this edition.)

REFERENCES

1. Singh. Khushwant and De Shobha (Eds.), *Uncertain Liaisons: Sex, Strife and Togetherness in Urban India.* New Delhi: Viking /Penguin India, 1993 pp. xxi, 208.
2. De Beauvoir Simone. *The Second Sex*, trans. and ed. H.M. Parshley, 1953, rpt. Harmondsworth: Penguin, 1983, p. 16.
3. *The Illustrated Weekly of India*, 06 Nov. 1992.
4. Foucault Michael, *The History of Sexuality*, Harmondsworth, 1984 p. 20.
5. *Uncertain Liaisons*, p. 4, XXV.
6. De Shobha, *Writing is Pure Sex*. Indian Review of Books. Vol. 3, No. 1, Oct 16—Nov 15, 1993. p. 30.
7. Freud's letter to Marie Bonaparte, quoted by Ernest Jones in *The Life and Work of Sigmund Freud*, New York: Basic Books, 1953, p. 421.

13

Travails of An Immigrant: A Study of Jhumpa Lahiri's *The Namesake*

SUSHILA RATHORE

Jhumpa Lahiri, Pulitzer Prize winner for her collection of short stories entitled *The Interpreter of Maladies* has created a specific niche for herself in the literary arena with her first debut novel *The Namesake* which has also got the 'best book of the year'[1] award. The novel has won critical acclaim overseas for its elegance, perception and compassion in identifying lives transported from India to America. *The Namesake is that rare thing: an intimate, closely observed family portrait that effortlessly and discreetly unfolds to disclose a capacious social vision.*[2] Lahiri an American born Indian, has portrayed very pragmatically the agonies of non-resident Indians. As we move through her novel, we get glimpses of her characters torn between America and India. *In The Namesake Lahiri enriches the themes that made her collection an International Best seller: the immigrant experience, the clash of cultures, the conflicts of assimilation, and most poignantly, the tangled ties between generations. Here again Lahiri displays her deft touch for the perfect detail-the fleeting moment, the turn of phrase-that opens whole worlds of emotion.*[3] They really find it difficult to get on easily with the people in America and in a strange backdrop find themselves alienated. When enquired, she explains this as an inheritance of her parent's ties to India:

> It's hard to have parents who consider another place "home" even after living abroad for thirty years. India is

home for them. We were always back so I never felt fully at home here. There's nobody in this whole country that we're related to. India was different—our extended family offered real connection. Yet her familial ties to India were not enough to make India "home" for Lahiri–*I didn't grow up there, I wasn't a part of things. We visited often but we didn't have a home. We were clutching at a world that was never fully with us* (Interview with Vibhuti Patel in *Newsweek International*, 9-20-99).[4]

Her novel *The Namesake* brings to fore many of the issues that Indians, settled in the promising land of opportunities, face in America. The narrative revolves around the difficulties faced by a Bengali couple in a different country—the clash of cultures, the relationship between parents & children, the generation gap, identity problems etc.

It talks about the journey of an Indian woman Ashima, the central character of the narrative, who moves from India to America after her marriage and in the process, suffers a lot by missing her country every now and then. She belongs to a traditional Hindu Bengali family, which lives in Calcutta. As the novel opens, we come to know that she is pregnant and is there in her house, *On a sticky August Evening two weeks before her due date, Ashima Ganguli stands in the kitchen of a Central Square Apartment, combining Rice Krispies and Planters Peanuts and Chopped red onion in her bowl.*[5]

After sometimes, she feels pain in her stomach and her husband Ashoke, an electrical engineer, takes her immediately to the hospital. In the hospital, she feels awkward when asked so many questions in a language with which she is not comfortable. Although, she has been a student of English literature, she can't speak or understand English with American accent with ease. A doctor comes to examine her progress and asks her something regarding her delivery, "She is told that she is still in early labor three centimeters dilated, beginning to efface," What does it mean dilated? She asks and Dr. Ashley holds up two fingers side by side, then draws them apart explaining the unimaginable thing her body must do in order for the baby to pass" (3).

Ashima, while staying in the Hospital really craves to talk with the other three women in the room. She is used to live in a joint family and is not in the habit of being lonesome without talking to each other. But now, she has to lie alone in her bed. Here, she really feels the ache in her heart as she is giving birth to her first child away from her home, "It is the first time in her life she has slept alone, surrounded by strangers; all her life she has slept either in a room with her parents or with Ashoke at her side. She wishes the curtains were open, so that she could talk to the American woman" (3). Being an Indian, she is in the habit of talking or sharing thoughts on such matters. She wants to communicate to an American who has given birth and wants to know what to expect at such a moment. But she is bereaved at the hypocrisy of the Americans, "She has gathered that Americans inspite of their public declarations of affection, inspite of their miniskirts and bikinis, inspite of their hand holding on the street and lying on top of each other on the Cambridge Common prefer their privacy" (3).

After the birth of the child, Ashoke visits her along with three other Indian visitors. But Ashima does not feel contended, as these Indians were merely substitutes for her family. She is all full of pain at the thought of her son being deprived the first look of his grandparents:

> Without a single grandparent or parent or uncle or aunt at her side, the baby's birth, like most everything else in America, feels somehow haphazard, only half true. As she strokes and suckles and studies her son, she can't help but pity him. She has never known of a person entering the world so alone, so deprived (25).

Both Ashima and Ashoke are Indians unaware of the custom of the Americans that they have to think of a name before going out from the hospital. As for the name, they have decided that they will wait for Ashima's grandmother's letter and name him as she suggests. They face lot of problems when they don't get the letter and face a dilemma when asked by the Doctor to name their son. As they don't have time to think they name him Gogol after the name of a Russian writer. At that time they don't know that this will cause so many identity problems in the life of their son.

The essence behind naming their son Gogol was very deep as far as Ashoke's life was concerned. Ashoke was a very well read person and extremely fond of reading. He used to read books of all kinds. His obsession with reading was so much that his mother was always convinced, "her eldest son would be hit by a bus or a tram, his nose deep into *War and Peace*. That he would be reading a book the moment he died" (13).

The same thing happened, the train in which he was traveling met with an accident and many people died. Ashoke was also severely injured in the accident and wanted to call someone for help but can't:

> Ashoke can still remember their shouts, asking if any one was alive. He remembers trying to shout back unsuccessfully, his mouth emitting nothing but the faintest rasp... The people were searching for the victims who were alive, when they were going after the search; Ashoke heard someone say, "Let's keep going" (18).

But the lantern's light lingered, just long enough for Ashoke to raise his hand, a gesture that he believed would consume the small fragment of life left in him. He was still clutching a single page of "The Overcoat," crumpled tightly in his fist, and when he raised his hand the wad of paper dropped from his fingers. "Wait," he heard a voice cry out. "The fellow by that book. I saw him move" (18).

After that he was dragged from that place on a cart and saved. This book by Nikolai Gogol saved his life and became a poignant but memorable experience of his life. Ashima shares her husband's acquaintance with the name and does not object to the name been given. For Ashoke "the name Gogol was more sacred than God. Instead of thanking God he thanks Gogol, the Russian writer who had saved his life, when Patty enters the waiting room" (21).

As far as the name Gogol is concerned, both Ashima and Ashoke name their son only to get a discharge certificate from the hospital and Ashima is convinced of the fact that as soon as her grandmother's letter comes with a name, they will change it. Ashima desperately waits for the letter from her grandmother. She feels so forlorn and cries throughout the day when she doesn't receive any letter. She receives letters from everybody at home except her grandmother. Later on, she comes to know that her grandmother has got paralyzed and is not in a position to suggest a name. She really feels unconsoled for many days, as she is very much attached to her. So ultimately they can't decide a public name and a name decided in haste takes its place:

> Ashoke and Ashima are not terribly concerned. After all, they both know, an infant doesn't really need a name. He needs to be fed and blessed, to be given some gold and silver, to be patted on the back after feelings and held carefully behind the neck. Names can wait..." (25).

According to a custom in Bengal there are two names, one is pet name a 'daknam' for home, and a good name, a 'bhalonam' for identification in the outside world. This idea also worked behind their casual attitude in deciding the name of their son. For instance both Ashima and Ashoke's names also contribute to the same thing. They have two names—one personal and the other public. "Bengali nomenclature grants, to every single person, two names. In Bengali the word for pet name is daknam, meaning, literally, the name by which, one is called by friends, family and other intimates, at home and in other private, unguarded moments..." (26). Both pet names and public names have their own uniqueness, "Good names tend to represent dignified and enlightened qualities. Ashima means—"She who is limitless, without borders." Ashoke the name of an emperor, means he who transcends grief Pet names have no such aspirations" (26).

Pet names have no such importance and they are considered insignificant and inane.

Ashima and her husband name their son Gogol not knowing the consequences that their son is going to face later. As he grows up, been brought up in a different country, he never likes going to his hometown and only wants to be in America. He doesn't like the change in the atmosphere and the surroundings in India, the relationships that he shares, he always feels uncomfortable in that environment which he considers to be unfamiliar. When his parents go to India for eight months both Gogol and Sonia don't like the idea. After reaching India, their parents start meeting their family members, which they didn't like, Ashima, *now Monu weeps with relief, and Ashoke now Mithu kisses his brothers on both cheeks, hold their heads in his hands. Gogol and Sonia know these people but they do not feel close as their parents do* (81).

Crisis related to names is very prominent in this work. Gogol Ganguli, a very important character in the novel always feels ashamed in front of his teachers and classmates because of his name. Everybody is curious about his name as if his name consists of a surprise element. In the initial phase of his life, he doesn't mind it:

> He recognizes Pieces of himself on the road signs: Go left, Go right, Go slow. For birthdays his mother orders a cake on which his name is piped across the white frosted surface in a bright blue sugary script. It all seems perfectly normal. It doesn't bother him that his name is never an option on key chains or metal pins or refrigerator magnets. He has been told that he was named after a Russian author, born in a previous century. That the author's name, and, therefore, his, is known throughout the world and will live on forever (66).

When he was a child everything was fine. But as he grew up he realized that there is some peculiarity in his name, more so when his teacher said in the course of his trip that his name is different. He never liked his name:

> For by now, he comes to hate questions pertaining to his name, hates having constantly to explain. He hates having to tell people that it doesn't mean anything in Indian. He hates having to wear a nametag on his sweater at Model United Nations day at school. He even hates signing his name at the bottom of his drawings in art class. He hates

> that his name is both absurd and obscure, that it has nothing to do with who he is, that is neither Indian nor American but of all things Russian...From the little he knows about Russian writers, it dismays him that his parents chose the weirdest namesake (76).

Whenever he uses to ask his father why he has chosen this name for him, initially his father didn't tell him the story behind his name but one night when he revealed this story to him, he became very emotional. Tears started flowing through his eyes. Still, he was adamant in changing his name and got it changed also. Again he faces so many problems while satisfying everyone's curiosity regarding his new name. On entering the University he introduces himself as 'NG' always afraid that if they find out about his previous name they will laugh at him. He hides this fact from his girlfriend Maxine and her parents also with whom he stays for a long time. He is all-full of fear when she requests him to visit his parents and tormented by the premonition of his name's revelation to her. He doesn't leave her alone so that she should not come in contact with his parents.

Gogol has always hated his name and his parents also for naming him in such a hurry. But when his mother was leaving for India, all of a sudden he becomes conscious of the sufferings his parents have undergone in this foreign country. The novelist describes his seclusion in the following lines:

> Nothing to signify the years his family has lived here, no evidence of the effort, the achievement it had been. It's hard to believe that his mother is really going, that for months she'll be so far. He wonders how his parents had done it, leaving their respective families behind, seeing them so seldom, dwelling unconnected, in a perpetual state of expectation, of longing. All these trips to Calcutta he'd once resented—how could they have been enough? They were not enough (281).

He now realizes the predicament faced by his parents in this remote ambience:

> Gogol knows now that his parents had lived their lives in America in spite of what was missing, with a stamina he

> fears he does not possess himself. He had spent years in maintaining distance from his origins; his parents in bridging the distance as best they could. And yet, for all his aloofness towards his family in the past, his years at college and then in New York, he has always hovered closed to this quiet, ordinary town that had remained, for his mother and father, stubbornly exotic (289).

Now the same Gogol Ganguli remembers his father, not with contempt on his face for his name but he feels himself complete with the name given to him by his parents, *The name he had so detested here hidden and preserved that was the first thing his father had given him* (289).

He feels a close association with his name Gogol. He feels an intimacy with his parents, recognizes the worth of his name, which he has ostracized throughout his life. He feels so much forlorn as his father is dead and his mother is also going to Calcutta. The name doesn't matter to him, now he craves for the love of his parents, and misses them a lot:

> The givers and keepers of Gogol's name are far from him. One dead. Another, a widow, on the verge of a different sort of departure, in order to dwell, as his father does, in a separate world. She will call him once a week, on the phone. She will learn to send e-mail, she says. Once or twice a week, he will hear Gogol over the wires see it typed on a screen. As for all the people in the house, all the mashis and meshos to whom he is still and will always be Gogol—now that his mother is moving away, how often will he see them, without people in the world to call him Gogol, no matter how long he himself lives, Gogol Ganguli will, once and for all, vanish from the lips of loved ones, and so, cease to exist. Yet the thought of this eventual demise provides no sense of victory no solace. It provides no solace at all (289).

Ashima Ganguli, an imperative persona in this work of fiction, is not a preacher but a practitioner and she has proved it in her long journey from India to America. Her grandmother with whom she is very close always believes in her and knows that she will not change even after living in a different culture:

> She had fed her sweets with her own hand. Unlike her parents, and her other relatives, her grandmother had not admonished Ashima not to eat beef or wear skirts or cut off her hair or forget her family the moment she landed in Boston. Her grandmother had not been fearful of such signs of betrayal; she was the only person to predict rightly that Ashima would never change (37).

Whenever she teaches her children the culture of their own country, it is because she has been very fastidious in practicing it. She guides them but she never forces her children to do, as she wants them to. She gives them full freedom to move out and explore the world and do the things according to their wishes. As far as the customs are concerned, she teaches them the norms and rules of a traditional family but never restricts them to her own orb.

Being a good mother she takes care of her children well. When Ashoke is not at home for instance, "She wanders around with Gogol, letting him run across the quadrangle, or sitting with him on rainy days to watch television in the student lounge" (50).

When Gogol starts going to nursery, she misses him badly, "She misses the sound of his fully, high-pitched little boy voice, telling her that he is hungry, or tired, or needs to go to the bathroom" (50).

Ashima along with her husband used to celebrate the festivals with great enthusiasm, but was also ready to celebrate Christmas, as her children were very fond of it. For instance she had decorated a tree along with her husband in their house just to give their children happiness. She had gained knowledge of these rules of giving gifts and decorating a tree from her children only but whenever the festival comes, she never forgets to give them gifts and do everything as they like her to do.

Nevertheless, she never forces her children to marry according to her wishes. Only once did Ashima and her husband told their son not to marry an American. *You're too young to get involved this way, Ashoke and Ashima tell him. They've even gone so far as to point out examples of Bengali men they know who've married Americans, marriages that have ended in divorce* (117).

In moments of her loneliness, she reads Bengali novels that she has read a thousand times, in order to have a feel of home.

In the role of a wife, Ashima is at her best. She loves her husband and is very careful in observing his preferences. Initially she faces some problems because her husband is a reserved person, not quick in expression. But with the passage of time, she comes to know his tastes:

> Eight thousand miles away in Cambridge she comes to know him. In the evenings she cooks for him, hope to please with the unrationed, remarkably unblemished sugar, flour, rice and salt she had written about to her mother in her very first letter home. By now she has learned that her husband likes her food on the salty side, that his favorite thing about lamb curry is the potatoes, and that he likes to finish his dinner with a small final helping of rice and dal (10).

There was a perfect harmonization between Ashima and her husband. He is also very caring and loving, "At night lying beside her in bed, he listens to her describe the events of her day; her walk along Massachusetts Avenue, the shops she visits the Hare Krishnas who pester her with their leaflets, the pistachio ice cream cones she treats herself to in Harvard Square" (10).

Ashima after the death of her husband gets really concerned about her son's marriage and she frequently asks her son about his plans for the marriage. Her son, Gogol Ganguli has got three affairs in his life, dates three different girls, but they were not successful. He breaks off his relation with Maxine because he doesn't like her interference in her family affairs. She doesn't like her going every week to visit his mother, at this he feels upset and breaks off the relationship.

Even after coming to know that her son has severed the relationship with his girlfriend Maxine, she insists him to continue with it but on seeing his adamant attitude regarding

Maxine she keeps quiet and asks his opinion about another girl Moushmi, a Bengali by descent. Gogol when being told by her mother about Moushmi starts meeting her and ultimately marries her.

At the outset everything went on well in their married life, but later on some misunderstandings creep in their life because of Moushmi's secret affair with a person Dimitri. On knowing this, Gogol feels very upset:

> They were in the middle of a conversation about how to spend the coming summer, whether to rent a house in Siena with Donald and Astrid, an idea Gogol was resisting, when she'd said, "Dimitri says Siena is something out of a fairy tale". Immediately a hand had gone to her mouth, accompanied by a small intake of breath. And then Silence. "Who's Dimitri?" he'd asked. And then! "Are you having an affair?" (282).

He felt humiliated and deceived and hence they got divorced.

In all these aspects discussed above Ashima Ganguli stands apart from all the other characters in her commitment towards her married life. She was fully dedicated to her husband when he was alive and even after his death. She does not like to sell the house, as she feels attached to everything in that house where she has spent her whole life with her husband, "Listening to their plans Ashima had felt a moment's panic a protective instinct, wanting to retract her offer, wanting the house to remain as it's always been, as her husband had last seen it..." (275).

She is a devoted Indian wife and is true to the meaning of her name, without confines. Initially this land, where she has spent thirty-five precious years of her life seems unusual to her, but now it seems an abode to her, just because her husband has worked here for such a long time and ultimately died. When she prepares herself to go to Calcutta, for her daughter's marriage, she suddenly feels warmth for this country:

> Ashima feels lonely suddenly, horribly permanently alone, and briefly, turned away from the mirror, she sobs for her husband. She feels overwhelmed by the thought of the

> move she is about to make, to the city that was once home and is now in its own way foreign. She feels both impatience and indifference for all the days she still must live, for something tells her she will not go quickly as her husband did. For thirty-three years she missed her life in India. Now she will miss her job at the library, the woman with whom she's worked. She will miss throwing parties, she will miss living with her daughter, the surprising companionship they have formed going into Cambridge together to see old movies at the Brattle teaching her to cook the food Sonia had complained of eating as a child....

She will miss the country in which she had grown to know and love her husband. Though, his ashes have been scattered into the Ganges, it is here, in this house and in this town, that he will continue to dwell in her mind (279).

Here we can see the striking contrast between two ladies Ashima and Moushmi who although belong to the same culture yet are entirely different. For Ashima, everything related to her husband is valuable or symbolizes her husband but for Moushmi the things related to Gogol are just commodities carrying no more connotation than what they stand for. Ashima also feels guilty, as she has encouraged her son to marry Moushmi. And as far as marriage is concerned, Gogol and Moushmi don't share their parent's thoughts on this institution. Moushmi, also being an Indian, is not so much devoted to her husband. She deceives him and even after revelation, there is no guilt on her face. She has got affairs before marriage also and after her divorce with Gogol, she is not that upset. Moushmi etiolates in front of Ashima.Ashima loved her husband when he was alive and even his death has not diminished it a bit, she feels incomplete without him. Even the walls of the house, and the place, which she has despised for all time, remains a source of involvement for her:

> The walls now remind her of the house when they'd first moved in bare except for the photograph of her husband which will be the last thing she will remove. She pauses for

> a moment, waving the remains of the incense in front of Ashoke's image before throwing the stick away (278).

All this is because of the different culture in which they have been brought up because the way she feels about her husband can't be expected from her children. As she thinks:

> But fortunately they have not considered it their duty to stay married as the Bengalis of Ashoke and Ashima's generation do. They are not willing to accept, to adjust, to settle for something less than their ideal of happiness. That pressure has given way, in the case of subsequent generation, to American common sense (276).

Ashima's life in America has brought a great change in her, not with regard to her mores but her independence in learning to do things on her own. Now she feels confident, she is not the same Ashima, always dependent on others for everything:

> For the first time since her flight to meet her husband in Cambridge, in the winter of 1967, she will make the journey entirely on her own. The prospect no longer terrifies her. She has learned to do things on her own, and though she still wears saris, still puts her long hair in a bun, she is not the same Ashima who had once lived in Calcutta. She will return to India with an American passport (276).

Further, on close observation, the writer has highlighted an immense difference between the two cultures very scrupulously. If we talk about the intimacy, there is a huge difference in the closeness shared by Gogol and his wife and his mother Ashima and her husband. For Ashima the closest intimacy between herself and her husband before marriage is that she just sets her feet once into her husband's shoes and takes it out quickly. But as far as Gogol's relationship is concerned, he shares a different proximity with his wife. They went to date each other, share all the dear moments, which is possible for their parents only after marriage. Moreover, Gogol also notices a sharp difference between his parents' treatment of Maxine and his own treatment by her parents. When he eats with them at the dining table, they are not at all bothered about what he is eating but at the same time his mother is so careful and spends her whole day cooking and keeps on asking Maxine persistently. He feels irritated with his parents when they tell him to be careful regarding his health etc. But he really feels relaxed at Maxine's house because her parents are not at all bothered about Maxine's friends, the way his parents do. He stays with her in the room, sleeps with her, which is not at all possible in his house. He feels disconcerted when his father instructs him about parking his car on the right side, his mother advising him to take care of his food etc. At that he really feels edgy but after the death of his father, suddenly he comes close to his mother and realizes his responsibility towards her. He misses every incident related to his father for instance, whenever he used to come home, he finds his father always waiting for him on the station.

Nonetheless, Jhumpa Lahiri uses food very explicitly in this venture to point out the customs, rituals and behavior patterns of a country. Even after going to America, Ashima never likes American food, *Though no longer pregnant, she continues at times to mix Rice Krispies and peanuts and onions in a bowl. For being a foreigner Ashima is beginning to realize, is a sort of life long pregnancy – a perpetual wait, a constant burden, a continuous feeling out of sorts (49).*

The food reminds her of her own country and her own flavor. Whenever Ashima used to invite her Bengali friends for dinner, she spent the whole day in cooking the Bengali food:

> She makes sure to prepare his favorite things; lamb curry with lots of potatoes, luchis, thick channa Dal with swollen brown raisins, pineapple chutney, sandeshes moulded out of saffron-tinted ricotta cheese. All this is less stressful to her than the task of feeding a handful of American children, half of whom always claim they are allergic to Milk, all of whom refuse to eat the crusts of their bread (72).

The writer has also used food to show the incompetence of Indians in America. For instance when Gogol was eating with another character Donald, he finds himself totally inept in front of him:

"Gogol does not find his observation particularly reassuring. He finishes plucking the last of the parsley leaves, watches as Donald grabs a knife and chops them expertly and swiftly, hand held flat over the top of the blade."

Gogol feels incompetent all of a sudden. "I've never quite figured out how to do that," he says.

> All you need is a really good knife. Donald tells him. I swear by these (242).

It can thus be observed that the writer has proficiently articulated the traumas of non-resident Indians, the identity crisis, the generation gap, and cultural differences immaculately. As said *In chronicling more than three decades in the Ganguli's lives, Ms. Lahiri has not only given us a wonderfully intimate and knowing family portrait, she has also taken the haunting chamber music of her first collection of stories and reorchestrated its themes of exile and identity to create a symphonic work, a debut novel that is as assured and eloquent as the work of a longtime master of the craft.*[6] Ashima, the character in this novel remains true to her name from the beginning till the end. She has proved the characteristics associated with her public name as being a person who takes everything in her stride as it comes. Born and brought up in India, Ashima continues to uphold Indian values, traditions and culture even in America after her marriage. She undergoes all the problems in the course of her journey from her own country to a different one very silently and learns to live life that way. She fulfills all the roles assigned to her as a daughter, a mother and above all, a wife and emerges as a winner in the end.

REFERENCES

1. http://www.houghtonmifflinbooks.com/readers_guides/lahiri_namesake.shtml#discussion.
2. http://www.nytimes.com/adx/bin/adx_click.html?type=goto&page=www.nytimes.com/search&pos=Ri.
3. http://www.amazon.com/exec/obidos/subst/home/home.html/102-0188170-0817702.
4. http://www.postcolonialweb.org/india/literature/lahiri/bio.html.

5. Lahiri, Jhumpa, *The Namesake*. New Delhi: HarperCollins Publishers, 2004, 1. All the quotes hereafter cited are from the same edition quoted along with page numbers.

6. http://www.nytimes.com/adx/bin/adx_click.html?type=goto&page=www.nytimes.com/search&pos=Ri.

14

A Blend of Magical, Devious and Divine: A Study of Siddharth Shanghvi's *The Last Song of Dusk*

GEETHA B.

Siddharth Dhanvant Shanghvi's debut novel *The Last Song of Dusk* is one of the most recent voices that have made an instant mark in the literary scene. The kind of deep understanding into the realm of intricate human relationships, of love and loss, of darker or shady aspects of human characters that he exhibits and the deft style of writing make Shanghvi's work a true winner. No wonder, the book has already won the first-novel Betty Trask Award for him. Through the explorations of love and loss, sexuality and innocence, friendship and solitude—it is surely another great debut from India. In the exotic technique of Magic Realism, Shanghvi weaves the tale of the Gandharvas in a combination of humour, darkness and exuberance. *The Last Song of Dusk*—a song of dawn for Shanghvi—has already won wide acclaim in the literary circles. It has received rave reviews like this one from *Booklist:*

> The vibrant, lush, and sometimes chaotic backdrop of post-colonial India has become fertile ground for a burgeoning circle of Indian novelists that Shanghvi now joins. His first novel blends biting social commentary with a sprawling family saga. ...In a narrative laced with poetic imagery, Shanghvi juxtaposes political commentary with magical realism.... Part fairy tale, part satire, part love story—all come together in a marvelously inventive debut.

Set in the 1920s the book mainly revolves round the lives of the Gandharva family, blessed and cursed, by magic: Anuradha, whose fabled beauty is such that the peacocks of Udaipur gather to bid her farewell when she leaves for Bombay to meet her groom, Vardhmaan. As the story unfolds, this woman of mesmerizing beauty and impeccable virtue is tossed and drifted by the ill fate that befalls upon her. A woman gifted with a voice that could make even the moon step out from behind a cloud in response to the 'opaque exquisiteness' of her melody fails to charm the ill fate away with her singing.

What happens to this woman of enchanting beauty and 'ingenuous unpretentiousness' forms the major part of the novel. Her marriage with Vardhamaan, their early married life filled with love and passion, the irrevocable fate that befalls on her, the loss of her first-born that results in a wide gulf between the loving couple, the solitude that she experiences henceforth, the second child with his genius for melancholy and then the life of an invalid that she is made to endure ...the story goes on and tragedies unfold one after another. To make matters worse and to strike with ill-founded vengeance at the most critical of moments there are a haunted house, an evil step mother-in-law and forces of nature. For all the dignity that she has, one wonders why she lacks the forbearance to handle her precocious children (one who could talk almost from the birth, while the other is born with a disquieting silence). It's difficult to understand why destiny has such an onslaught in its design. Only answer perhaps is in what Anuradha's mother had whispered in her ears as she left Udaipur to meet her future husband: *In this life, my darling, there is no mercy.*

What initially has all the ingredients of a beautiful marriage, before long, turns to be a succession of misfortunes. How the deep love and the passion that the newly weds have for each other turns into a relationship shorn of the feeling of companionship is perhaps the most unfortunate aspect of the tale. Shanghvi tells how they gradually lose sight of each other, how their relationship flounders as they are unable to cope with tragedy after tragedy. There is a poignancy about the story of Gandharvas that deepens as we are told how the chasm between the two widens as both of them lose their ability to comprehend the joy derived from life's small redemptions, how the storyteller-doctor finds it impossible to cope with the losses of his mother and son. Whether it is the growing solitude that the couple experience or the sense of loss that Anuradha experiences, Shanghvi treats it with utmost sensitivity. The changing landscape of love is movingly told and one wonders at Shanghvi's penchant for melancholy without which such a feat would not have been possible.

Somewhere in the middle of the book we are introduced to the exploits of a seductive artist Nandini, Anuradha's orphaned cousin. Anuradha brings this cousin of hers to live with her when she returns to live with Vardhmaan. Nandini—a very talented albeit eccentric artist has a penchant for panthers and can walk on water. Product of an unhappy marriage, she is abused as a child. Still in her early teens, Nandini happens to be a precocious lover, muse to India's greatest artists and fiancée of the son of the Governor. A fable goes that one of the women on her mother's side loved a leopard. Her feline stride, her fetish for panthers and her feline ferocity in lovemaking can only be attributed to this quirk in the family. It is said that seven generations back, on Nandini Hariharan's maternal side, a woman had coupled with a leopard in the mountains of Matheran, and to this day the family could not rid the bane of cat's blood in their veins—the blood that made the women in the family gorgeous, selfish and recondite.

The novel is told in the exotic technique of Magic Realism. To tell the extraordinary stories of Nandini Hariharan and other female members in her family, the magic of music that Anuradha's family has inherited, the powers of their music, the evil spirits at work whether it be in Dwarika house or Dariya Mahal, Shanghvi couldn't have thought of any better technique. Magic realism being a mode suited to explore and transgress boundaries; it empowers the writer to fuse the mundane with the extraordinary. According to Zamora and Faris, Magic Realism,

> often facilitates the fusion, or coexistence, of possible worlds, spaces, systems that would be irreconcilable in other modes of fiction. The propensity of magical realist texts to admit a plurality of worlds means that they often situate themselves on liminal territory between or among those worlds—in phenomenal and spiritual regions.... So magical realism may be considered an extension of realism in its concern with the nature of reality and its representation, at the same time that it resists the basic assumptions of post-enlightment rationalism and literary realism (5-6).

The mode of Magic Realism in literature is traced back to Latin American writers like Guatemala's Miguel Ángel Asturias, Argentina's Julio Cortázar, and Mexico's Carlos Fuentes and the like. The movement's best-known proponent is the Colombian novelist Gabriel García Marquez who has used the technique many times, most famously in his novel *One Hundred Years of Solitude (1967)* of the writers of Indian subcontinent, Sulman Rushdie has been much talked about for his use of Magic Realism. When writers initially adopted this mode of writing, it offered a new style that at once celebrated the mundane, and yet was alien to the then idea of Realism by altering the boundaries of the acceptable. It employed various techniques that endowed all things with a deeper meaning and reveal mysteries that always threaten the secure tranquility of simple and ingenuous things. Works of magic realism mingle realistic portrayals of ordinary events and characters with elements of fantasy and myth, creating a rich, frequently disquieting world that is at once familiar and dreamlike. As critic Franz Roh noted:

> This [art offers a] calm admiration of the magic of being, of the discovery that things already have their own faces, [this] means that the ground in which the most diverse ideas in the world can take root has been reconquered—albeit in new ways. For the new art it is a question of representing before our eyes, in an intuitive way, the fact, the interior figure, of the exterior world (19-20).

In the Magic Realist novels the recognizably realistic merges with the unexpected and the inexplicable. Here, elements of dreams, fairy story, or mythology combine with the everyday, often in a mosaic or kaleidoscopic pattern of refraction and recurrence. And that is what exactly Shanghvi manages to do. With the blend of mundane with the magical and extraordinary in the tradition of other renowned magic realist writers, he uses this technique to make his readers willingly enter and tread between the realistic and the magical worlds that he creates. His success in this mode of writing perhaps can be gauged by the way in which he manages to blur the difference between the two worlds. As Peter Gordon puts it:

> There is rather more magic than realism in the style of Shanghvi, but in what struck me as a very Latin American deftness of touch, Siddharth Dushyant Shanghvi has been able to get his reader to suspend disbelief and accept the rules of this universe where girls walk on water, malicious parrots spout venom and houses are haunted by dead gay lovers.

Magic Realism perhaps is not new to Indian storytellers. If one recalls how as children we were fed with folklores and mythological tales that traversed through known and unknown universes with ease. In fact, for long, it has been so much of our story telling tradition that we have forgotten to note where realistic ended and magic began. Shanghvi has an interesting point to make when he says how much of our Bollywood too is replenished with elements of Magic Realism! He observes how magic realism is our very way of perceiving:

> Life does not occur in India: it is an event. Life tears at its seams in the old country, it gapes out of the skin of time, it stands up and sings, it sits down and weeps: how can you not write when you have known this?

Another important aspect of the book is its deep relationship with music. From the very title to the last page of the novel, music plays a very important role. There is the beauty and magic of music that one constantly comes across. As is clear after reading the book, the tale of Anuradha is completely entwined with this last song of dusk. It becomes a metaphor for life—life with all its joys and sorrows, life that is a result of the magical, the divine and even the devious. Even when there are forces and powers that plot against individual lives, their music never fails. It offers a balance, a harmony and an austerity even in madness.

As we are told early on, the magical powers of music have been inherited by generations of women in Anuradha's maternal side. It is passed on to her and to her children. Anuradha herself once relates to Vardhmaan the stories about what magic music had in their lives. She had an aunt who could sing a song that lit up all the oil lamps and another who knew a song that brought the monsoon on time. When she sang, rain gushed down into the deep draught of Rajasthan. As Anuradha puts it:

> ...the songs are a dowry of magical arias handed down in my family. Each woman came with her own tune. My mother knew a song that made the trees flower (45).

If for Shanghvi, the last song of dusk is the whole story of Gandharvas, the story for Anuradha is Shloka, the child born with a disquieting silence; Shloka—the one who 'would carry the Story everyone else had lived.' For Shloka, it is an evening song that returns no echo:

> A melody released with a volcanic contralto, it rises up reaches far and it touches the blue bells hiding and the weasels and smallest harvester ant that ever breathed. But it returns no echo... this last song of dusk, now it demands no reply nor permits imitation simply because it is full in itself: a breath that will never be breathed again. All things under its bough will be healed and returned to the place they came from: silence (295).

The gift of music has come to the family with its own stake: a genius for melancholy. That perhaps is the only justification and only consolation for the Gandharvas. Why otherwise should such a plethora of tragedies befall on them? Why life is snatched away from Mohan—their first-born with his genius for music. Why the second child is born with a 'disquieting silence?' Why Vardhmaan dries up of all tokens of his affection for Anuradha? How does his tales dry up giving space for only silence? Is it Vardhmaan's defence mechanism to cope up with whatever life has had in store or is it that couple has now grown acutely afraid of loss and thus is scared of loving?

The foundation for the tragedy that unfolds in the life of Anuradha and her husband is laid out in the very beginning of the novel. She, a woman of enchanting beauty and mesmerizing voice is too perfect to be ordinary. Vardhaman, the handsome young husband, is too virtuous to be ordinary. The first-born Mohan, who at the age of seventeen months could reproduce the 'arc of her melody, the hauteur in it, without a single error' is too precocious. All these perhaps are portentous of the tragedies that are to strike. Even Anuradha herself gasps at the prescience that for such depth of talent the price would be 'ferocious.' At one level the whole family is blessed, at another it is terribly cursed.

The Dwarika home of Gandharva's, the forces of nature and then the Dariya Mahal- *the castle of the sea*—at Juhoo all seem to plot against the Gandharva's throughout the book, as though they had to pay a price for all the talent, beauty and virtues they were blessed with. The Dwarika Mahal, with the domineering presence of the step-mother-in law Divi bhai with her vicious tongue, crushes not only the dream of Anuradha, but also her first-born son. The house that gave Anuradha a slightly daunting feeling the very first day of her entry, the window and the shingh tree arching up to it, the scary height it stood at that 'formed a viscious, bubbling terror at the base of her long neck had suggested her about the Mischief it could unravel with impassioned deviousness' proves to be calamitous. When the tragedy strikes, it leaves scars that can never be healed, haunting their lives forever.

As circumstances force Anuradha to leave the Dwaraka home and to live in Udaipur with her mother. When she comes back with Vardhmaan, it is to the beautiful, haunted mansion Dariya Mahal. Dariya Mahal has its own mind; it is filled with some kind of Hardian 'imminent will' that intensifies the misfortune, which strikes the Gandharva family. As they navigate the ever-changing landscape of life, the old villa that has been impregnated with the sorrow of Edward accentuates their ill fate. There lives the ghost of the love of Edward—the Englishman who had built Dariya Mahal with the sole purpose of living there with his lover Raghuvir Singh before dying of waiting. Shanghvi attributes now a villainous intent to the Dariya Mahal. With the death of Edward it had taken a fetish for sorrow, a hatred for joy, love and happiness. As Shanghvi puts it,

> a breathless, crazy, deceived sadness oozed out of his flesh and seeped into Dariya Mahal: it tricked into the spaces between the flat stoning, swam into dusty corners wove around the rafters, until the house and Edward's waiting grief were one single monument to heartbreak (76).

The scheming Dariya Mahal strikes Anuradha and her valued ones at most importunate of moments. The dark house with its own designs is portrayed to be scheming to bring more ill fate to the household. The house with the echo of the cry of the unrequited love of the Englishman can't stand any strain of optimism or joy. When Anuradha becomes pregnant with her second child, it is perturbed that her annoying optimism might infect Vardhaman and so has taken things to its own hands; its "Bitter hands. Cold hands. Hands that held a whiteman waiting for the brown one... who never came."

And the Dariya Mahal chooses a rainy afternoon to strike. As pregnant Anuradha, alone one afternoon, bends to knife away the lemongrass sheaves the haunted house strikes. What exactly happened that made her fall on her navel hurting herself and the baby inside her—she too couldn't make out. Her water bag had burst "giving worries to her and to the unborn...worries for the well being of each other." We are told, Dariya Mahal, if it had had legs, "would have slipped on its dancing shoes, clicked its knees, and done a hurrah" at its success.

Dariya Mahal has more such designs to bring woe to this family. Anuradha, now in bed, has to put her feet tied up to stop the baby falling prematurely. One month into the accident and the baby could no longer endure its captivity. She bleeds profusely, so much so that 'her shadow on the wall seemed to melt in shape and size.' Even the rain Gods seemed to work in tandem with Dariya Mahal in adding to their difficulties. As Anuradha bleeds, the roads are flooded and taking her to the hospital becomes out of the question. Vardhaman now is forced to give a snake venom injection to Anuradha in a desperate attempt to stop her from dying of bleeding. Perhaps it is this venom injection that brings baby Shukla quietness in his eyes and a silence that is hard to be broken. It is as though the melancholy of Dariya Mahal had swept into the child and would remain with him forever. One wonders why Anuradha herself could not foresee or avoid making Dariya Mahal their home; even though she had realized the beauty of the house must have been the result of some 'endless sorrow' in the beginning itself? Perhaps fate has power over one's judgments and reason.

There are certain aspects that strike us about Shanghvi's writing. He doesn't stop at being just another over ambitious beginner who adopts the technique of magic realism to suit his own purpose, to bring people who can walk on water or sing songs to bring rain into the desert. His knack for story telling doesn't stop with the tale of wandering spirits of an unrequited love. Nor does it stop with fatalistic overtones. There is a remarkable maturity in his understanding of the inner life of his characters. His novel has a strong narrative drive and a deep sorrowful song that sings of love, loss and solitude. The lyrical quality of his prose makes the book win raving reviews. The *Times Literary Supplement* had this to say about the book:

> What begins as an erotic fairy tale grows into an exploration of love and loss, sexuality and innocence, friendship and solitude.... Shanghvi's loose poetic style [is] cut with a dash of magical realism... [and his] story has eloquent insights into the nature of love.

What exactly Shanghvi intended in this book? Perhaps to come to terms with what he tells in the book: 'it is so strange that love and loathing, joy and distress, quietness and noise, all eventually blur and one is left wondering where one started and the other ended.'

In *The Last Song of Dusk*, Shanghvi handles multiple themes: at one level he explores different facets of love, at another he transgresses the social constructions of sexuality. Whether it is the conjugal love between the husband and wife that evolves into a more sublime love before the setting in of solitude, or the affection of Gandharva couple towards their children, or even the longing of that English man who spent years waiting for his homosexual partner or even the innocent love of Sherman for the not so innocent Nandini, Shanghvi has an inkling of the workings of love, its different shades. As he tells in one of his interviews, this book was mainly an exploration of how love lights up our lives in the ways we seldom ever imagine. He also sees it as his own attempts to come to terms with his solitude. The process of writing the novel, he says, had been a process of gathering his own solitude. He tells us how the liquid ache in his chest seemed to melt as he wrote:

> the fist in my heart opened up and became an embrace. And, over time, this embrace grew to become my first novel. A novel about Anuradha, Gandharva and her magical, healing songs; about Vardhmaan, her husband, hostage to his secret losses; Nandini, the dazzling, devious artist and her scandalous sexual liaisons; and about Shloka...I don't know why tears reeled down my face.

What ultimately Shanghvi succeeds in is telling the strange truth that 'love and loathing, joy and distress, quietness and noise, all eventually blur and one is left wondering where one started and the other ended.'

The most striking aspect of the book is the author's ability to delve into the deeper recesses, the inner life of human beings. Be it Anuradha, Vardhamaan, Edward or even the eccentric Nandini—they are only symbols of those who are thrown to the mercies of fate—surfing through the canvas of life. Even the most idiosyncratic of characters suffer from or in the absence of a very human need with a divine name-love.

The variegated manifestations of love and tenderness and also the sense of loss, a feeling of solitude that always lurks behind, have a profound impact. The deep understanding that he has into the nature of love touches the reader, lends gravity to the book, as can be seen from the following passage from the book:

> Even love comes with its own season...and relationships with their own kismets. They start through us and love loves through us. And when the give-and-take between two individuals is over, the relationship fades. Like a fruit that must fall from the bough if it is to carry its life into its next avatar. There is nothing more critical than to exercise the generosity to let something end with the grace that it started with (264).

As Anuradha tries to come to terms with this sad reality, she also realizes that whatever her heart attaches itself to is taken away from her. And she has now come to understand that Dariya Mahal has such a heinous heart that it is ever ready to pounce upon whatever she values. She has to send her young son Shloka before he is lost forever. The hard lessons of life now have made Anuradha realize that all that her heart affiliates itself with will be taken away from her. What she writes in her letter to Radha Mashi is a clear expression of her fears of the fate that could take her young son Shloka away forever if she doesn't send him away herself:

> Many years ago, I accepted Mohan's leap into his own destiny, so much braver, with so much more velocity... I saw Vardhmaan move away into his own world and I told myself: 'Yes, in this too there is the hand of something larger than me. Something which will not allow me to lose myself in my love for him.' So I stepped back, and then I saw him for the first time: vulnerable and broken and true. I suppose life is a process of looking clearly at things. But this will find its greatest trial when I send my little Shloka away (274).

As we go through the novel, the liquid ache that escapes Anuradha takes hold of the reader too. Vardhmaan, too, is not unruffled by this ache. With the drying of his stories he has lost all means of expression. Even when the longing for Anuradha, for the feeling of togetherness that he had once shared with Anuradha becomes acute, he punishes himself by not submitting to the feeling. Mohan's death, thus, haunts him throughout. Shanghvi gives expression to what Vardhamaan goes through beautifully there are times when he misses her familiar sweet humming, her simple presence. Sometimes,

> he wanted nothing more than to run down the path on which he'd left her behind. With a frangipani braid in his hand. With an unremembering heart. He saw, however, that he hadn't merely left her; rather, she too had wandered away into a geography of such physical agony that it would take an entirely different map to reach her (248-249).

Anuradha, who once entered Vardhmaan's life thinking that she would age in the friendship of this man, had been evicted from the reverie somewhere, somehow. Call it fate, destiny or powers with devious intent; pitted against its powers, magic of her benign self does not have a chance. Perhaps the only consolation to the reader is she has now come to accept it, has learnt to live with her solitude. She finally has understood that "the street slang of life was one word alone: irony."

As we approach the book there is a solemnity, a dignified silence that slowly set in about the Gandharvas. Now, sometimes, they would continue staring at each other in the knowledge that,

> the endurers of a common fate have an association that outlives calamity and joy, strengthens over time, and deepens into a clarity that allows them to accept that love was nothing but the fragile excuse that enjoined them, and after its cessation, after the haunting emptiness of its passing, this silence they were now sharing was, in fact, nothing short of divine eloquence (283).

The Last Song of Dusk—a tale of exquisite friendships, immense sacrifices and dangerous desires—is told with tenderness and with brilliant wit. The novel with its exquisite beauty moves the reader, allows one to experience the terrific beauty of a sad tune. No wonder, it haunts one for long. Even though the exploits of some of the eccentric characters become bizarre at times the underlying themes, the finesse of approach and the poetic sensibility of Shanghvi make the novel carry itself with poise. The raving national, international reviews and the already won Betty Trask Award are indicative of the power of this vibrant new voice from India.

REFERENCES

1. Afzal-Khan, Fawzia, *Cultural Imperialism and the Indo-English Novel: Genre and Ideology in R.K. Narayan, Anita Desai, Kamala Markandaya, and Salman Rushdie*, University Park, PA: Pennsylvania State University Press, 1993.
2. "Magic Realism," *The Columbia Encyclopedia*. 6th ed. 2004.
3. Shanghvi, Siddharth Dhanvant: *The Last Song of Dusk*. New Delhi: Penguin Books Ltd., 2004.
4. Wilson, Rawdon, "The Metamorphoses of Fictional Space: Magical Realism." *Magical Realism: Theory, History, Community*, (Eds.) Zamora, Lois Parkinson and Wendy B. Faris. Durham, NC: Duke University Press, 1995. 209-233.
5. Zamora, Lois Parkinson and Wendy B. Faris, (Eds.) *Magical Realism: Theory, History, Community*. Durham, NC: Duke University Press, 1995.
6. http://www.arcadepub.com.
7. http://www.asianreviewofbooks.com/arb/article.php?article=418.
8. http://www2.britishcouncil.org/india/india-connecting-2004/ india-connecting-east http://economictimes.indiatimes.com/ articleshow/746925.cms.
9. http://www.siddharths.com/acclaim.htm.

15

Ambiguous Divinity in Manil Suri's *The Death of Vishnu*

R. SWARNALATHA

What if God were one of us
A Slob like one of us
A stranger on the bus
Trying to make His way home
(John Osborne's song "One of Us").

Manil Suri's much acclaimed debut-making novel, *The Death of Vishnu* revels in the dialectic tension between omnipotence and powerlessness—of man as God and God as man. Suri effortlessly weaves thumbnail sketches of the idiosyncratic residents of a crowded Bombay apartment into the rubric of Hindu philosophy. The eponymous hero of the novel is a drunk who lies dying on the landing of the apartment while the residents argue ferociously about who has to pay the ambulance charges. The author presents Vishnu through two viewfinders; the first foregrounds the all-pervading God of the Vedas and Upanishads whereas the second subtly hints at the human God who could be just any of us.

The early reviewers of this novels like Elise Mignon have commented on the novel's metaphorical matrix which is capable of multiple interpretations: The building becomes a metaphor for the social and cultural division existing in contemporary India and Vishnu's later ascent of the building's steps parallels the soul's progress through the Hindu stages of existence. Commenting on the elusive nature of the text, Kuritzky writes, "Like cloud formations and constellations,

Manil Suri's novel, *The Death of Vishnu*, can be interpreted as any number of things, read and enjoyed in many different ways, with each way as fulfilling as the others. There is no clear entry point here."

The novel itself houses many quests; starting from the self-flagellating religious quest of Mr. Jalal, the romantic quest of Kavitha and Salim gilded by the glitter and vacuousness of romantic love and the minor quests of the likes of Mrs. Pathak who hanker after social eminence in the kitty party circles. Even Short Ganga, the charwoman dreams of high recognition for her self-styled scientific discoveries. The dying Sheetal Taneja longs to make it to the hall of fame in the Guinness Book of World Records by memorising all the dialogues of a Hindi movie. After Sheetal's death, her husband Vinod's quest centers round freeing himself from the ghosts of her memories and recovering from the zombie-like existence which his bereavement forces him into. Vishnu, the drunken handyman, who lies dying also does not seem to have any grandiose quest. His consciousness throws up snippets from his past life. It is lit up with the memories of his mother who entertains and encourages him with stories of Jiv, the allegory of the soul who evolves from an insect to a grand being. The other focus of Vishnu's ebbing consciousness is Padmini, the prostitute, and the memories of his days of love with her.

Ironically Vishnu, who is Suri's only candidate for manifestation of divinity, is dying. The dying Vishnu is witness to all the events happening around him in the apartment. He is the center around which the events of the novel mysteriously arrange themselves. As an act of penance Mr. Jalal curls up under the blanket with the filth-covered Vishnu and is rewarded by a 'Vishvaroopa darshana' of Lord Vishnu. Mr.Jalal is so overcome by this epiphanic vision that he spreads the message that Vishnu is a God. Vishnu is a witness to his own deification and later to the communal tensions which spring between the Jalal family and the Hindu residents of the neighbourhood. Vishnu, once the aider and abettor of the Kavitha-Salim romance, is now the passive witness to their elopement which provides the initial impetus to the communal tensions in the apartment. Vishnu, for the major part of the novel, does not act but instead is acted upon. The novel, as Dave Weich puts it, "is part-sitcom and part-meditation, a brilliant counterpoint of action and stillness."

This paper seeks to explore the philosophical vision that emerges from the rich resonances of Hindu thought and mythology in this novel. The most obvious starting point is the philosophy of perennial evolution which emerges from the stories of "Jiv," which are narrated to Vishnu by his mother: "A yogi-spirit named Jeev born nine hundred and ninety thousand times" (148). The slow evolution through the transformation of life from one species to another in its journey to perfection is addressed in the Yoga Sutras of Patanjali. The ancient Puranas, especially the *Brihad Vishnu Purana* states that there are a total of 8,400,000 species which includes plants, aquatic creatures, amphibians, birds, anthropoids after which the human species of 200,000 varieties come into being, and Man then engages in purposeful activity to attain perfection.

Jeev starts off on the lowest ladder of evolution; he is an insect "smaller than a banana seed." It takes him many lives to reach the level of a human. In one of his incarnations Jeev is born as a little sparrow who is accidentally wounded by Arjuna's arrow. Arjuna nurses the bird back to health and as per his mother's injunctions is ordered to share the bird with his four brothers. However the sparrow becomes unduly attached to Arjuna, who one day sets it free in the thick forest with the advice that each creature has its own karma to follow. As Arjuna's handsome face disappears from sight, the little bird realizes that it is rising beyond the earth and even beyond the trinity, "with Brahma reclining in the chariot of the seven swans, and Vishnu rising in all his brilliance into the sky, and Shiva at the edge of the world, getting ready to do his dance (151)."

The Jeev Chronicles also warn that it is possible to step down the ladder of evolution as quickly as it is possible to climb up. In one of his incarnations, Jeev is a Brahmin who is very severe towards a sweeper woman who has committed the heinous crime of gazing at him directly in the eye. Indra, the God who is passing by comments that a stick is not really necessary when mere words are enough. As a result, Jeev is sent back to the earth as a monkey with his Brahminical mind intact.

The stories of Jeev are mirrored in the characters in this novel who are at different levels on the ladder of perfection. Bill Duryea writes that "Each character in an Indian building dances to the music of his/her position in life, caught up in the daily squabbles and sensuous pursuits that Hindu religion teaches are necessary until one becomes sated by that lifestyle and moves on to another stage."

Manil Suri playfully hints at the latent divinity in his characters. The Jeev chronicles gently lead the reader to the Vedantin's world-view. According to Vedanta, both the soul and God belong to the same category of Self—the former is the individual self (Jivatman), whereas the latter is the Supreme Self (Paramatman). God in Vedanta, is not only the creator, but also the created. The divine power is not a mere formless, impersonal material principle. It is a living dynamic conscious force that can assume a concrete personal form. Vishnu is given this truth at a very early age by his mother. She tells him that he is Vishnu of the ten avatars, "Rama and Krishna are part of you...You are Vishnu...keeper of the universe, keeper of the sun. What would be the world without you?" (21).

The same idea is mirrored in the religious quest of Mr. Jalal. His initiation by Vishnu in the epiphanic dream is almost a parody. Vishnu offers him a walnut from a bowl, cracks the shell and sifts through the pieces to offer it to Mr.Jalal, who is infuriated by the triteness of the act. Vishnu challenges him by posing the question, "And what do you think—this enlightenment that you are seeking- it comes in a nut?" Infuriated by the question, Jalal goes on to expound why he is the right candidate for enlightenment. After all those months of sleeping on the ground without a pillow and starving himself, Jalal feels that he has a right to enlightenment. When Vishnu asks him to calm down in order not to miss the significance of the present moment, he reacts by calling Vishnu a miserable drunk and retorts that all religion is a hoax. It is precisely at this moment that the revelation takes place. Vishnu's fist swings up through the air and smashes the walnut into his skull. Jalal's mystic third eye opens up and through it he sees a sun emerge from behind Vishnu; the suns multiply until the whole sky is covered with them. Vishnu's body metamorphoses into a limitless form with innumerable limbs, glittering with divine ornaments, brandishing heavenly weapons, wearing celestial garlands, anointed with scents of heavenly weapons, wearing celestial garlands, anointed with scents of heavenly fragrances. The terrifying faces spouting flame where human forms are crushed to death. The form keeps expanding until the terrified Jalal is made to ask, "Tell me, who are you in this terrible Form?" (156). The answer that he gets is identical to what Arjuna hears from Krishna in Chapter 11 of the Bhagwad Gita. Arjuna is made to see that the Absolute is the animating force behind everything. It penetrates into material, emotional and intellectual qualities of the manifested objects. The formless Brahman through its magical form of Iswara creates everything and remains immanent in it. The formless Brahman is difficult to comprehend and cannot be seen. The manifold manifestations of the Lord induce Arjuna to see for himself the cosmic form of Ishwara, who is the creator, sustainer and destroyer.

Manil Suri's Vishnu in his awesome manifestation defines his role as both preserver and destroyer of the universe:

> I am all living things, I am creation itself. Look at me and see in my body the whole Universe...I am the aging of time, the beginning and end of the universe. As each day ends, all creatures are renewed and destroyed in me (156).

In this Visvarupa Darshana Yoga, Jalal is made to realize the highest Advaitic truth that all things emerge from the Brahman and withdraw into the Brahman, like the spider, which creates a web and withdraws it too (Mundaka Upanishad 1.1.7). The vision ends with a terrifying injunction to Jalal. He is asked to spread the message of Visnu's divinity: "Tell them down there to recognize me for who I am...Before it is too late, too late for all." Jalal finds himself getting absorbed into the body of

Vishnu and he is overcome with the bliss of the Samadhi-like oneness. The concept of salvation in time before the ultimate annihilation is the prelude to the apocalyptic vision of the Kalki avatar which Suri stages in a surrealistic yet contemporary setting.

Vishnu's main task is to preserve the divine order. If this is disturbed, he descends to the earth, taking the form required by the occasion. This is the concept of the avatar in Hindu philosophy. The development of the ten avatars of Vishnu from Matsya (the fish) to man, passing by the Varaha (the Wild Boar) and Vamana (the Dwarf) symbolizes the transformation of mankind. The tenth avatar of Vishnu epitomises his fearsome role as destroyer who engages in the purgatory annihilation of evil in order to bring about good. The Vishnu Purana gives a graphic description of the function of the Kalki avatar:

> He will be born as Kalki in the family of an eminent Brahmin...endowed with the eight superhuman faculties. By his irresistible might, He will destroy all the barbarians and thieves, And all whose minds are devoted to iniquity. He will then reestablish righteousness upon earth (Vishnu Purana 4,24).

The Kalki avatar as portrayed by Suri is a controversial surrealistic picture. Reviewers like Anna Skea have found the section disturbing because there is a clear injunction to kill infidel barbarians, especially barbarian children. The possible implication of this section in a country where religious fundamentalism is making its appearance is rather frightening. She writes, "The fact remains that the position of that passage from Hindu mythology made me uncomfortably aware that of all the families in the book, the Muslim family came off worst in the end." Kai Friese does not find any philosophical depth in the novel. On the other hand, he compares it to the flippant approach of Rushdie's *Midnight's Children*. "Where Gibreel Farishta falls to his doom, Vishnu ascends to his rebirth. Similarly, while Rushdie chanced his hand by prostituting the wives of the prophet 'Mahound' Suri chooses a whore as the consort of the terrestrial Vishnu. More generally, the Bhagavad Gita is to Suri's book what the Koran is to Rushdie's."

The dying Vishnu has a host of avatars to choose from. He could be Narasimha, Vamana, Rama or Krishna. However, he decides that he cannot become an avatar that has already lived so he decides in favour of Kalki, the last and unmanifest avatar of Vishnu who is "destined to cut the thread of time and purify all of mankind." The avatar manifests itself in Vishnu's consciousness at a critical moment when the cigarettewalla and the panwallah of the neighbourhood are gathering people to seek justice for the missing Kavitha, whom they think has been abducted by the Jalal family. Vishnu becomes Kalki, the white horse, wielding his burning sword, riding a horse that carries his name. From the dim corridors of memory, scenes flash wherein his mother goes down on all her fours imitating the horse of Kalki. When the child demands to know who she is, the mother replies: "I am your horse, O great Vishnu...Together we will descend on earth to battle the wicked" (239). Memory transports the consciousness of Vishnu into a surrealistic moment outside Jalal's door. He finds himself metamorphosing into the avatar. His mother disappears and in her place there is a real horse, which is pristine white. His stick becomes a flaming sword and he finds himself astride the horse, which leaps into the air taking him on a strange journey.

The first person narrative of the white horse of Vishnu is a disturbing discourse on the balance of good and evil in the universe. It is in a way a reversal of the scenario of Bhagavad Gita, wherein the Lord urges the guilt-ravaged Arjuna to carry on the war against the elders and evil doers of the Kaurava clan, keeping his mind steadfast only on the right action. In Suri's novel, Vishnu as Kalki avatar is as averse to blood shedding and gore as Arjuna is. The white horse exhorts Vishnu to take action against the infidels and barbarians who have "buried the teachings of the Vedas" and "poisoned the air with their alien ways." Vishnu, the God, does not see this as an invasion and points out that "evil springs up from inside the hearts of people, it needs no external source to appear."

The horse persistently quotes the Puranas and reminds Vishnu that there is divine sanction to kill the barbarians in order to restore the Vedic order to the land. The horse who also calls itself Kalki, forces Vishnu to ride along the banks of the Ganga, butchering and killing infidels as they ride along. Vishnu follows his horse helplessly: "A rider can only journey where his horse conveys him". The white horse is also a ruthless agent of destruction. It proclaims lustily, "If Vishnu falters, if he leaves a job half done, a barbarian half alive, I finish things off myself" (241). When Vishnu balks at killing barbarian children, the horse reasons that by killing them, they will be sent to less ignoble births and even if they are allowed to live, it would be an act of cruelty because they will develop into full-fledged barbarians. As Vishnu weeps at the immensity of his act, the horse reminds him, "It is your sacred duty...Your dharma, as foretold in the Agni Purana...Accept the dharma you must perform, O Vishnu. For there is nothing more dishonorable than failing in your sacred duty" (242). In Suri's version, the Kalki avatar is both God and beast, the masculine and feminine principle, kindness and ruthlessness—the contraries coexist. The dialogue between Vishnu and the horse are strikingly parallel to the third chapter of the Bhagavad Gita. Lord Krishna chastises Arjuna when he laments about why the Lord wants him to indulge in the ghastly warfare and stresses about the importance of karma yoga: "Perform your prescribed duty, for action is better than inaction" (Bhagavad Gita, Verse 8). Lord Krishna insists that Arjuna should do his allotted work of a warrior without resorting to escapism. Work should not be given up capriciously without purification of materialistic propensities. Karma yoga is all about the relinquishing of private ownership and the surrendering of action to the Supreme Intelligence. But in Suri's novel, there is a role-reversal. Godhead does not lead but instead is led. The horse of Kalki proudly proclaims, "In his heart, he knows I am right. That is why he does what I say" (243). As Vishnu's sword flashes and mows down the barbarians, the horse is elevated by the vision of a civilization, which has been restored to its primordial greatness. The horse's vision is both beautiful and chilling. In the cleansed country rites and rituals are preserved, children respect their elders and wives obey their husbands. At the same time castes do not intermarry and there is an almost fanatical insistence on maintaining the purity of the race. And the chants of the Rig Veda are heard suffusing the air. Meanwhile, Vishnu who is oblivious of the newness of the cleansed society weeps. The horse does not allow the God to linger in his emotional states and urges him with these words, "Arise O Great Warrior and let us be on our way!"

The Kalki avatar manifests itself in the consciousness of Vishnu when an enraged gathering of Hindu neighbours bang on Jalal's door demanding to see Salim. Vishnu who wants to test his new found powers as God, decides to test them on a group of ants. He wills them to be immobilized. But when nothing happens and he wonders in what sense he is Kalki if he cannot even dispatch an ant. So he does not concern himself with the commotion at Jalal's and ascends to the landing between the second and third floor where Thanu Lal, the miraculous ash-producer, is curled up fast asleep. Vishnu is overcome by the urge to wake up Thanu Lal and hold a conversation with him about God. But he finds that he is unable to do so because he has lost his sense of touch. He again starts doubting his divinity: "How can he be a god if he has no power? Could he just be a man, the man he has been his whole life?" (254). But there is no time to think about answers because he knows intuitively that there is no other way but to keep ascending until he reaches the top.

The top of the landing is metaphor, not just for the most elevated state of consciousness but also for death. As he ascends to the terrace door, he can see and hear a cluster of cheering Gods waiting to welcome him into their celestial brotherhood. His eyes seek his divine consort, Lakshmi and he eagerly anticipates the cosmic magnitude of their moment of union. But with every step that he takes, the question "God or man, man or God" looms large in his mind. As he climbs up the last stretch, he realizes that it is a path of no return. Although his imagination struggles to hold a vision of Lakshmi and his divine vehicle, Garuda, he finds Yama, the God of

Death blocking the entrance at the uppermost part of the landing. Yama becomes omnipresent, blocking out the other divine entities. He waves his mace and tells Vishnu that it is time for him to sleep. Vishnu tries not to succumb to Yama, but his efforts are futile. Lakshmi and Garuda leave and the order of Yama keeps echoing in his ears. His mother's voice also flows into his soporific consciousness but the words are different this time. She says, "When the age of Kaliyuga is drawing to a close, then my little Vishnu will take a rest...The sun will go down and the seas will die as Vishnu closes his eyes...For eons will he sleep on Ananta, regaining his strength. Opening his eyes when it is time to begin the cycle again" (304). It is tempting to find echoes from Indian religious texts while reading this passage. At the end of the Kali Yuga which lasts for 432,000 years, there is an abundance of strife, ignorance and vice which reach a crescendo. Then the Kalki avatar vanquishes the negative forces and commences a golden age called Satya Yuga. When Kalpas end, even the Gods like Brahma are not exempt from death because they form part of the material universe. In the Bhagavad Gita, Lord Krishna defines himself as both life and death because in the Absolute Unity the contraries co-exist. Chapter 9 talks about the end of a Kalpa where Krishna says: "At the end of a kalpa, all beings merge into my nature, then, at the beginning of the next kalpa, I emit them again." The reader is tempted to believe that Suri's Vishnu is falling into one such slumber, which marks the interregnum between the dark age of human foibles and a golden age of awareness. But the envisaged end is totally reversed. Mr. Jalal is hounded by an angry mob because they feel that he has committed the heinous crime of mouthing the sacred message of the Gita. His son has also had a hand in defiling the religion because he dared to elope with a Hindu girl. Arifa, Jalal's wife has to pay for her husband's unusual religious quest with her life and Jalal himself is hurt. In the hospital a bemused Jalal wonders whether the slew of unfortunate events could be a result of his undertaking the faith.

As Vishnu crosses the threshold of the final step the lights dim, his eyes close and he feels that he is about to see a movie.

The movie is appropriately titled "The Death of Vishnu." The story has all the spicy ingredients and the run of mill song and dance sequences of Hindi movies. Vishnu and Padmini comprise the enthusiastic audience who watch the movie while slurpily enjoying their ice cream. The story proceeds from the scenes of childhood; warm memories of his mother and it gradually progresses to his romantic episodes with Padmini, Vishnu's relationship with Kavitha and suddenly the movie focuses on Vishnu's ascent up the flight of stairs to the terrace door. At this juncture Vishnu wishes the movie gives clear directions about what he is climbing towards and equally clear answers to the question whether he is man or God. The climactic moment of the film coincides with the opening of the terrace door. Vishnu watches with bated breath at this unrevealed part of his life. At this juncture he realizes that the entire theatre is empty and that even Padmini has left. Vishnu walks to the center of the stage and faces the projector. The screen is a giant lit field extending all around him. The light from the projector is so bright that it blurs everything around him. The light enters him and his body becomes incandescent and he merges with the light.

The entire movie is a modern rendering of an eschatological experience. It could be compared with the role of Chitragupta, the accountant of Yama, the God of Death, in Indian mythology. Chitragupta [from the Sanskrit *chitr* to depict, color with various colors + *gupta* hidden] is the secret recorder who paints the picture of the person's life on the astral light and allows the departing soul to see his entire life episodes in a flashback. He is a deva-scribe in the abode of the dead, who records human virtues and vices and reads out the account of every soul's life from his register when the excarnate soul arrives in the kingdom of Yama, the god of death. The giant white screen of the theatre which Suri uses as a symbol of all-pervading light is a metaphor used by advaitins to initiate the course of self-enquiry. Advaitins use the example of the screen and the myriad images it throws up to demonstrate the relationship of the unity consciousness which expresses itself in all created objects. In his book, *From Science to God*, Peter Russell writes:

> The faculty of consciousness can be likened to the light from a film projector. The projector shines light onto a screen, modifying the light so as to produce any one of an infinity of images...The light itself, without which no images would be possible, corresponds to the faculty of consciousness. We know all the images on the screen are composed of the light, but we are not usually aware of the light itself...We are seldom aware of consciousness itself" (32).

Realisation involves disengaging identification with the illusory objects and realizing the source. Manil Suri's Vishnu reaches the threshold of this awareness. At the end of the movie show, when Vishnu looks at himself, "he can no longer tell where the light ends and his body begins" (311).

Vishnu dies without saving any of the inhabitants. The Jalals are still in hospital, Kavitha comes back to her home after she realizes the practical implications of her elopement with Jalal. A police inspector arrives to get a first-hand report from the inhabitants about Vishnu's death and the mundane everyday scenario is repeated with the familiar quarrels about how much each family spent on the ailing Vishnu.

The concluding chapter deconstructs the ascension patterns of the soul's journey which the novel had built up so far. The excarnate soul of Vishnu is enveloped in darkness and suddenly the darkness is pierced by the sweet sounds of a flute, notes so moving that they guide him like a strand through the darkness. The darkness fades to reveal the blue-skinned Krishna who invites Vishnu to join his pranks of stealing and eating butter. The divine child frolics through the forest and Vishnu follows him until he drops asleep tired. The exquisite melody of the child's flute wakes him and he asks the child whether he is Krishna. The wise child points out that Vishnu knows it already. Vishnu is given the permission to rest for a night but the child firmly points out, "Tomorrow, you go back" (329). Manil Suri introduces the Krishna avatar towards the end of the novel. This avatar is renowned not only for its marvellous deeds but also as the Universal teacher of Wisdom. Krishna, as a human avatar of Vishnu also symbolizes love. Maybe Vishnu has to go back to the earth to perfect himself through love before he can save the society and regenerate the world. Touching on the same point, reviewer Susy Hansen writes, "Suri has created an endlessly complex world that both breaks its inhabitants' heart and occasionally holds out the prospect of redemption."

This novel suggests a divinity quest which is both a perennial and perpetual becoming as well as an immanent, in-the-moment 'suchness,' a journey which is both forward and backward on the ladder of evolution and at the same time is also a journey to nowhere gripped by the statis of an imminent death. Trapped in between the space of these paradoxes, the reader is forced to think of answers . Though there are no ready solutions offered, the novel offers love as the only antidote for the all the foibles, petty hatreds and communal tensions found in the microcosm of Vishnu's apartment. And the microcosm is the macrocosm.

REFERENCES

Duryea, Bill, Review. *The Death of Vishnu* <http://www.sptimes.com/News/022501/Perspective/Hindu_theology_in_an_.shtml>.

The Bhagavad Gita, Trans. Sri Aurobindo <http://intyoga.freeserver.com/the_gita.htm>.

Russell, Peter, *From Science to God*, Mumbai: Yogi Impressions, 2003.

Skea, Ann, Review. *The Death of Vishnu*. <http://www.eclectica.org/v5n2/skea_suri.html>

Suri, Manil, Interview. By Suchitra Betal. *The Hindu*, January 21, 2001.

——. *The Death of Vishnu*. London: Bloomsbury, 2001.

Friese, Kai, "We are so Sari: Indian Expat Novelists evoke the Homeland". <http://www.villagevoice.com/vls/172/friese.shtml>

Hansen, Suzy, Review. *The Death of Vishnu*, <http://dir.salon.com/books/review/2001/01/11/suri/index.html>

Johnston, Charles, Trans. *The Yoga Sutras of Patanjali: The Book of Spiritual Man.*
<http://www.gutenberg.org/dirs/etext01/patan10.txt>

The Upanishads, Trans. Max Muller
<http://www.sacred-texts.com/hin/upan/index.htm/>

Kuritzky, Joshua, Review. *The Death of Vishnu.*
<http://www.cnn.com/2001/SHOWBIZ/books/05/17/review.vishnu/index.html>.

16

The Novels of Shobha De: A Feminist Study

SHIVIKA VERMA

Shobha De, a super model, celebrity journalist and the best selling author, stands as "a pioneer" in the field of "popular fiction" and ranks "among the first to explore the world of the urban woman in India."[1] As a writer she is gifted with extraordinary ability to discuss very sensitive aspects of human life tactfully. The way she narrates each and every aspect of human relationships is really wonderful.

Shobha De has acclaimed her popularity of novel-writing which are rich in contents as well as she has mastered the art of story telling with a viable use of language. In fact, as a writer she differs considerably from other Indian women novelists. She believes in frank narration of incidents and situations with a touch of open-heartedness. She concentrates on problems of women and deals with psychology in her style of intimate understanding. Her novels indicate the arrival of a new Indian woman, eager to defy rebelliously against the well-entrenched moral orthodoxy of the patriarchal social system.[2] As a result, her women characters are modern, strong and they take bold decisions to survive in society, which makes her essentially a feminist novelist.

The term 'feminism' has been derived from the Latin word 'femina' which means women. It was used with regard to the issue of equality and women rights movement. Feminism means a rebellion wherein she struggles to achieve racial, social, econmic and spiritual equality with man.

The French dramatist Alexander Dumas first coined the term feminism' in 1872 which has been used and interpreted with numerous shades and colours, with different texts and contexts at present. In 1928, Virginia Woolf delivered a modest lecture—*A Room of One's Own* which had unforeseen results and interpretation even today regarding the status and role of women. *Simon de Beauvoir's The Second Sex* (1949-50) deals with the feminist ideology and concentrates on facts and myths about woman. Elaine Showalter has written *A Literature of Their Own: British Women Novelist from Bronte to Lessing* (1977) and a lecture delivered by her entitled "Towards a feminist poetics" has discussed 'feminist writing.'

Shobha De in her novels and essays has shattered patriarchal hegemony in Indian society fed on well- known injunctions of the Manusmriti.[3]

Pita rakshati kaumarya, bharta rakshati yauvane
rakshti athavire putrah, nastri svatantryam arhati.

The father protects her adolescence, and the husband in her youth, and when she becomes old, her sons protect her, a woman does not deserve freedom.

Virginia Woolf would put it, "imaginatively she is of the highest importance, practically she is completely insignificant...some of the most inspired words, some of the most profound thoughts is literature fall from the lips in real life she could hardly read could hardly spell and was the property of her husband"[4] (*A room of one's Own*).

Shobha has raised sexuality as a weapon and as a problem for the women in the traditional Indian society. She feels that most of the problems of women are sex-oriented and sex-centered in the male-dominated society. Her women characters are free from the chains of husband and society, reactionary and rebel, and 'new woman' and 'a liberated human being.'

Her novels are not a series of *bodice ripper*[5] but as David Davidar observed, they are serious attempts at "discovering India through Indian eyes."[6] She just demands the sense of justice, equality and liberty of woman in society and regarding women question, as she seriously thinks and says, *I write with a great deal of empathy towards women. Without waving the feminist flag, I feel very strongly about the woman's situation.*[7]

Shobha De believes in power and women power as a trend-setter of society. Money to the novelist is the greater leveler. As a result, Aparna in *Snapshots* is a *corporate woman, an Indian corporate woman. A businessman* (180). *Rashmi* and Swati are leading 'liberated life'. The 'new Indian women have attained economic independence and they are "a breed apart" who are characterized with "a rare seriousness." Even after approving economic freedom, her characters are not money-maniac. Asha Rani in *Starry Nights* bursts out on her overpowering mother:

> Money, money, money that's all you think of. Well, I'm fed up of your money machine. I have done enough for everybody...now I want to live for myself and enjoy my life (106).

Shobha De's another important issue is marriage as an institution, which provides to the society the needs for love, security and children. *Dharmashastras* consider marriage as a sacrament. Simon de Beauvoir also writes, "Marriage is the destiny traditionally offered by society."[8] But on account of growing sexual encounters and promiscuity of economically independent women, they are leading towards divorce, ego-crisis, restlessness and historical ethos. But the change in attitude towards marriage, according to De is, "a big step forward" towards freedom of women. In *Shooting from the Hip, De* advocates,

"If a self-sufficient woman with a roof over her chooses to marry, it is because she wants to share her life with someone in the fullest sense, not because she is looking for a lifelong meal ticket" (112).

Shobha De has created a world of characters that have a diverse marital status .In *Snapshots,* Reema and Surekha are married housewives, who have had arranged marriages as "a prize catch" in "the highly competitive marriage market" (104). Rashmi is an unwed mother with a responsibility of a bastard son. Swati and Aparna are divorcees. Swati still enjoyed with her former husband in London, they led "separate but friendly lives... we loved each other dearly but we led strictly individual lives" (189). She now lives as "a liberated woman." Aparna is not mentally prepared to marry again and to her, the term "husband" is "an awful word" (24).

Marriage is not essential in the fictional world of Shobha De. Deb in *Sultry Days* says, "who knows about marriage-sharriage... I am happy as I am" (27). When he agrees to marry Nisha, it is meant for his "daal-roti, a warm bed, twice-a-week maalish and a daily screw" (159-60).

According to Shobha De, sex is the need of all people and that "sex is no longer the most dreaded and despised three-lettered word in India" (*Uncertain Liaisions,* xxi, 208). There is nothing derogatory in sex as it is the bedrock of all relationships.[9]

Shobha De has shattered the image of respectability in marriage. Rashmi treats sex as "mutual need, mutual dependency" (49) and for Swati, sex is "a hobby and regarding her affairs, she feels that there is nothing to be ashamed of" (164). She does not find sex as dirty (164). She highlights the importance of sex as art and religion:

> Sex is not filthy...our minds make it so. Look at Khajuraho, Konark...have any of you studied the *Kama Sutra?* Fascinating. It's a pity we got brainwashed by some frustrated, repressed idiots. I think sex is a celebration—the highest form of religion (164).

As a feminist concern, Shobha De deals with the plight of woman as a favourite theme in her novels. In her novels, we can witness "neglected wives of men too busy, making money to bother with making love to the beautiful women with cold bodies they'd abandoned back at home" (57).

Shobha De has highlighted 'Indian male' as a counterpart of her female characters who have been painted with murkiest colours. In *Uncertain Liaison*, De has revealed, "Indian men make the world's lousiest lovers" as "they are high on ego, low on performance" (4, xxv).

They behave like animals as Malini in *Starry Nights* opines that "men are all animals, and we women such fools" (150). In *Snapshots*, Rashmi believes that men lead "petty, self-obsessed lives" and "they preferred flirts and flatterers. Even manipulators" (49). She feels that men are all "intrinsically, instinctively, intuitively dishonest" (46).

We can find a world of male characters in Shobha De's novels that are viewed from the eyes of her female characters. Karuna in *Socialite Evenings* finds her husband "unexciting, uninspiring, untutored" and feels that she had "married the wrong man for the wrong reasons at the wrong time." She sums up the Indian woman's marital life as "an exhausted generation of wives with no dreams left" to whom, marriage is "like a skin allergy, an irritant right" (65). Karuna plays different time to quench her emotional and psychic thirst. In *Starry Nights*, Iqbal is a "shrewd man" who knows "how to market himself" as he is "exceedingly handsome" with "the most incredible stories" of his exploits. Thus, the image of a man in her novels is generally negative, sexy, homosexual, heterosexual, weak-willed person who is also a product of her feminine treatment of her male characters.

Shobha De is truly a painter of modern men and women of Indian society. *Sisters (1992)* deals with the fabulous and intriguing corporate world of business tycoons with notes of suspense, romance imported locales and sex. It is based on the psychic conflict of a liberated woman, who is divided between a personal self and that of a social self. She is called "Pulp Queen" and "Desi Jackie Collins" by critics. But she is read both by men and women from sixteen to ninety. She has provoked the hot sex in novel but she is definitely a writer of feminist leanings. *Strange Obsession (1992)* is the explosive novel about the lustful relationship of two young women—Amrita and Meenakshi who have a lesbian relationship. *Second Thoughts (1996)* deals with a young middle class Bengali girl, born and bred in Calcutta, who makes an arranged matrimony alliance with a Bombay-based foreign returned Bengali. Maya, the young bride is more fascinated and in love with Bombay than with the prospect of having married Ranjan. It is an explosive tale of love and betrayal, which exposes the hollowness of marriage system In *Small Betrayals (1995)* and *Shooting From The Hip* (1994) Shobha De ventures to handle other genres of literature. It has presented the different snapshots of life with variety of sex. *Shooting From The Hip* presents Shobha De as a versatile writer with diverse areas like politics, media, food, festival films, books and personalities and in her writing, she is straightforward and original. In *Why I Write*, she feels, "writing is pure sex." *Selective Memory: Stories from My Life* (1998) is a story of candid writing of autobiography in which Shobha De appears as a daring daughter, a wife and a worried mother, an audacious, utterly liberated woman of post-independence generation. In her *Selective Memory*, she writes, *The woman you meet in selective memory may not be the woman you think you know* (528). The image of person in her autobiography establishes her as a skilful writer, deeply conventional, highly devoted and a shrewd judge of people.

Shobha De has been labelled as an evergreen Queen Pornography, a master of "pulp fiction," "a vamp of feministic ideals," "an experimenter of feminism" or "a mere peddler of pornographic fiction"[10] by critics. Her women characters are not only "the sex-starved unsociables"[11] as S.P. Swain observes but they are also sensitive and sensible human beings of metropolitan society with a cosmopolitan culture. As critical opinion has it, theme is in De *much that is amusing, outrageous, thought-provoking, even shocking*[12] and *rarely does one see an Indian author writing with such frankness and obvious feeling.*[13]

No wonder then that Shobha De has aroused a veritable storm and that fiery debate rages around her. Shobha De undoubtedly is a talented writer and one comes across some original insights and brilliant strokes in her works. Shobha De's characters are spokespersons of her feminine ethos which will certainly establish her as a feminist novelist in the real perspective and it will definitely rank her among the leading stars in the galaxy of feminists in Indian writing in English literature as well as in the world literature as her three novels have been selected by the reputed school of oriental and

African studies of London which identified her as a literary figure.

REFERENCES

1. C.P. Surendran, "Just Another De," *The Illustrated Weekly of India*, 6 November, 1992.
2. R.S. Pathak, "Feminist Concerns," in the *Fiction of Shobha De* ed. Jaydipsinh Dodiya, Prestige Books, New Delhi, 2000, pp. 35-36.
3. Jaydipsinh Dodiya, "The Fiction of Shobha De."
4. Virginia Woolf, "A Room of One's Own."
5. Sunil Sethi, "De in and De out," *Seminar*, 384, August, 1991, p. 40.
6. Sarita Vellani, Interview with David Davidar, *Seminar*, 384, August, 1991, p. 43.
7. *The Hindustan Times Magazine*, 12 February, 1995, p. 3.
8. Simon de Beauvoir, *The Second Sex*, trans. H.M. Parshley (Penguin, 1983), p. 445.
9. Shobha De, *The Illustrated Weekly of India*, Nov. 1992.
10. Sudhir Kumar, "Artist as a vamp: A Feminist Approach to Shobha De's Starry Nights," ed. Jaydipsinh Dodiya, *op cit.*, p. 140.
11. S.P. Swain, "Socialite Evenings: A Feminist Study," ed. Jaydipsinh Dodiya, p. 140.
12. *The Hindustan Times*, qtd. Small Betrayals (New Delhi: OBSPD, 1995).
13. *Business Standard.*

17

From Clarity to Chaos: A Complex Pattern of Journey in Manju Kapur's *Difficult Daughters*

PUSHP LATA

The seeds of Modem feminist fiction lie in fact in the struggle that has been commenced half a century ago in its full swing, against patriarchy and sexism, particularly by female writers. ***Sexual Politics,*** a phenomenal study, critically explores the task of feminist critics and also explores the ways of male dominance over females. It is envisaged that male dominated ways of looking at things have been deconstructed and questioned by these feminist writers. In the galaxy of Indian feminist fiction writers, Manju Kapur has secured a niche for herself by adding her much acclaimed debut novel *Difficult Daughters*. The paper attempts to study how Virmati, the female protagonist, is a character designed to evoke complex feelings in the reader. In Virmati the novelist has remarkably blended the complex and convoluted emotions of guilt and ambition, drive and regression, clarity and confusion. It certainly mirrors the predominant characteristics of modern Indian woman. The paper attempts to explore how *Difficult Daughters* is in fact the story of social struggle in which the educated Indian woman has launched herself in order to emancipate herself from the confinement of patriarchal Indian social structure that circumscribes her being. The paper also examines how Virmati's journey of realization and freedom scrambles into incoherence and aggravates her misery of life and closes all the doors of happiness. In the intricate odyssey of her life the novel depicts the shattering of all her romantic illusions of equality which ultimately force her to lead the role of a second wife in a man-made society.

Manju Kapur's *Difficult Daughters* can be considered a chronicler since it serves as a mirror to reflect times, places and people of India at the time of freedom struggle and immediately after independence. Thus, she tries to capture the historical enigma and bafflement that exists in this eon. The debut novel unfolds the story, where the narrator laboriously attempts to reveal the 'truth' that Indian women are breaking the shackles of male hegemony and are striving hard to realize their own self. In a social milieu, which continuously demands some kind of balance and social discipline to survive, Virmati, the protagonist, like emotionally starved being, lives in a world where the rightness of her approach is questionable. She attempts to enunciate the societal norms and follows her instincts and agrees to become a second wife. While comparing the two works '*Where Shall We Go This Summer*' and *Cry, the Peacock,* Sanjay Kumar has aptly written that "Sita, the protagonist of *Where Shall We Go This Summer* manages the disaster by running into it while Maya, the protagonist of *Cry, the Peacock* on the other hand, reels under it and fails to do anything until it envelops her." Though Virmati and Maya are two different kinds, yet from this particular angle they seem to cherish some resemblance in their character. The crisis comes in her life at an early age as she is headed towards an illicit love for Prof. Harish, a married man who tries to seduce her at the outset, yet later it becomes an obsession for her. In fact, at the start of the story she is a harmless, innocent and docile girl who simply cannot understand the subtle 'designs underlying the professor's looks and enticing talks. It is only this time when the tragic dimension creeps into her un-disturbing life. After her association with professor, she happens to live in a situation, which does not allow her any ordinary options, which generally are acceptable to society. Thus Virmati's life becomes a series of perpetual struggle against all odds and she happens to become a second wife of the professor. Thus, Virmati tries to adopt the unconventional ways, as she crosses the patriarchal threshold. Manju Kapur as a novelist does not try to establish the rightness of her doing, but rather projects the inner sufferings and confusions that keep engulfing her mind ceaselessly after she becomes the co-wife.

Looking back at the events of her unmarried life we find she comes from an affectionate and well-protected family. When she has to go to Lahore for further studies, the question arises who will go along with her. Suraj Prakash cannot leave his shop, Kailash Nath is too young to accompany her and Somnath seems to be irresponsible. Shakuntala Pehanji has offered, but how can Kasturi expect a young unmarried niece, already corrupted by Lahore to recognize any lurking invitation to sin. Therefore Kasturi, Virmati's mother herself decides to go with Virmati. She makes her one last attempt to make Virmati understand the ways of the world and the so-called right path. She says:

> If you cannot consider your duty to us, at least consider yourself. There is a time in the cycle of life for every thing. If you willfully ignore it like this, what will happen to you?

She further adds:

> A woman without her own home and family is a woman without moorings (111).

Kasturi is a little apprehensive about her daughter's intentions after she refuses her engagement with Inderjeet, a decent boy. Harish is in fact, responsible for this kind of bi-directional pull in her life, as she is caught subtly in hopeless illicit love. At the beginning of her love, Virmati-feels that *Professor Sahib was not formidable* (40) but later she finds *her life in difficulty oscillating between education and marriage* (38). After she becomes the second wife of the titular hero of the novel, Harish, she turns into a block of wood even before the first year of her marriage lapses. Though the social opprobrium is not expressed openly, yet she becomes isolated, silent and withdrawn. However, her mind and her heart are constantly agitated, rippled and tumultuous with thoughts of her freedom and position in the society and family. All the time she feels left out and unwanted. This is because from washing his clothes to polishing his shoes, to tidying his desk , dusting his precious books, filling his fountain pens with ink, putting his records back in the jackets, mending his clothes, hemming his dhotis, seeing that they are properly starched, Ganga, the first wife does it all. Observing all this, the questions regarding her own peripheral existence_crisscross her mind, as the novelist writes her mind in the following words:

> And what about her? What kind of wife was she going to be if everything was to be done by Ganga? (216).

For Virmati the days keep passing , empty like the day before. She tries to become friendly with Guddiya, her sister-in- law but she pretends to be busy with her homework and other household works. Manju Kapur appositely projects her position in the family:

> Though not overtly hostile, in the warring factions that existed in the house, she belonged to the opposition side (219).

On her arrival in Amritsar, she writes and tells her own family that she is married but nobody comes to see her. Not even the young ones to whom she has practically been a mother. She realizes that she has transgressed. However, one day she decides to make amends and pay visit home with this feeling in her heart. The novelist describes her movement:

> Full of desperate hope, Road. Virmati shuffled down Lapel Griffin road (220).

All blood relations seem cold and barren. Nobody wants her, nobody likes her. They are certainly contorted with rage and implacably hostile. When she reaches home she does not dare to enter into the house from the front door. However, she goes from the backyard, where the cows are kept. It is very symbolic, the very core member of the family loses the right to enter into the house unhesitatingly. Moreover when her mother happens to see her standing there, she hurls all possible harsh words and asks her to get out of the house:

> You've destroyed our family you badmash! ... You have blackened our face everywhere! For this I gave you birth? Because of you there is shame on me, shame on Bade

Pitaji! But what do you care, brazen that you are! (221).

Virmati's false hopes are finally shattered. She realizes that all ties between herself and her family are broken. Despite all care and concern, all sacrifice and responsibility that she carried out being the daughter of the family, they have flung her away. The relations are strained and broken to the extent that she is not even invited to her brother's marriage, though even most remote relatives are passed to come. She feels wretched and lacerated. She remains aloof and unattended. That is the reason when Harish takes pride in discussing the political scenario at national and international level, she is worried about her own freedom. Conversation that takes place on 8 May, Harish tells Virmati:

> Now it's our turn next. Now they will have no excuse. Cripps had given a commitment. At the San Francisco Peace Conference the eyes of the world will be on Britain. There will be pressure put on her recognize our sovereignty ... No, Britain is now finished, Viru, finished (254-255).

She does not respond to the above statement coming from Harish's lips, but she thinks herself—

> And me, thought Virmati, what about me? The war, or the end of it.... Suddenly he is transformed. He becomes visionary.... I feel so utterly left out, so utterly cold. Will there be any change in my life, I wonder? (255).

She rather starts delving deep into her self. She wants her needs to be acknowledged. This is the reason when she refuses to go back home and she tells herself bluntly:

> I will relate to you with dignity or not at all. None of this hiding and whispering and keeping my voice down and struggle over who is going to wash your underwear and who is going to clean your shoes. None of this for me (155-156).

The marital home and bed that she seems to have craved for years, she is ready to renounce and look for an opening.

Virmati gets enrolled for masters degree in Philosophy. She hates this subject very much, Harish calls Philosophy a noble subject, on the contrary she finds this to be dull, abstract and meaningless subject but considers it as her only means of escape. As readers we are startled at her state of mind that ,gets reflected in her monologue on 12 Nov. 1944, the INA Day:

> The child shows such courage, while I fret about my petty domestic matters, at a time when the nation is on trial. I too must take a stand. I have tried adjustment and compromise, now I will try non- cooperation (159).

Corollary to this thinking of hers, the battle of her independence that she started in her youth she takes it up again with full vigour. This voyage of her own liberation has created irrevocable lines of partition, pain and suffering around her, as the freedom movement of the country results in India-Pakistan partition, affliction, anguish and agony of millions of homeless, lifeless, tortured souls of the country. Virmati feels stronger with the certainty of the nascent life with in and when it is considered safe, she wants to help in the camps. On the contrary, Harish does not allow her to do so. According to him she must think of the baby as she already had an abortion and one miscarriage. However, she has already given away all the clothings left unused in the house for the unclad and the begging inhabitants of the city.

In another incident we, as readers, can easily envisage her struggle clearly, when Virmati gives birth to a girl, she suggests 'Bharti' as a name, since she feels that God had blessed her with the child at the dawn of freedom of the country. But this is outrightly rejected by Harish and he names the child as 'Ida' which sounds as a Persian name to Virmati. Over this, Harish irritatingly remarks:

> Let anybody think what they like for us it means a new slate, and a blank beginning (277).

With the advent of freedom for the country, it can be easily realized that the man who talks about freedom, does not provide freedom to his wife even for such a trivial matter like keeping the name of the newly born child at her choice.

The sum up, Manju Kapur has been keenly perceptive, sensitive, imaginative and intelligent while portraying the tribulation of Virmati, the protagonist who suffers endlessly when she gets trapped in the illicit love and becomes a second wife. The novelist has successfully projected the painful isolation and separation from her roots which she experiences during the complex journey of her life. It appears that Virmati's drive for emancipation derails miserably for she ends up being nothing. Glancing back it seems that the clarity in her mind, witnessed by the reader in the initial phase of her life—which of course is to achieve equality and dignity in a patriarichal Indian society—deserts her and she meets her end looking all the more clouded and confused. Probably Manju Kapur belongs to the group of women who wish to create a world free of dominance and hierarchy, a world that rests on the principles and equality and is truly human.

REFERENCES

1. Manju Kapur, *Difficult Daughters* (New Delhi: Penguin), 1998, p. 14. All subsequent textual references are to this edition only. The page numbers are given in parenthesis immediately after the quotations.
2. Sanjay Kumar, The Reverse Patterns of Journey in *Cry, the Peacock* and *Where Shall We Go This Summer? The Fiction of Anita Desai* ed. Suman Bala and D.K. Pabby (New Delhi: Khosla Publishing House) p. 122.

18

Walking on Her Own Road: Modern Indian English Woman Poet

RASHMI BAJAJ AND APARNA BATRA

Eunice De Souza, a noted critic and herself an Indian English poet avers, *What I am as a poet is a result of what I am in all the aspects of my life*[1]. In male writers the crises do not have any gender-dimension with gender-specific angst and agony whereas in women littérateurs gender generated crises are an overwhelming reality. Arriving in the world as an undesirable creature, uprooted in the middle of life and transplanted in a new soil, struggling against odds, which may befall her for being a woman, a woman feels like an eternal diasporic and expatriate.

The gender-generated crises of womanhood and quest for identity are dominant preoccupations in women's writings. Cutting across the boundaries of class, caste, religion and nation, women writers strongly articulate these crises of being. Sylvia Plath moans, *I am nobody,*[2] Elinor Wylie regrets *being alone and hard beset,*[3] Margaret Atwood *clamours for pure space,*[4] Christine Gomez *feels nothing, no body, non-worthy*[5] *and* Rukmini Nair *is all pain to be a lower case letter, lost.*[6]

Much of the gender-specific crises of women seem to be not God-made but man-made and in a traditional country like India, society continues to be formidable force to contend with. Unlike in Nissim Ezekiel *where Home is the place to gather grace*, in women writers 'Home' often becomes the microcosm of the callous macro world where many social evils and ills find a respectable shelter and patronage. The outcome is the inextricable mingling of the personal and the social in writing of these Indian women poets. In the case of these women who fall in the category, Gayatri Spivak terms as *third world women*,[7] the personal writing invariably becomes a kind of social commentary also. In an endeavour to set their land in order, these writers re-evaluate the entire gamut of experience, examine the imposed identity and reassess the 'given' in relationship and roles.

As perceived by these poets Indian society is sexist, discriminating and in fact, inhuman in its attitude towards women. For all her touted humanistic values, spiritual heritage and high-flung philosophy, India continues to be a dreadful land where in Vijaya Goel's words:

No invaders needed
For killing Laxmibais
We are strong enough to do so
Now we need only excuses
To poison Meera
Each time she is born.[8]

These poets have suffered the unmitigated pain of arriving in this world as unwelcome beings. This traumatic feeling of being unwanted haunts the writers all through their lives. Lakshmi Kannan movingly expresses a girl child's first tryst with this agonizing reality as her cries mingle with:

The moans of the women around
Lamenting the birth
Of a baby girl
Uninvited guest.[9]

In young Eunice De Souza such a disgusting parental attitude led to rebellion and embitterment. Having known that her parents wanted a boy, she made *words the weapon to crucify*.[10]

A servere identity crisis is experienced as the growing-up girls are coaxed and conditioned into stereotyped roles. Growth of a real self and complete personality are invariably thwarted by a plethora of do's and don'ts. Kamala Das feels the tyranny, *Tragedy is not death, but growth*. As she grew up, the categorizers cried:

Dress in saree, be girl
Be wife, be embroidere, be cook
Be a quarreller with servants, fit in, oh
Belong.[11]

This crisis has been experienced and expressed by poet after poet. Lakshmi Kannan in *An Omen* angrily recalls her childhood full of instructions: *No, Don't run/don't take long strides/ don't raise voice/be a woman, be moderate in everything.*[12] Even a poet like Monika Varma, who avowedly is not a feminist, articulates the pressures of being a woman. When as a child she indulged in activities like tree climbing, she was told to get down at once, as "it is most unsuitable for young ladies."[13] In fact, all natural or spontaneous expression of feelings is denied to a woman. Imatiaz Dharker finds 'purdah' to be an eternal condition and damnation of a woman's life:

Mouth must be watched, especially
If you are a woman. A smile
Should be stifled with Sari-end
None must see your serenity cracked
Even with delight.[14]

A girl is made conscious of her peripherality and centrality of male right *ab initio*. The entire rearing and gearing up of a girl is male-oriented as her salvation, unlike men's, lies in marriage. Fathers, mothers, grandmothers, grandfathers all prepare her for this ultimate cherished destiny. When Sujatha Modayil was seventeen, her grandmother raised a hue and cry: *Get her married/before the light/goes out of her face.*[15]

In our marriage-obsessed society, relationship with a male in marriage has been considered to be an all important step in a woman's self-realization. This traditional prop however seems to rather aggravate the identity crisis. Kamala Das went to her man to learn, "What I was and by learning to grow" but instead she became a dwarf:

Lost my will and reason, to all your
Questions I mumbled incoherent replies[16]

Sunita Jain in her poem 'A Song for Us' Seeks a relationship where she *will be to myself/in me fulfilled*[17] but what happens is just the opposite. Lalitha Venkateswaran, at seventeen, had many ambitious plans and worth fulfilling dreams:

All learning would be stormed by me
I would sing, make speeches, read the news
Write, act, run office & marathons.[18]

But then entered man. The poet mourns:

You did not belong in my plans
My house broke up to keep you whole
The construction costs were terrible[19]

In the Poem 'Sea Changes' Margaret Chatterjee feels constrained to protest: *Have I no existence of my own*?[20] Taking stock of her life after her man's parting, Mamta Kalia feels bereft as she realizes:

In reality
All our friends were your friends
All our ideas your ideas
All our projects your projects
I followed you like a corollary[21]

In a society that sets such a high premium on marriage, double life is the fate of many a married woman. As her husband arrives, the lady feeling all 'disjointed inside' pretends to be happy and wears a smile 'eternally saying cheese'. A married daughter chooses not to unburden her heart even before her parents for the fear of hurting their sentiments. One who wanted to talk of 'suicidal despair' ultimately

Swallowed everything
and smiled a smile of great content[22]

The role expectations from a wife are largely stereotyped and any deviation can be unpardonable. In Sujata Bhatt's 'She Finds Her Place' the husband

Wanted a wife
Not a poet
So he burnt Anna's poems
In a Samovar[23]

The traditional image of woman is that of an 'Angel in the

house' whose world is of 'Kinder, Kuche, Kirche'. The women find the endless drudgery of household chores oppressive. This 'dreadful litany' of 'Jhadoo, pocha bartan, Kapade' makes Sujatha Modayil feel *Koel's song is Dead.*[24] The unshared thankless burden of what Spivak calls 'Zero work', gradually reduces even a techanically qualified, accomplished and talented woman to a non-entity:

> I no longer feel
> I am Mamta Kalia
> I am Kamala
> Or Vimala
> Or Kanta or Shanta
> I cook, I wash
> I bear, I wash
> I bear, I rear
> I sulk, I sag.[25]

All these conditions are the 'normal' life conditions of a woman. The whole truth is more frightening. A woman is a victim of many atrocities. Domestic violence and wife-bashing are the ugly realities of our families. Sujata Bhatt's poem 'A Story for Pearse' narrates the sad saga of her aunt Hiraben who was beaten with bamboo-pole and whipped all over. The only consolation was: *at least they did not set her ablaze.*[26] Imtiaz Dharker's woman was not so lucky; she was burnt alive and on the top of it she did not find this burning unusual:

> It was the only choice
> She had ever known
> Another torch blowing in the dark
> Another woman.[27]

Dowry deaths and 'satis' are the shameful truths of 21st century India. In her poem 'Flame,' Rukmini Nair ironically calls Prometheus an Indian for his pyromania (love of fire) as only in India fire is put to such a varied use. From our beloved Ram in antiquity we have used it to 'test involvement, chastity:' "we burn brides , and we burn widows."[28]

A woman in herself is not much of a prized person. She is an agent or an instrument of procreation. High rate of mortality during childbirth is an accepted thing. For the modern women poets, Taj is a living monument of the tragedy of young empress:

> Light of the world
> Who died bearing a fourteenth child.[29]

Condition of a widow is pathetic due to the inhuman treatment she receives at home and outside. Her only identity is widowhood. Forced to live a listless life of an accursed being, she is:

> Forbidden to see the sun for a year
> Allowed to crap only at night
> When the pure were out of the way.[30]

The poet's widowed mother travels in third class, with her in-laws traveling first class in the same train. Enormous is the crisis of womanhood that finds expression in the writing of these modern Indian English Poets. To Imtiaz Dharker, a woman looks like a "creek where happiness forgot to shine." Unlike the romantic 'laden eyed despair' of Keats here:

> Stone lay upon her eyes
> And each day tears fell
> Upon her face, a river bed
> With fine lines carved by misery.[31]

In the writings of these women poets, the female persona seems to be very vulnerable and the victim of a too powerful patriarchal system. However, these poets epitomize not only the crises of womanhood but also the emergence of a New Indian Woman. Their poetry evinces a strong protest, questioning, questing, and a growing assertion and celebration of their identity as a woman. In Rukmini Nair's words:

> Soft that is the word
> You'd choose her
> And later knowing
> Better-Survivor.[32]

Even Kamala Das, who thinks she could find her 'peace' only in her lover's arms, feels tormented by doubts:

Woman, is this happiness
This lying buried beneath a man.[33]

Sujatha Modayil's spirit craves for freedom:

Oh, when
Will she be free
To be herself.[34]

and to achieve this freedom she wonders:

What should a woman do?[35]

In these poets, female personae evolve their strategies to survive and prevail. In Shanta Acharya's poem *A Giddy Mannequin the persona acquires from her man an attitude of discerning unconcern and she perfects it to an art of survival.*[36]

Poets like K.K. Dyson make a direct passionate appeal to readers to lend their support and sympathy to the cause of women:

I implore you
All who read my lines
If you have mothers
Sister, wives or daughters,
Remember those
Who have been forced to pay
In the high-inflated currency of pain
For being born women.[37]

Realization of being powerful and being rendered powerless grows and the poets jolt fellow-women out of their complacency:

You are the power of this earth
The creator of man
Yet you live at his feet
Begging to survive![38]

Another bold strategy with these women poets is conversion of 'Aesthetics of Marginality' into 'Asesthetics of Body.' They realize that the first step is validation of material itself—the lives and experiences of women. Challenging the male dictum: what wisdom lies in menses, deliveries & milk-filled breasts?' These women go on to celebrate their intimate female experiences of ovulation, child-birth and sexual 'jouissance'. Sujata Bhatt's 'Udalyee,' 'Little Asparagus,' Sunita Jain's 'The Moon Months' are a few of such examples. Body that has been an instrument of subjugation since antiquity, is now sought to be made into an instrument of power. This process of empowerment has been powerfully captured by Lakshmi Kannan in her poem 'Draupadi:'

> The pain was more tangible years ago
> When she was a mere palpitating
> Beaten and kicked about
> Not beaten anymore
> Draupadi stands bare of bruises
> *** *** ***
> She has done it
> Has offended the supreme male
> Into a sudden silence
> By her terrible nakedness.[39]

This new woman is a woman who is not an eremophobic or loneliness-phobic creature. Increasing self-assurance and confidence bolden her to reassess the almost unquestionable issue of relationship with male. Uma Parmeswaran in her poem 'I Wish I Knew What to Tell you, My Daughter' examines the pros and cons of man-woman relationship. She is well aware of the hazards—lonely remembrance, promiscuous abandon, lonely aloneness, yet she knows that a woman can go her way *from strength to strength even without a male.*[40] In other poets like De Souza, Malavika Sanghvi, Rukmini Nair, Sujata Bhatt, Achla Bhatia we do not have a central male referent and the poets reveal new concerns and a wide canvas.

Relationship with a male is now a choice and not a compulsion or a panicky antidote to insecurity. Sujatha Modayil realizes:

> She who seeks light
> Must learn to walk in
> Darkness on her own road[41]

Sujata Bhatt's 'tall woman walks alone' and finds her place' 'among a crowd of trees.' It is no more an insecure clutching and kowtowing to the male but a relationship on equal footing where they demand equal respect and dignity:

It must meet you
It must be half the way.[42]

Suniti Namjoshi sets the terms clear:

Do no make me beg
Nor ask for more than you would give.[43]

However, the poet in whom this pride in identity as a woman is fully realized and womanhood celebrated is Rukmini Bhaya Nair. In her book *The Hyoid Bone* she makes not the 'rib-caged bird' *i.e.,* heart but a detached bone, the metaphor of a woman's existence. The agenda of this new woman is:

Not a fresh lover, strong man
Or clown, but a new language
In which to hold her own.[44]

With her motto "Tears are not our style, erudition says it better," she sets out on her subversive journey. The myth of a male writer's superiority stands shattered as she throws a challenge to Shankara, the eighth century Hindu philosopher and reformer:

We have wrung poems from our household tasks
Carrying water child sorrow can you do as much.[45]

Undaunted the poet goes on to subvert the myth of a male God and the male as the super creation:

Every man has memories of being a woman
And women know they have been gods,
At one time or another........................
Ardhanarishwara.[46]

A perusal of these women poets' writing offers a revealing insight into the ongoing transition in female psyche. Their assertive and defiant writing jolts readers out of their complacency, reorients sensitivity and sensibility, and seeks to create a more democratic, equal and gender-friendly world where a woman could 'hold her own.'

REFERENCES

1. In an interview with Arlene R.K. Zide, Eunice De Souza stresses the point that women's experiences and socialization as a whole being different, their writing is bound to be different. See Introduction. *In Their Own Voice* ed. Zide (Delhi: Penguin Books, 1993) p. xix.
2. Sylvia Plath, "Tulip," *Collected Poems*, ed. Ted Hughes (London: Faber & Faber, 1981) p. 148.
3. Elinor Wylie, "Alone and Hard Beset," *Psyche: The Feminine Poetic Consciousness*, ed. Barbara Signitz and Carol Rainey (New York: The Dial Press, 1973), p. 57.
4. Margaret Atwood, "Song of the Hen's Head," *Canadian Literature in the 70's,* ed. Paul Denham and Mary Jane Edwards (Toronto: Holt, Rinehart and Winston 1980), p. 102
5. Christine Gomez, quoted by R.K. Singh, *Indian English Poets*, ed. R.K. Singh (New Delhi: Bahri Publication, 1992) p. 5.
6. Rukmini Nair, 'Five Uneasy Pieces', *The Hyoid Bone* (Delhi: Viking Books, 1992), p. 73.
7. Gaytri Spivak in her article "Poststructuralism, Marginality, Post-Coloniality and Value" talks at length about 'third-world women' and the gender-generated identity crises. See *Literary Theory Today*, eds. Peter Collier, Helga Geyer-Ryan (New York: Cornell University Press, 1990), p. 219.
8. Vijaya Goel, "Martyr," *The Autumn Flowers* (Calcutta: Writers Workshop, 1990), p. 8.
9. Lakshmi Kannan, "Woman with a Past," *Exiled Gods* (Calcutta: Writers Workshop, 1985), p. 22.
10. Eunice De Souza, "De Souza Prabhu" *Twelve Modern Indian Poets* ed. A.K. Mehrotra (New Delhi: Oxford University Press, 1922), p. 119.
11. Kamala Das, "An Introduction," *The Old Playhouse and other Poems* (Madras: Orient Longman, 1973), p. 27.
12. Lakshmi Kannan, "An Omen," *The Glow and the Grey* (Calcutta: Writers Workshop, 1976), p. 27.
13. Monika Verma, "disremember Me Doves," *Green Leaves and Gold,* (Calcutta: Writers Workshop, 1970), p. 31.
14. Imtiaz Dharker, "A Woman's Place," *Purdah and Other Poems* (Delhi: Oxford University Press, 1989), p. 32.

15. Sujatha Modayil "Light," *The Attic of Night* (Delhi: Rupa and Co., 1971), p. 27.
16. Kamala Das, "The Old Playhouse," *Tonight This Savage Rite* (New Delhi: Arnold Heinemann, 1990), p. 14.
17. Sunita Jain, "A Song for Us," *Silences* (New Delhi: National Publishing Hous, 1982), p. 31.
18. Lalitha Venkateswaran, "Building," *Declarations* (Calcutta: Writers Workshop, 1970), p. 18.
19. *Ibid.*
20. Margaret Chatterjee, "Sea Changes," *Towards the Sun* (Calcutta: Writers Workshop, 1970), p. 10.
21. Mamta Kakia, "Sunday Song," *Tribute to Papa and Other Poems* (Calcutta: Writers Workshop, 1978), p. 25.
22. Mamta Kalia, "Eight Years After Marriage," *Poems 78* (Calcutta: Writers Workshop, 1978) p. 28.
23. Sujata Bhatt, "She Finds Her Place," *Brunizem* (Delhi: Penguin Books, 1993), p. 38.
24. Sujata Modayil, "Between Two Worlds," *The Attic of Night*, p. 57.
25. Mamta Kalia, "Anonymous," *Hers: English Verse by Indian Women*, (ed.) Mary ann Dasgupta (Calcutta: Wirters Workshop, 1969), p. 66.
26. Sujata Bhatt, "A Story for Pearse," *Monkey Shadows* (Delhi: Penguin Books, 1993), p. 66.
27. Imtiaz Dharker, "Another Woman," *Purdah and Other Poems*, p. 88.
28. Rukmini Nair, "Flame," *The Hyoid Bone*, (Delhi: Viking Books, 1992), p. 84.
29. Sujatha Modayil, "Written in Hospital," *Crucifixions,* (Calcutta: Writers Workshop, 1970), p. 71.
30. Eunice De Souza, "Transcend Yourself You say," *Women in Dutch Painting,* (Bombay: Praxis 1988), p. 32.
31. Sujatha Modayil, "Stones," *The Attic of Night*, p. 23.
32. Rukmini Nair, "Female Line," *The Hyoid Bone*, p. 79.
33. Kamala Das "The Conflagration," *The Descendants*, (Calcutta: Writers Workshop, 1967) p. 20.
34. Sujatha Modayil, "Voice & Tradition," *We the Unreconciled*, (Calcutta: Writers Workshop, 1967), p. 43.

35. Sujatha Modayil, "All Alone," *We the Unreconciled*, (Calcutta: Writers Workshop, 1967), p. 48.
36. Shanta Acharya, "A Giddy Mannequin," *In Their Own Voice*, p. 1.
37. K.K. Dyson, "After Reading Nawal El Saadwi's Book" *In Their Own Voice*, p. 72.
38. Vijaya Goel, "She," *The Autumn Flowers*, p. 15.
39. Lakshmi Kannan, "Draupadi", *In Their Own Voice*, p. 97.
40. Uma Parmeswaran, "I Wish I Knew What to Tell You My Daughter," In *Their Own Voice*, p. 173.
41. Sujatha Modayil, "Light," *The Attic of Night*, p. 29.
42. Melanie Silgardo, "A Memory," quoted by Bruce King, *Modern Indian Poetry in English* (Delhi: Oxford University Press, 1987), p. 157.
43. Suniti Namjoshi, "Grace," *More Poems* (Calcutta: Writers Workshop, 1971), p. 26.
44. Rukmini Nair, "Five Uneasy Pieces," *The Hyoid Bone*, p. 74.
45. Rukmini Nair, "Gender Role," *The Hyoid Bone*, p. 54.
46. Rukmini Nair, "The Hermaphrodite Longings," *The Ayodhya Cantos*, (Delhi: Penguin Books, 1999), p. 134.

19

Reading Literature from the Margins

P.S. RAMANA

Literary works like Bapsi Sidhwa's *Ice-Candy-Man*, Arundhati Roy's *The God of Small Things,* Naipaul's *A Bend In the River* and Taslima Nasrin's *Lajja* (Shame) raise some important questions about the validity and usefulness of theoretical categories of national 'English' literature as well as some other popular and broader descriptive labels like Commonwealth Literature', Third World Literature' 'Post-colonial Literature and New Literatures in English used for referring to literatures in colonial languages originating from former colonies. The site of origin of a literary work determines much of its thematic, aesthetic and ideological emphasis and implications; there is no doubt that these labels relating literary works to their geographical locations and historical backgrounds serve, mostly for the benefits of the 'centre' as very convenient ways of describing and classifying literature originating from the countries representing the margins or the periphery. With the global literature publishing, distributing, establishing and canonizing industry, shifting its focus somewhat from the European/white center to the margins consisting of former colonies, an increasing number of authors and literary works, originally published or translated into colonial/neocolonial languages like English and French are gaining audience, recognition and appreciation in many parts of the world. Naturally, these terms are proving more than handy in introducing and describing such works as well as for pointing out their difference from the mainstream literatures in English or French. Much of contemporary western literary theory and criticism focuses on cross-cultural readings and foregrounds language over all other aspects of literature. Ashcroft *et al* often credited to be founders of post-colonial studies with *The Empire Writes Back* club literatures of former Asian and African colonies together under the term post-colonial and declare that all such literatures "emerged in their present form out of the experience of colonization and asserted themselves by foregrounding the tension with the imperial power, and by emphasizing their differences from the assumptions of the imperial center" (Ashcroft, 2). The problem is that for most readers of Arundhati Roy, Bapsi Sidhwa or Taslima Nasrin, located in the Indian subcontinent, neither such cross-cultural perspective involving imperial center is required nor past colonial experience nor English language is the central issue.

The categories stemming from the implicit assumption of the 'authenticity and 'centrality' of the dominant canon, approach, organize and grade literary works from the hegemonic perspective as they point out the 'otherness' of literary works in terms of the established and governing, predominantly White Eurepean traditions and preoccupations. It is a fact that in contemporary scenario, most literary works in 'English,' representing the margins, are brought into public notice by the hegemonic publishing and establishing industry with its own economic and political agenda. Nevertheless, irrespective of their absorption into the dominant canon or not, these works have an appeal and significance in concrete socio-cultural environment they portray. And the prevalent labels fail to give much significant or relevant information about the works themselves, about their aesthetic/thematic orientation or ideological/political significance in the socio-cultural contexts they depict. To make such literature relevant for the culture and societies it represents, it needs to be reappropriated by those cultures and interest groups and individuals, studied and evaluated using their own parameters; in short, rather than, talking back to the empire' it has to be made to talk to its own people whom it depicts and who as target audience can lead to the best aesthetic, cultural and ideological communication.

Classifying literary works in terms of the national identities of the authors involves two basic theoretical problems. It implies, on the one hand, an abstract homogenization of the country a work comes from, which is highly reductive and problematic, particularly in case of a vast and diverse country like India; and the other, it suggests a binary division between that site and the rest of the world. Apparently not even a very small state can have such a homogeneous and unique identity that differs from that of everyone else. The problem is even more complicated in case of migrant, exile or diasporic writing with a Naipaul, Rushdie or Sidhwa almost permanently leaving the countries of their birth and early development as creative writers, on their own volition or forced by circumstances beyond their control, to settle in the developed world. Often they earn most of literary reputation and celebrity status by writing about the countries left behind and, consciously or unconsciously, targeting as consumers of their work the reading public of their adopted countries and continents. The categorization becomes even more artificial and vague in case of broader labels like 'postcolonial literature' or Third World literature which while apparently clubbing together diverse cultural political and ethnic identities spread over vast geographic space, forground only one feature, like appropriation of a non-native language, colonial past or economic backwardness, of that large and complex assemblage.

Literary works reflect, probe and critique different socio-cultural identities and ideologies in many and unique ways. Clubbing them together under categories foregrounding one aspect of their background not only simplifies the complex cultural and ideological practices that go into the production of a literary work, but also tends to limit the arena of their emotional appeal and political impact. "Literary texts are produced in highly differentiated, usually over determined contexts of competing ideological and cultural clusters, so that any particular text of any complexity will always have to be placed within the cluster that gives it its energy and form, before it is totalized into a universall category" (Ahmad, 121). These works are consumed too in similarly complex ideological and socio-cultural environments. Neither literature nor culture, defined "as a constitutive social process, creating specific and different ways of life" (Williams, 19) can be described in terms of the limits imposed by state borders, colonial/ post-colonial history or linguistic features alone.

With the increasing realization of the ideological role of culture and literature in establishing and maintaining (and even challenging) hegemonies, the study of culture and literature has been institutionalized, promoted and used by powers that be. It has become an academic discipline as well as business the world over. And with globalisation of publication and distribution industry, an increasing interest is being shown in the study of works originating from different geographical and cultural sites due to easy availability of such works and their ideological/political potential in different socio-cultural environments. Taslima Nasrin's *Lajja* (Shame) is a case in point. Specifically and in a documentary manner dealing with and condemning communal violence against minorities in Bangladesh, it was banned in the country of its origin while the novel was translated into many Indian Langauges and widely distributed by agencies and groups in India who are closely associated with forces responsible for communal riots in India. Consequently, a novel apparently condemning communal frenzy targeting minorities (particularly women) in one social formation was used to rouse communal hatred and to justify sactarian violence in a different community with minority group in the one becoming majority in the other and vice versa.

The literary works that are selected, distributed, studied and even canonized from 'other' cultures are not 'innocently' or 'neutrally' chosen on some 'aesthetic merit' alone. Terry Eagleton argues in a slightly context, about the theoretical underpinning of the concepts of literature and value: The so-called literary canon, the unquestioned great tradition of the national literature, has to be recognized as a construct, fashioned by particular people for particular reasons at a certain time. There is no such thing as a literary work or tradition, which is valuable in itself, regardless of what anyone might have said or come to say about it. 'Value' is a transitive term: it means whatever is valued by certain people in specific situations, according to particular criteria and in the light of given purposes....All literary works... are rewritten, if only unconsciously by the societies which read them; indeed there is no reading of a work which is not also a re-writing [italics in the original] (Eagleton, 10-11). This explicit theoretical emphasis on socio-cultural and ideological construction of literatures as well as the parameters of their analysis and evaluation is nowhere more obvious than in some of the popular contemporary literary critical theories. The Feminist and Marxist literary theories and criticism openly flaunt their gender and class-based conceptions of societies, academic and cultural institutions and scholarship. Other theories that profess neutrality or proclaim to limit their concerns to literature or culture alone, refusing to have anything to do with broader social or political domain simply attempt to camouflage their ideological implications.

Edward Said whose work inspired colonial discourse analysis observes: "The development and maintenance of every culture require the existence of another different and competing alter ego... Each age and society re-creates its 'Others.' Far from a static thing then, identity of self or of other is a much worked—over historical, social, intellectual and political process that takes place as a contest involving individuals and institutions in all societies. The construction of identity is bound up with the disposition of power and powerlessness in each society, ... Human identity is not only not natural and stable, but constructed, and occasionally even invented outright" (Said 332). All cultural identities differ from one another in one way or the other. Every perceptive consciousness is rooted in its own socio-cultural, racial, class and gender identity. Naturally, all multicultural readings and criticism have a definite element of this construction and even invention of the culture inevitably studied as the other. It is also a fact that the hegemonic socio-political dispensations dominate and control most of the sites, perspective and parameters of cultural and literary studies. Consequently, despite the different cultural identities, 'marginalized' cultures tend to be further marginalized or ignored altogether with the governing interests determining what should be read and how.

Apparently, the question of a work's ideological/political significance or its author's cultural identity is, by no means, unproblematic. It cannot be decided simply in terms of his/her 'national' background or colonial/post-colonial past, which, as in case of authors like Naipaul or Sidhwa, is often difficult to define. The appropriation of a former colonial language like English by an author belonging to the 'margins' representing the former colonies in order to talk back to colonial centre is not a factor significant enough to define all such art because much of such art, often attempts to reach out to its own people too: the reading public belonging to the cultures and geographical areas dealt with in that work, whose problems and concerns it raises and where it can have most ideological/ social relevance and aesthetic appeal because of shared cultural and social background.

Despite English language and native 'English' literatures apparently having elitist status in South Asian countries like India, Pakistan and Bangladesh, and despite native 'english' literatures in these countries being largely restricted to comparatively privileged sections of society, the cultures that they portray, the thematic and ideological orientations they have, relate them more closely to native language literatures than to the dominant colonial canon, at least for reading public belonging to cultures and regions of such work's origin. Most of such work in 'English' may be initially established and popularised by the global publishing and distributing industry, as in case Arundhati Roy, Jhumpa Lahiri, Taslima Nasrin and Bapsi Sidhwa, such is seriously studied, discussed and critically evaluated in universities and colleges located in south Asia. Naturally enough reading of The *God of Small Things or Ice-Candy-Man* in some part of the Indian sub-continent would not involve a multicultural perspective that it does when the work is studied in the Western academic institution by western intellectuals or even by diaspora scholars like a Bhabha or a Spivak.

Two things appear to be certain: study of a work of art, however complex, multifaceted or problematic, in its own culture would involve a different set of parameters and attitudes from the situation when it is studied in an 'other' environment and subjected to a multicultural analysis; secondly, the sociocultural significance and ideological impact of a work is much greater if it is studiéd in its own or similar sociocultural environment, which often cannot be homogenised into its national or post-colonial/ third world identity without losing some of its active ideological impact. This is not to suggest that appeal of literature should be or can be limited to specific geopolitical spaces but that caste and gender bias portrayed in *The God of Small Things* or barbaric face of communal divides created and exploited by politicians and the woman-as-victim paradigm evoked in *lce-Candy-Man or Lajja* would lead to much more than a merely academic activity when these works are studied by readers and scholars of whose experiences and sociocultural and historical background such incidents form a part. The all-important question is to what use literature and its study is put, by whom, where and in whose interest?

The literary significance, aesthetic appeal and political message of *A Bend In the River, lce- Candy-Man, Lajja or The God of Small Things,* irrespective of their geographic location in the 'margins' in terms of the world portrayed, depends as much on their authors' own ideological location and conscious/ unconscious intentions about the role and, purpose of their work, as on the nature, location and cultural orientation of reading and interpretive communities.

V.S. Naipaul, one of the most celebrated post-colonial writers, more than protesting against or writing back to the colonial centre appears to be professing doom for 'marginalized' cultural and political formations and implicitly speaking for the inevitability of a neo-colonial global empire by castigating formerly colonised and plundered cultures and nationalities for their corruption, lawlessness, violence, unpredictability and absence of socio-political institutions. He orientalises Africa in *A Bend ln the River* in a way no white orientalist could ever hope to do. The worst possible and hopeless social, political and economic scenario is evoked for the unnamed African country devastated by the colonial rule, from which the empire has visibly withdrawn relinquishing responsibility but retaining control through a despotic dictator and continuing military intervention. The novel written from the perspective of a completely alienated, rootless drifting 'outsider' can certainly not evoke sympathetic involvement or acceptance from the native Africans that serve as the geographical background of the novel. Salim, the narrator-protagonist, is a 'voluntary exile' who calls himself a Muslim of Indian origin. But both culturally as well as religiously he is completely alienated and does not belong anywhere or to anyone. He does not have any national identity either, except that of a migrant who feels like a total outsider in the post-colonial environment he is in: "with no family, no flag, no fetish." *A Bend In the River* focusing on the lives and problems of migrants and exiles, rather than the natives, in a world of increasing ethnic intolerance and persecution, reflects a perspective more akin to the colonizers thån to their victims. How can this novel portraying life in a very poor, economically backward and plundered African ex-colony, from the perspective of an unsympathetic and persecuted 'outsider,' written by an author who grew up in another former colony (Trinidad), who claims ancestry to a third former colony (India) but who has earned his living and made his literary reputation while residing in the colonial centre (London), be divined in terms of its national, third world or post-colonial identity? And what would such labels reveal about the political vision presented or the ideological implications of the book?

In sharp contrast to nihilistic pessimism and detached cynical attitude of Naipaul about the present and future of nascent ex-colonial nationalities and states, Bapsi Sidhwa, while vehemently condemning communal violence and anarchy in such newly independent nations, expresses a vision of hope, viability and commitment through her involvement and concern for the nation and the culture portrayed in her novels. She attempts, in *Ice-Candy-Man,* to present a 'Pakstani' version of events related to partition of Indian sub-continent and to write an alternative history to the one written "in books by British and Indian scholars"who "caricatured and portrayed" Jinnah as a *monster (Ice-Candy-Man, 160).* A feminist social worker belonging to microscopic Parsi minority community in constitutionally Muslim republic of Pakistan with an orthodox patriarchal cultural background, Sidhwa can in no way be taken as a 'typical' Pakistani. Her minority status both in terms of gender and religio-cultural background impinges visibly upon all her work. The central thematic paradigms in *Ice-Candy-Man* are feminist issues: 'woman-as-victim' and 'women-as-saviour' of women and the weak, Condemning male chauvinism and violence-mongering, callous selfishness of the politicians and barbaric nature of communal frenzy in targeting hapless minorities and women, Sidhwa artistically juxtaposes the incidents on both sides of the border to go beyond narrow national commitments. Consequently, the appeal of her novel is not constrained by her Parsi or Pakistani background.

The story of gradual communalisation of peaceful Lahore at the time of partition and, specifically, of abduction, humiliation and exploitation of a Hindu Ayah by a chameleon-like unnamed Muslim manipulator, is juxtaposed with even more brutal and heinous crimes against Muslim minorities on the Indian side of the border in villages like Pir Pindo. Unlike *Lajja*, *Ice-Candy-Man* depicts rising communal passions, dubious role of politicians, brutalities and victimisations of innocent minorities on both sides of the border, Naturally, the narrative moves beyond narrow national identities. A positive feminist vision, consciousness of the vulnerability of women and the weak, and belief in the ability of women to act and to come up as saviours of the victims of selfish manipulations and socio-cultural exploitation gives Sidhwa's novel its special moral appeal that goes well beyond the national, third world or post-colonial descriptions. Sidhwa and Nasrin's novels explicitly dealing with communal riots seen from feminist and liberal democratic perspectives evoke much more than an academic analysis when communities closely related to the 'world' presented in the fictional narrative study them. The banning of *Lajja* and persecution of its author in Bangladesh is as much indicative of socio-political significance and role the of fiction in society it portrays as it is of an intolerant regime and fundamentalist clerics ruling those societies.

Arundhati Roy's novel, *The God of Small Things* is another socially relevant work that has received great appreciation for its aesthetic qualities: innovative and creative use of language and narrative technique. Most of its reputation is based on 'language in the book' rather than 'book in the language.' Thematically, it is deeply located in the 'margins,' while in novelistic technique it bears a close affinity to the 'centre.' It processes serious socio-cultural and political issues: the injustice being perpetrated through different hegemonic cultural and economic practices and the role and significance of the sociocultural and family environment in construction of the individual subjectivities. In terms of the socio-cultural environment presented, this highly realizable narrative tells a potentially dark tale of human suffering brought about by casteism and ideologies. The novel particularly exposes the caste/class based, gendered and biased social system manifestly operational, in Indian society that gives privilege to the higher castes, upper classes over lower castes, poor classes and women. In portraying the fortunes of a particular family, Roy highlights the inferior position of women in the 'male chauvinist society.' *The God of Small Things* is thematically a complex, tension-filled, family drama with strong socio-cultural and political implications. The evocative tale of the discrimination, exploitation and humiliation of the underprivileged individuals in different circumstances and situations in the traditional South Indian society pits natural human urges and needs like right to life, equality, dignity and personal freedom, along with innate individual desires for love and affection, social and financial security against a man-made but deeply-entrenched culture that has different codes of conduct, privileges and laws for individuals belonging to different sexes, social and economic classes, castes and religions.

To tell her story, Roy uses a highly innovative and experimental narrative strategy with verbal experimentation, innumerable flashbacks and flash-forwards and recurring references to the same events and objects time and again, like the multiple refrains in a musical composition. One of the best artistic accomplishments of Roy lies in her very careful manipulation of English-language lending a very special style and idiom to the novel. The playful and meticulously planned narrative technique with its deliberate discontinuities, digressions, repetitions, philosophising, irony and humour, gives a distinctive flavour to the novel. Linguistic and technical innovativeness is often foregrounded, drawing attention to language itself and making it non-referential. Both in theme and technique, *The God of Small Things* is explicitly anti-establishment, highlighting their liberal ideals of personal freedom and challenging the brutal power of existing ideological, social and aesthetic institutions. In terms of appropriation of 'english' as a resistance or subversive strategy in a 'post-colonial' novel, *The God of Small Things,* despite a sprinkling of Malayalam words, phrases and names throughout the text, is very much an 'English' novel. Though Roy calls herself 'the worst-read person, she knows,' her novel reveals a scrupulously designed and executed narrative structure that attempts to carefully integrate contemporary artistic and narrative techniques and styles used by well- known authors like Gabriel Garcia Marquez, Salman Rushdie and Vikram Seth, with the exotic experience and flavour from the 'periphery' for the Western and westernised international readers. Rather than being an attempt at rejection of the dominant literary canon, Roy's narrative experimentation appears to operate under the control of canonized 'western' texts and styles. That is perhaps one of the reasons for the exceptional commercial success of the novel and its stupendous reception by international media.

Cultural identity of an author involves much more than the question of citizenship of a particular state or region. Still, national or cultural background of an author cannot define or limit the aesthetic appeal or ideological impact of a work. An author's relationship to a particular nation or to a third world or post-colonial state, by birth or citizenship, or one being an exile or a migrant representing a particular diaspora cannot determine the nature, appeal or aesthetic merit of a work.

It is obvious that creative writing today is a professional activity influenced among other things by economic interests as well as a desire to be popular and to be appreciated by a wide section. These pragmatic and material considerations influence almost all writing from the centre' as well as the 'margins'. Except for *Lajja,* originally published, in Bangla and naturally targeting native readership, all the other three novels discussed above were written with international English.

There is no objective aesthetic value that determines a work being incorporated into the literary canon. Complex socio-cultural and ideological practices, interests and parameters influence a work being regarded as a significant literary product to be accepted, studied and analysed by literary/ cultural establishment. Marginalized interest groups and communities are more or less excluded from the validating and canonizing institutions. They can at best use and re appropriate available works for consciousness raising activities and subject them to analysis based on alternative parameters allied to the suppressed perspectives. For feminists, choosing to work on female authors may be first important libratory step, but it has to be followed up with readings and analysis from an anti-patriarchal perspective. Similarly, only focusing on already established 'Third World,' post-colonial, or diasporic writers without exposing the socio-political and economic systems and ideologies operative in the world and reflected in literature is not going to help the cause of the marginalized.

REFERENCES

1. Ahmad Aijaz (1992) in *Thoery: Classes, Nations Literatures*, Delhi: OUP.
2. Ashcroft, Bill, Grffiths, Gareth and Tiffin, Helen (1989), *The Empire Writes Back*, London: Routledge. 2002.
3. Eagleton, Terry (1983), *Literary Theory: An Introduction*, Delhi: Maya Blackwell. 2000.
4. Naipaul, V.S. (1979), *A Bend In the River*, London: Oxford.
5. Roy, Arundhati (1997). *The God of Small Things*, New Delhi: IndiaInk.
6. Said, Edward (2001) *Afterword to Orientalism*, New Delhi: Penguin.
7. Sidhwa, Bapsi (1988), *Ice-Candy-Man*, New Delhi: Penguin.
8. Taslima Nasrin (1993), *Lajja* (Shame). Trans. Tutul Gupta. New Delhi: Penguin, 1994.
9. Williams, Reymond (1977), *Marxism and Literature*, OUP.

List of Contributors

K.C. Mishra, Senior Grade Lecturer, Deptt. of English, Government College, Bomdila-790001 (Arunachal Pradesh).

Mansing G. Kadam, Lecturer, Deptt. of English, Sadguru Gadage Maharaj College, Karad, Dist. Satara (Maharastra).

Sanjay Kumar, Reader, Deptt. of English, Chaudhary Devilal University, Sirsa (Haryana).

Nandini Sahu, Assistant Professor, Deptt. of English, ICAR, Raygada (Orissa).

Sathyaraj V, Research Scholar, Deptt. of Humanities & Social Sciences, IIT, Kanpur-208016 (Uttar Pradesh).

Joe Verghese Yeldho, Research Scholar, Deptt. of Humanities & Social Sciences, IIT, Kanpur-208016 (Uttar Pradesh).

Shubha Mishra, Lecturer, Deptt. of English, P.W.S. College of Arts and Commerce, Nagpur (Maharastra).

Kanhaiyajee Jha, Reader, Deptt. of English, Marwari College, Darbhanga-846004 (Bihar).

Umed Singh, Lecturer, Deptt. of English, Chaudhary Devilal University, Sirsa (Haryana).

Binod Mishra, Assistant Professor, Languages Group, BITS, Pilani-333031 (Rajasthan).

Devika, Lecturer, Languages Group, BITS, Pilani-333031 (Rajasthan).

Ashok Kumar, Lecturer, Deptt. of English, IMS Engineering College, Ghaziabad-201009 (Uttar Pradesh).

S.S. Kanade, Lecturer, Deptt. of English, S.M.P. College, Murum, T.Q. Omerga, Dist. Osmanabad-413605 (Maharashtra).

Sushila Rathore, Lecturer, Languages Group, BITS, Pilani-333031 (Rajasthan).

Geetha B., Lecturer, Languages Group, BITS, Pilani-333031 (Rajasthan).

R. Swarnalatha, Lecturer, Languages Group, BITS, Pilani-333031 (Rajasthan).

Shivika Verma, Research Scholar, K.N. Govt. P.G. College, Gyanpur, Bhadohi (Uttar Pradesh).

Pushp Lata, Assistant Professor, Languages Group, BITS, Pilani-333031 (Rajasthan).

Rashmi Bajaj, Lecturer, Deptt. of English, Vaish P.G. College, Bhiwani (Haryana).

Aparna Batra, Lecturer, Deptt. of English, Adarsh Mahila Mahavidyalaya, Bhiwani (Haryana).

P.S. Ramana, Reader, Deptt. of English, Punjabi University, Regional Centre, Bhatinda (Punjab).